MW01137610

Creole Cookery

Edited by
The Christian Woman's Exchange

PELICAN PUBLISHING COMPANY
Gretna 2005

The word "Pelican" and the depiction of a pelican are trademarks of Pelican Publishing Company, Inc., and are registered in the U.S. Patent and Trademark Office.

ISBN-13: 978-1-58980-342-8

This 2005 edition is a facsimile of the original 1885 version and is an exact reproduction in all respects.

This reprint is a joint project of the Hermann-Grima/Gallier Historic Houses and The Historic New Orleans Collection.

Printed in the United States of America

Published by Pelican Publishing Company, Inc.
1000 Burmaster Street, Gretna, Louisiana 70053

THE

CREOLE COOKERY BOOK.

EDITED BY THE

CHRISTIAN WOMAN'S EXCHANGE

OF NEW ORLEANS, LA.

———

The object of the Christian Woman's Exchange, in the publication of this volume, is
to provide funds for the purchase or erection of a building to meet the
demands of their constantly increasing business. The recipes
which make up the collection are the contributions
of housekeepers experienced in the science of cookery as practiced
throughout the
South, and
more particularly as it is understood and applied by the Creoles of Louisiana.

———

NEW ORLEANS:
T. H. THOMASON, PRINTER, 36 NATCHEZ STREET.

———

1885.

PREFACE.

The literary world has for years been replete with the economical and successful experiences of the thrifty Northern housewife, while New Orleans, where, as Thackeray says, "you can eat the most and suffer the least, where claret is as good as it is at Bordeaux, and where a bouillabaisse can be had, than which a better was not eaten at Marseilles," has heretofore appeared indifferent to this laudable ambition of her distant neighbors in thus neglecting that all important addition to her literature.

The moral influences of good cooking have been too frequently and forcibly put before us in works of a weightier character, too amply illustrated by historical facts, to necessitate anything here but a passing notice to that effect.

In this time, glorious with the general diffusion of learning, it is befitting that the occult science of the gumbo should cease to be the hereditary lore of our negro mammies, and should be allowed its proper place in the gastronomical world.

The time is now ripe for a new "Almanach des Gourmands," and the following collected recipes, with their prestige of great names, including what is best in the Creole and American cuisine, are introduced, with the modest hope that they may prove to both public and publisher a source of rich, practical benefit.

CHRISTIAN WOMAN'S EXCHANGE

OF NEW ORLEANS.

BOARD OF MANAGERS.

Mrs. R. M. Walmsley,
" T. G. Richardson,
" Theo. Auzé,
" E. J. Wharton,
" S. H. Davis,
" S. H. Kennedy,
" S. Delgado,
" F. N. Griswold,
" C. W. Wood,
" John G. Parham,
" T. J. Carver,
" P. N. Strong,
" K. Fuhri,
" Arch. Mitchell,
" H. J. Leovy,
" E. Ranlett,

Mrs. M. W. Bartlett,
" D. A. Given,
" John R. Juden,
" J. H. Allen,
" Fred. Wing,
" S. Landrum,
" M. C. Jennings,
" B. D. Wood,
" A. Brittin,
" Percy Roberts,
" G. W. Pritchard,
" L. P. Wayne,
" T. H. Holmes,
" J. B. Wallace,
" Albert Baldwin,
" J. M. Parker.

[*Extract from Charter.*]

ARTICLE SECOND. The purposes and objects of said corporation are de-
clared and specified to be the amelioration of the condition of needy and
worthy women by enabling and assisting them to earn a livelihood, and pro-
viding the means and opportunities of disposing of the products of their
labor and of other property to them belonging; and in furtherance of such
charitable purposes to establish and maintain a depot for the reception and
sale of any marketable articles that a woman can make in her own home,
or any valuable articles which her necessities may oblige her to dispose of,
thereby assisting a needy woman to turn to personal profit whatever useful
talent she may possess.

CONTENTS.

SOUPS—

    Crab Soup.. 2
    Gumbo D'Herbes—Green Gumbo............... 2
    Turtle Soup..................................... 2
    Gumbo Aux Herbes............................ 3
    Terrapin or Gopher Soup 4
    Clear Soup..................................... 4
    Pea Soup....................................... 5
    Clear Gravy Soup.............................. 5
    Corn Soup...................................... 5
    Vegetable Soup................................. 5
    Potato Soup.................................... 6
    Cocoanut Soup................................. 6
    Groundnut Soup 7
    Chestnut Soup................................. 7
    Crab Soup..................................... 7
    French Soup................................... 8
    Oyster Soup 8
    Oyster Soup for Six Persons 8
    Oyster Soup................................... 8
    Oyster Soup................................... 9
    Mrs. Coolidge's Oyster Soup................... 9
    Okra Soup..................................... 9
    Okra Soup..................................... 10
    Okra Soup..................................... 10
    New Orleans Gumbo........................... 10
    Calf's Head Soup.... 10
    Balls for Mrs. Ames' Calf's Head Soup......... 11
    Lamb's Head Soup............................. 11

SHELL FISH—

    Terrapins 12
    Terrapin Pies.................................. 12
    To Dress Turtle Steaks 12
    Clam Pie 13
    Clam Fritters.................................. 13
    Clam Chowder................................. 13
    To Pickle Shrimps 13

Baked Shrimps 14
To Dress Shrimps in Tomato Catsup 14
To Dress Shrimps......... 14
A Nice Way To Serve Crabs 14
Stuffed Crabs.................................. 15
Stuffed Crabs.................................. 15
Stewed Crabs.................................. 15
Pickled Oysters.... 15
To Dress Oysters in Cream 15
Fried Oysters.................................. 16
To Stew Oysters............................... 16
Stewed Oysters................................ 16
Epicurean Oysters............................. 16
Scolloped Oysters 16
Stewed Oysters (Very Delicate) 17
Oyster Sausage................................ 17
Cooking Crabs.... 17
Baked Clams 17
To Batter Oysters............................. 18
Pickled Oysters 18
Stewed Oysters (French) 18
Scolloped Oysters............................. 18
Oyster Pie.................................... 18
Fried Oysters 19
Fried Oysters................................. 19
Scolloped Oysters............................. 19
Shrimp Pie 19

FISH—

French Fish................................... 20
Baked Fish................... 20
To Stew Red Fish............................. 20
Boiled Trout.... 21
Boiled Mackerel.............................. 21
Fried Cod Fish 21
To Boil Salmon............................... 21
To Roast a Fish 22
Roasted Salmon.............................. 22
Fried Cod Fish 22
Flounders Sauté............................. 22
Cold Red or Other Cold Fish.................. 23
Fish Cake.................................... 23
Fish au Gratin............................... 23
Baked Fish a La Crême 24

To Stew Fish.................................... 24
To Dress Sheephead........................... 24
To Bake Red Snapper.......................... 25
Baked Red Fish............................... 25
Turbot, Hallibut and other Fish a la Crême....... 25
Courtbouillon of Red Fish..................... 25
Courtbouillon of any Sort of Fish............... 26
Courtbouillon of Perch........................ 26
Broiled Fish.................................. 26
Sour Stew.................................... 26
To Pot Fish.................................. 27

SAUCES—

Ragout Souse.................................. 28
Onion Sauce................................... 28
Celery Sauce.................................. 28
Egg Sauce.................................... 28
White Sauce for Veal or Lamb.................. 28
Sauce Piquante............................... 28
Tomato Sauce................................. 29
Mayonnaise 29
Fish Sauce................................... 29
White Sauce.................................. 29
White Sauce for Fowls 29
Oyster Sauce for Boiled Fowl or Turkey.......... 30
Egg Sauce.................................... 30
Egg Sauce.................................... 30
Oyster Sauce................................. 30
A Cream Sauce for Fillet...................... 30
Brown Roux.................................. 31
White Roux.................................. 31
Cullis 31
Tomato Sauce 32
Sauce Flamande 32
Tartar Sauce................................. 32
Venison Sauce 32
Salmi of Ducks, Venison or Birds 32
Cream Sauce................................. 33
Apple Sauce for Roasted Goose................. 33
How to Make Curry 33

FOWL—

Wild Ducks or Teal 35
Roast Fowls 35

Roast Fowls.. 35
To Stew Partridges 35
Brown Fricasse 36
Stewed Ducks 36
Stewed Pigeons 36
Stewed Rabbits or Ducks...... 37
Ducks a la Mode.................................. 37
Roast Ducks 37
Boiled Ducks 37
To Hash Ducks 38
To Stew Ducks............. 38
Stewed Ducks 38
Battered Chicken.............................. 38
Fried Chicken 39
To Make a French Pilau 39
Poulet a la Eugenie 39
White Fricasse of Chicken........................ 39
Boiled Fowls 40
Cold Fowls......... ,. 40
Potted Piegeons....... 40
To Dress a Goose ....,........ 41
Broiled Chickens 41
Coquilles de Volaille 41
Coquilles de Volaille 42
Coquilles de Volaille 42
Croquettes, Chicken 43
Croquettes............ 43
Sweet Breads.......... .... ·· 43
To Roast A Turkey................................ 43

MEATS—

Broiled Venison............................ 45
Stewed Venison.............................. 45
Venison Steak 45
Venison (The Haunch)........... 45
Cotelettes En Chevieuil (Cutlets, Venison Style)... 46
Bœuf Roulé (Rolled Beef)....................... 46
Foie de Veau En Sauté (Daube of Veal Loin)..... 46
Paté de Veau (Veal Pie)......................... 47
Terrine de Bœuf (Potted Beef) 47
Stuffed Ham 47
Stuffing for the Ham 47
Bouillé 48
Stewed Rump of Beef............................. 48

Beef Steak Pie 48
Potted Beef 49
Beef a la Daub................................. 49
Beef Steaks... 49
Beef Stewed with Oysters 49
Irish Stew 50
Stewed Smoked Beef 50
Beef Patties 50
Potato Beef 51
Cold Brisket of Beef............................... 51
Spiced Beef 51
Veal Paté to Serve Cold........................ ... 51
Pressed Beef.................................. 52
Corn Jelly Daube................................... 52
Raviolé a la Avegno............................... 52
Fare or Stuffing...................................... 53
Croquets of Cold Meat............................ 53
To Make Sweet Breads 53
Fried Lamb... 54
Veal Olives... 54
Spiced Beef.. 54
Corn Beef.... 54
To Pickle Tongues................................ 55
Boiled Beef... 55
A la Mode Beef 55
A Cold Dish for Lunch........................... 56
Ham Toast......... 56
Bouillé 56
Beef Balls.. 56
Beef Steak Pie 57
Spiced or Smoked Beef 57
To Stew Beef... 57
To Pickle Beef....................................... 58
Beef Ham.......................... 58
Ronfolk Cured Ham............................... 58
To Cure Bacon:...................................... 59
To Cure Beef..... 59
Fillet de Bœuf 59
Minced Meat.. 60
Curing Hams 60
Apple Pork 61
How to Boil a Ham 61
Pickled Beef.. 61
Pickled Chine... 61

Veal Loaf.. 61
Spiced Tongue.................................... 62
Bewitched Beef or Veal........................ 62
Pot au Feu....................................... 62
Roly Poly.. 62
Daub... 92
Cold Hash 63

VEGETABLES—

Boiled Potatoes.................................. 64
Irish Potato Snow Balls.......................... 64
Roast Potatoes................................... 64
Baked Irish Potatoes............................. 64
Potatoes in Cream 64
Potato Snow...................................... 65
Boiled Potatoes 65
Fried Potatoes................................... 65
Potato Balls 65
Potatoes With Thick Batter. 65
Fried Irish Potatoes 66
Irish Potatoes Mashed............................ 66
Potato Balls for Breakfast....................... 66
Sweet Potatoes 66
Fried Sweet Potatoes 66
Green Peas 66
Green Peas a la Bourgeoise....................... 67
Green Peas 67
Potato Salad 67
Jumballaya (A Spanish Creole Dish) 67
On Cooking Tomatoes.............................. 67
To Keep Tomatoes 68
Tomato Omelette 68
Stewed Tomatoes 68
Stuffed Tomatoes 68
Tomato Omelet 69
To Bake Tomatoes................................. 69
Tomato Soup 69
Fried Tomatoes 69
Baked Tomatoes 70
Stuffed Tomatoes................................. 70
To Prepare and Boil Rice......................... 70
How to Wash Rice 70
Preparing Rice or Hominy 70
Egg Plants 71

Stuffed Egg Plants 71
Turkish Egg Plants 71
To Cook Salsify 71
Salsify Oysters 71
Salsify Fritters 72
Carolina Boiled Rice 72
Rice as Cooked in Japan 72
Corn Baked in a Dish 72
Corn Fritters 73
Corn Oysters 73
Corn Oysters 73
Very Healthy Slaw 73
Warm Slaw 74
To Boil a Cauliflower 74
Stewed Spinach 74
To Boil Artichokes 74
Stuffed Macaroni 74
Baked Macaroni 75
Cauliflower Omelet 75
Stewed Carrots 75
Parsnip Fritters 75
Dried Okra 75
Boiled Okra 76
Fried Cucumbers 76
Fried Plantains 76
Onion Custard 76
Asparagus (Italian Fashion) 77
Toasted Cheese 77
Stewed Beets 77
Cold Slaw 77
Fonds L'Artichoux—Stuffed 77

BREAD—

Family Bread 79
Lightened Loaf 79
Tea Rolls 79
Spanish Rolls 79
French Rolls 80
Sponge Bread 80
Family Bread 80
Brown Bread 80
Rolls with Milk 80
Diet Bread 80
Diet Bread 81

Economical Muffins............................ 81
Hampton Muffins.............................. 81
Indian Muffins................................ 81
Water Muffins................................ 81
Cornmeal Muffins............................. 82
Egg Muffins.................................. 82
Plain Muffins................................ 82
Risen Muffins................................ 82
Corn Bread................................... 82
Molasses Toast............................... 82
Sweet Journey Cake........................... 83
Bread Cake................................... 83
Corn Bread Rusk.............................. 83
Corn Bread................................... 83
Corn Cake.................................... 83
Virginia Egg Bread........................... 84
Potato Corn Bread............................ 84
Sweet Corn Bread............................. 84
Corn Wafers.................................. 84
Hoe Cake..................................... 84
Soda Bread................................... 84
Potato Bread................................. 85
Batter Bread................................. 85
Cornmeal Rusk................................ 85
Risen Corn Cake.............................. 85
Dried Bread Crumbs........................... 85
Cornmeal Bread............................... 85
Corn Bread................................... 85
Cornmeal Bread............................... 86
Muffin Bread................................. 86
Hominy Cakes................................. 86
Gruel Batter Cakes........................... 86
Virginia Corn Cake........................... 86
Virginia Cakes............................... 87
Lapland Cakes................................ 87
Flannel Cakes without Yeast.................. 87
Sweet Flannel Cakes 87
Flannel Cakes 87
Bermuda Johnny Cake 87
Buckwheat Cakes 88
Cream Cakes 88
Steeven Cakes 88
Whigs.. 88
German Waffles 89

Sweet Potato Waffles 89
Rice Waffles.................................... 89
Rice Waffles.................................... 89
Waffles 90
Potato Waffles 90
Bread Cake..................................... 90
Rice Bread 90
Flannel Cakes 90
Milk Biscuits 90
To Make Rolls.................................. 91
Crumpets....................................... 91
Pan Cakes 91
Sweet Wafers 91
Tavern Biscuits................................ 91
Breakfast Cakes 91
Buttermilk Bread 92
Rice Bread 92
Potato Bread 92
Yankee Biscuits 92
Suffolk Cakes 92
Butter Biscuits................................ 92
Clareville Biscuits 93
Thin Biscuits 93
Sweet Potato Buns 93
Virginia Buns 93
Richmond Muffins 93
Maryland Biscuit 94
Sally Lunn..................................... 94
Washington Loaf 94
Bachelor's Loaf................................ 94
Warsaw Breakfast Cake.......................... 94
Buttermilk Rolls............................... 95
Light Cakes 95
Cream Cakes 95
Sally Lunn or Tea Buns......................... 95
Naples Biscuit................................. 95
New York Rusk 96
Sponge Biscuit................................. 96
Zouave Rusks................................... 96
Raised Waffles................................. 96
Indian Bread 96
Indian Meal Griddle Cakes 97
Dyspepsia Bread................................ 97
Dyspepsia Bread................................ 97

Tancredi Cake........................ 97
Egg Toast 97
Tongue Toast 98
Ham Toast 98
Home Made Crackers 98
Bannock 98
Rusk........... 98
Corn Bread 99
Brown Bread 99
Mrs. Meyer's Muffins 99
Mrs. L. Wayne's Bread Receipt.................. 99
Paste...... 99
Pyramid of Paste........................... 100
Paste for Croquants 100
Bread Dough Paste.......................... 101
Patent Flour.............................. 101
Very Light Paste 101
Potato Paste..... 101
Poor Man's Paste.......... 102
Rice Paste................................ 102
Puff Paste 102
Hop Yeast................................. 102
Patent Yeast............................. 102
Potato Yeast......... 103
Baker's Yeast............................. 103
Country Yeast............................. 103
Norfolk Yeast............................. 103
Milk Yeast 103
Williamsburg Yeast........................ 104

CAKES—

Cream Puffs.............................. 105
New York Cup Cake. 105
Indian Pound Cake 105
Marbled Cake 106
Savoy Biscuits 106
Aberdeen Crulla Cake.... 106
Sontag Cake............................. 106
Family Cake......... 107
Cocoanut Cake........................... 107
Cottage Cake 107
Carraway Cakes 107
Hampton Cakes 107
Cream Cakes............................ 108

Cake Without Butter..........................108
French Cake 108
Common Cake..........................108
Oak Hill Cakes..........................108
Black Cake (Plain)..........................108
Black Cake..........................109
Sweet Biscuits..........................109
Spring Cake..........................109
Love Knots..........................109
Spanish Cake..........................109
Sugar Cakes..........................109
Shrewsbury Cake..........................110
Sponge Cake With Butter..........................110
Sponge Cake..........................110
Commencement Cake..........................110
Cumberland Cake..........................110
Benton Tea Cakes..........................110
Orange Cake..........................110
Reddie Cake..........................111
Drop Biscuits..........................111
Lemon Pound Cake..........................111
Brown Cakes..........................111
Silver Cake..........................111
Gold Cake..........................112
French Cake..........................112
Almond Cakes..........................112
Brown Cakes..........................112
Cocoanut Cake..........................113
Meringues..........................113
Derby Cake..........................113
Rosa Cake..........................113
Shrewsbury Biscuit..........................113
Charlotte Cake..........................114
Victoria Buns..........................114
Norfolk Black Cake..........................114
Almond Cake..........................114
Indian Pound Cake..........................114
Sugar Biscuits..........................114
Doughnuts..........................114
Brown Cakes..........................115
Orange Cakes..........................115
Sugar Cakes..........................115
Holiday Cake..........................115
Scotch Bread..........................115

Express Pudding..116
Premium Cake 116
Spice Cake..116
Silver Cake..116
Wafers 116
Kendall Cakes..117
Tea Cakes..117
Oatland Cakes..117
Plain Cake 117
Cup Cake 117
Jelly Cake..117
Lemon Jelly Cake..118
Angel's Food 118
Naples Biscuit..118
Cake for Sauce..118
Coffee Cake..119
Spice Cake..119
Snow Balls..119
Cup Cake 119
Pearl Cake 120
Portsmouth Cakes 120
Jenny Linds 120
Thompson Cake..120
Crullers 120
White Cake..120
Almond Balls..121
Nut Cakes..121
Pound Cake 121
Mrs. Clay's Premium Cake..121
Cocoanut Cake..121
Berwick Sponge Cake 122
Tea Cakes..122
Charlotte Russe Without Cream..122
Ginger Bread Nuts 123
Winter Ginger Cakes..123
Royal Ginger Cakes 123
Soft Ginger Bread..123
Jelly Sponge Cake 123
Light Ginger Bread 124
Ginger Cakes 124
Ginger Nuts 124
Light Ginger Bread..124
Dickson Ginger Bread..124
Light Ginger Cakes 124

Niagara Ginger Bread...........................125
Ginger Cup Cake...............................125
Soft Ginger Bread.............................125
Ginger Bread 125
Sponge Ginger Cake.. 125
Sugar Ginger Bread 125
Jumbles.......................................125
Jumbles 126
Cocoanut Jumbles..............................126
Jumbles.......................................126
Federal Cake 126
French Jumbles................................126
Tea Cake......................................127
Harrison Cake.................................127
Whigs...127
Common Cake...................................127
Curd Cakes....................................127
Japan Cake....................................127
Cake Without Eggs 128
Lancers Cake 128
Chocolate Macaroons...........................128
Orange Cakes..................................128
Jumbles 129
Sponge Cake...................................129
Peach Leathers 129
Ginger Cookies 129
Filling for Chocolate Cake 129
Ginger Bread..................................129
Macaroons.....................................129
Cinnamon Cakes................................130
Callers 130
Roll Jelly Cake...............................130
Delicate Cake 130
Sweet Wafers 130
Sponge Cake 130
Strawberry Cake 131
Cream Puffs...................................131
Angel's Food..................................131
Almond Biscuits...............................131
Cousin Jane's Buns............................132
Silver Cake...................................132
Tea Cakes 132
Silver Cake...................................132
Gold Cake.....................................132

Icing 132
Sunshine Cake................................. 132
Marble Cake (Dark Part).....................133
Marble Cake (Light Part)....................133
Strawberry Short Cake.......................133
White Sponge Cake..........................133
Lady Cake 133
White or Silver Cake........................134
White Fruit Cake.............................134
White or Bride's Cake.......................134
Fruit Cake...................................134
Spiced Ginger Cake..........................135
Economical Sponge Cake.....................135
Domestic Fruit Cake.........................135
White Fruit Cake............................135
Filling for the Above.........................135
Jelly Cake...................................136
Ginger Cake.................................136
Angel's Food................................136
Icing..137

ICES, ETC.—

Ice Cream 138
Milk Sherbet 138
Velvet Cream................................138
Ice Cream 138
Lemon Ice Cream............................ 138
Frozen Tapioca Cream......................139
Mock Charlotte Russe.......................139
Charlotte Russe, Hotel Splendide, Paris. 139
Ice Cream 140
Charlotte Russe.............................140
Cocoanut Cream............................140
Seasoned Cream 140
Caromel Ice Cream..........................141
Vanilla Ice 141
Chocolate Ice...............................141
Strawberry Sherbet 141
Strawberry Cream........................... 142
Peach Ice...................................142
Blanc Mange of Moss.......................142
Coffee Jelly.................................142
Blanc Mange 143
Apple Float 143

Orange Whips 143
Apple Island...................... 143
Rice Blanc Mange 143
Sugar Candy Custard..................................144
Lemon Ice Cream................... 144
Carrageen Moss.. 144
Wine Cream...144
Icing...... 144
Boiled Icing..... 145
Custard Ice..145
To Clarify Sugar 145
Apple Float.......................................145
Ice Cream 145
Almond Cream...................................146
Orange Cream 146
Currant Cream...... 146
Rice Milk 146
Spanish Flummery...................................146
Stone Cream...147
Lemon Jelly...147
Bavarian Cream. 147
Almond Custards ....,.............147
Trifle... 147
Cocoanut Custard........................148
Baked Custard...........................148
Cottage Custard...................... 148
Almond Custard........................148
Whips....................................148
Apple Meringue............. 148
Apple Trifle 149
Damson Cheese........................149
Noyeau Cream...... 149
Blanc Mange.......................149
Biscuit Glacé...... 150
Biscuit Glacé 150
Richmond Maids of Honor...................150
Chocolate Cream.............................151
Ice Cream............ 151
To Make Slip..............................151
Raspberry Cream...........................151
Arrowroot Jelly........................ 152
Orange Peel Syrup 152
Charlotte Russe.............................152
Italian Cream.......................,...........152

Dutch Blanc Mange............................153
Syllabub and Cream...........................153
Macaroon Cream..............................153
Chocolate Cream......... 153
Italian Cream..... 153
Biscuit Ice Cream......... 154
Angel's Repast................... 154
Apple Snow 154
Ornamental Dish.............................155
Kisses 155
Almond Ice..................................155
Matrimony 156
Pineapple Sherbet.........   156
Peach Sherbet..............................156
Lemon Sherbet..............................156
Baked Custard..............................156
Chocolate Mange............................ 156
Whip for a Trifle...........................157
Gateau de Pommes........ 157
Lemon Salad 157
Snow Cream 157
Charlotte Polonaise 158
Eugene Cream...............................158
Lemon Cream 158
Mock Ice.....................................159
Devonshire Cream 159
Chocolate Custard...........................159
Almond and Macaroon Custard 159
Creamed Pineapple..........................159
Creamed Strawberries 160
Noyeau Cream.............................. ... 160
Jelly 160
Potato Soufflé 160
Cocoanut Sherbet 160

PUDDINGS—

Cocoanut Pudding 161
Ice Pudding.... 161
The Famous Bakewell Pudding 161
Famous Apple Pudding 161
Fig Pudding.................................162
Windsor Pudding............ 162
Plum Pudding 162
Bird's Nest Pudding........ 162

Cheese Pudding 162
Snow Pudding 163
Breeze Pudding................................163
Berryman Pudding 163
Savoy Pudding 163
Fancy Pudding 164
Custard and Apple Pudding 164
Apple Batter Pudding................................164
Queen Mab's Pudding................................164
Potato and Raisin Pudding 164
German Pudding................................165
Rice Pudding................................165
Almond Pudding................................165
Eve's Pudding................................165
Bread and Butter Pudding................................165
Ground Rice Pudding 165
Fancy Pudding................................166
Cabinet Pudding 166
Almond Cheese Cakes................................166
Sweetmeat Pudding................................166
Governor's Pudding 166
Sweet Potato Pudding................................166
Arrowroot Pudding................................167
Indian Meal Pudding................................167
Boiled Cake Pudding 167
Lemon Pudding................................167
Tapioca Pudding................................167
Potato Pudding 168
Quince Pudding................................168
American Pudding................................168
Walterian Pudding................................168
Chancellor's Pudding................................168
Ginger Cake Pudding................................169
Transparent Pudding................................169
Orange Pudding................................169
Gooseberry Pudding................................170
Pumpkin Pudding................................170
Baked Apple Pudding................................170
Danish Pudding................................170
Cocoanut Pudding................................171
Cocoanut Pudding................................171
Sweetmeat Pudding................................171
Adelaide's Pudding................................171
Plum Pudding................................171

Soda Cracker Pudding 171
Orange Pudding 171
Victoria Pudding 172
Peach Pudding 172
Fruit Pudding 172
Lemon Pudding 172
Almond Pudding 173
Murangue Pudding 173
Nutmeg Pudding 173
Flirtation Pudding 173
Aunt Mary's Pudding 173
Ginger Pudding 174
Plum Pudding 174
Domestic Pudding 174
Cheap Pudding 174
Almond Gust 175
Riz au Lait 175
Apple Cornmeal Pudding 175
Swiss Pudding 175
Lemon Pudding 176
Soufflé Pudding 176
Biscuit Pudding 176
Hindoo Balls 177
Elysian Pudding 177
Wellington Pudding 177
Southern Pudding 177
Hominy Pudding 178
Sponge Cake Pudding 178
Almond Florendine 178
Baked Arrowroot Pudding 178
Baked Batter Pudding 179
Almond Pudding 179
Bread Pudding 179
Sauce for Batter Pudding 179
Potato Pone 180
Apple Pie 180
Lemon Mince 180
Custard for Pies 180
Apple Fritters 180
Cocoanut Tarts 181
Baked Apple Dumpling 181
Mince Meat 181
Mince Pies without Meat 181
Cheese Cakes 182

Lemon Cheese Cakes 182
Mince Meat 182

PRESERVES, ETC.—

Preserved Pineapple...........................183
Jelly 183
Preserved Cranberries 183
Preserved Orange Peel...........................183
Pineapple Syrup for Ice Cream. 184
Lemon Citron.......................184
Rich Syrup 184
Baked Quinces...................................184
Orange Wafers...............................184
Preserved Figs 185
Preserved Tomatoes....... 185
Quince Cheese 185
Preserved Peppers 186
Tomato Jelly 186
Grape Jelly 186
Peach Jelly...................................186
Raspberry Jam 187
To Stew Apricots 187
Stewed Apples 187
White Compote of Pears...........................187
White Compote of Apples.. 188
Dried Cherries.............................188
Cherry Jam 188
Baked Apples.............................188
Baked Pears 189
Charlotte Des Pommes 189
Peach Tart 189
To Preserve Strawberries 190
Quince Jam 190
Preserved Apples 190
Preserved Figs..............................190
Preserved Tomatoes...........................191
Orange Marmalade.............................191
Apple Jelly... 191
Mixed Marmalade...........................191
Strawberries Whole...........................192
Strawberry Jelly...........................192
Raspberry Jelly...........................192
Quince Jelly...........................192

Orange Jelly...............................193
Peach Jam..................................193

PICKLES—

Pickled Cucumbers......................194
Pickled Cherries.......................194
Pickled Lemons 194
Pickled Damsons........................195
Pickled Cauliflowers 195
Nasturtion Seeds.......................195
Sweet Pickle Tomatoes..................195
Augustine Mangoes......................196
To Pickle Walnuts White................196
Pickled English Walnuts................196
Tomato Catsup (French).................197
Pickled Peaches........................197
Pickled Onions.........................197
Spiced Peaches.........................198
Pickled Cucumbers......................198
Pickled Tomatoes.......................198
Oil Mangoes............................198
Pickled Cucumbers......................198
Pickled Plums..........................199
Button Tomatoes........................199
Tomato Catsup..........................199
Winter Tomatoes........................200
Tomato Catsup 200
Green Tomato Soy 200
Pepper Mangoes 201
A Quick Way of Pickling Cabbage........201
Sweet Damsons..........................201
Sweet Plums............................201
Lemon Pickle...........................201
Cider Apple Sauce......................202
German Pickle 202
Sweet Pickle Peaches...................202
Sweet Peaches..........................202
Pickled Cabbage........................203
Pickled Radish Pods 203
Soy....................................203
Pickled Cabbage 203
German Pickle..........................204
Creole Sauce...........................204
Chickens Royal 204

Fowls in Fillets With Pistachoes. 205
Mrs. Joy's Chow-Chow Pickle 205
Stuffed Peaches................................. 205
Oil Mangoes 206
Yellow Pickle.................. 206

CONFECTIONERY—

Chocolate Caromels 207
Candy 207
Chocolate Caromels............................ 207
Cocoanut Drops................................ 207
Brown Taffy 207
Cocoanut Meringue............................ 208
Cocoanut Drops 208

MISCELLANEOUS—

Reiz de Veau 209
Cotelettes en Papilottes....................... 209
Curry 209
Bisque Potage—Mme. Eugène................... 210
Spiced Peaches...... 210
Herb Gumbo................................... 210
Croquettes 211
Savory Friar's Omelet.......................... 211
To Boil Hams..................................211
Fig Pickles 212
Potato Salad................................... 212
Mangoes. 213
Useful Receipts 213
Sponge Cake.................................. 214
Omelette Soufflé 214
To Boil Fish 214
Neutralizing Poison with Sweet Oil............. 215
Drawn Butter................................. 215
Beef Tea for Invalids 215
Home Made Yeast Powder..................... 215
Kentucky Corn Pudding.... 215
Weights and Measures......................... 216

CONTRIBUTORS.

To Miss Mary Pannell special thanks are due for her liberal contributions, which she was many years in collecting from the colored "Aunties" of Virginia.

Mrs. R. M. Walmsley,
  ·· S. H. Kennedy,
  ·· A. V. Davis,
  ·· J. B. Wallace,
  ·· D. A. Given,
  ·· M. E. Simpson,
  ·· J. G. Parham,
  ·· Theo. Auzé,
  ·· A. J. Tebo,
  ·· T. H. Holmes,
  ·· G. A. Vincent,
  ·· R. Pritchard,
  ·· H. J. Leovy,
  ·· H. M. Smith,
  ·· J. M. Parker,
  ·· W. Dickson,
  ·· Dugué,
Miss C. Carter,
  ·· M. Eggleston,

Mrs. T. G. Richardson,
  ·· Jefferson Davis,
  ·· B. M. Palmer,
  ·· S. Delgado,
  ·· M. C. Jennings,
  ·· J. Gasquet,
  ·· P. Werlein,
  ·· Fred. Wing,
  ·· L. P. Wayne,
  ·· E. J. Hart,
  ·· W. C. Clark,
  ·· Preston,
  ·· S. McCutcheon.
  ·· M. Henderson,
  ·· M. Richardson,
  ·· L. L. Reid,
  ·· Randolph,
Miss I. E. Leovy,
  ·· K. A. Monroe,

Madame Eugène, Mrs. Morris, and others.

# SOUPS.

SOUP MAKING.

Some one has said, ".that a well made soup is not only one of the most wholesome forms in which food can be taken, but it is also one of the most economical." Take for example our New Orleans Gumbo, which can be made of scraps of cold meat or fowl, a few oysters, crabs or shrimps, and, with a couple of spoonfuls of well cooked rice, is a very satisfying and economical dinner. Even a rich soup is less expensive than almost any other dish. It seems to us, that this branch of cooking has been rather neglected by our southern housekeepers, so we have given a larger number of receipts for soups than will be found in other cookery books. In colder climates, soup stock can be made and kept for several days, but in our warm, moist climate, it would become sour, so must be prepared each day.

In making soup, special care should be taken of the vessels, to have them perfectly clean; the meat and vegetables well washed and carefully prepared. Soup should be boiled slowly for four or five hours; skimmed thoroughly when it first begins to boil, for it cannot be easily made clear afterwards, and no grease should be left to float on the top. Add vegetables and herbs as soon as the soup has been well skimmed and the grease ceases to rise. When the meat and vegetables have been fried or browned, boiling water must be added in small quantities, but otherwise, always use cold water. For thickening soups, use arrowroot, rice flour, or corn starch, mixed with a little cold water, and stirred in about ten minutes before the soup is dished. The soup should boil quickly after the thickening is added. Use very little salt, as the lack of it can be remedied—spices should be used whole and sparingly. All soups must be served very hot.

CRAB SOUP.

Have ready one dozen large crabs; separate the fat from the back shell and bodies; cleanse them from the dead men's fingers; boil the claws and pick the meat from them; have ready a large stew-pan, into which put one tablespoonful of lard, two of butter, one large onion; cut up into not very small pieces; one clove of garlic; allow this to brown a little, then add one whole can of tomatoes, or 18 or 20 fresh ones; after they have stewed 10 minutes, add the meat from the crab claws, then the crabs; season with salt and black and red pepper, the rind of a lemon, and one tablespoonful of the juice; sift over this about one-half dozen grated soda crackers; then add boiling water to make the required quantity of soup, and allow it to boil moderately for two hours; a little while before serving, add the fat from the crabs and a little thyme, parsley and sweet marjoram. This receipt will serve soup for about 12 persons.

GUMBO D'HERBES—GREEN GUMBO.

Take equal portions of young cabbage leaves, beet leaves, turnip leaves, mustard leaves, spinach, cresses, parsley, green onions, and place them in boiling water; when well boiled, chop them fine; make a good soup (brown gravy) in which you put beef and ham to fry a little; then add your vegetables (or herbs); stir often and let them fry about one hour, keeping the pot well covered; then add the required quantity of hot water, and let it all boil gently for about two hours. By adding hot pepper, you will have a real "Creole Gumbo."

TURTLE SOUP.

Take the whole of the turtle out of the shell; cut it in pieces, that it may be more easily scalded. Throw these pieces, with the fins, into the pot, and when scalded, take off the coarse skin of the fins and lay them aside to make another dish. The thick skin of the stomach must also be taken off: under it lies the fat, or what is termed the citron. Thus prepared, it is ready for making the soup. Cut up the turtle in small pieces, throw them into a pot. But before doing this, take a leg of beef and boil it to a gravy; then put in the pieces of turtle, adding as *much* water as will cover the whole, about 2 inches. Let it boil slowly for 3 hours. The seasoning and the citron should be put in when the soup is half done. To 2 quarts and a half of soup add ½ an ounce of mace, a dessertspoonful of allspice, a teaspoonful of cloves, and salt, black and cayenne pepper to your taste. Use parsley, thyme, and onions in the soup while boiling; when nearly done thicken with 2 tablespoonfuls of flour. To give it a good color, take a tablespoonful of brown sugar and burn it; when sufficiently burnt add a wineglass of water; of this coloring use 2 tablespoonfuls in the soup. The forcemeat for the balls may be made with a bit of the turtle, a small piece of ham, and seasoned highly with sweet herbs; add the yolk of one egg, roll it into the balls, fry them and put them into the soup; boil ½ a dozen eggs hard, slice them and put them in after adding ½ a pint of Madeira wine. After the wine cooks a little, the soup will be ready for table.

GUMBO AUX HERBES.

Take equal parts of cabbage leaves, beet leaves, turnip leaves, mustard leaves, spinach, cresses, parsley and green onions; soak them and wash them thoroughly, and trim them by taking off the coarse mid rib of the leaf; boil them for at least two hours; add to the water a teaspoonful of cooking soda, strain them and chop up as you would spinach. Take a piece of veal brisket and a slice of ham, which should be cut into small pieces, add a large onion, chopped fine, salt and pepper; fry all in a heaping spoonful of lard to a rich brown; now add the greens, stirring with a wooden spoon, and then add as much hot water as will make sufficient gumbo for the family. Serve with boiled rice.

TERRAPIN OR GOPHER SOUP.

Take a large fresh water terrapin, clean and place it in a digester with 2 quarts of water, a slice of bacon, 2 dozen cloves, 3 dozen allspice, salt, black and red pepper; boil this for 3 or 4 hours; thicken and brown it, before serving it up; throw in a glass of wine, in which has been grated half a nutmeg.

CLEAR SOUP.

Have 5 or 6 pounds of lean beef from above the knee cut into small pieces, and the bones chopped; add a slice of ham cut fine; put this on in about 6 quarts of cold water. Let the soup come to a boil and skim it well; throw in a tablespoonful of salt and a half tea cup of cold water, to help the soup to throw up the scum better, which must all be carefully taken off until it ceases to rise; now add one large or two medium sized onions, two carrots, cut fine, and one or two pieces of celery; let this boil slowly from 6 to 8 hours, or until the broth is reduced to one-half the quantity; your meat should be cooked to pieces; pass all through a cullender and strain all through a coarse cloth; put this in a cold place until the next day, when it will be jellied, provided the weather is sufficiently cold; skim all the grease carefully from the top; take the jelly, or soup as it may be, and pour it carefully into another vessel without disturbing the bottom, and heat it well; have a bowl of ice water with a piece of ice in it to keep the water cold; have a clean flannel cloth, or bag, well wet, which dip in the ice water, and pass a small quantity of the broth at a time through the bag, constantly shaking the dregs from the flannel and wetting it with ice water; season highly with cayenne pepper, and salt to the taste; heat it now to serve, adding vermicelli, maccaroni or pates, as you like. If the meat is good and the soup is made properly it will be perfectly clear, but if cloudy before you strain it, beat the whites of three eggs stiff, and pour them into the soup. and let all come to a good boil; let it set about five minutes before you strain.—*Mrs. R. Pritchard.*

PEA SOUP.

To 2 quarts of split peas, put 2 gallons of water, a handful of parsley, a little cayenne pepper, salt and celery seed, to suit taste. Put the peas in soak the night before, and after boiling pass through a sieve; then add a large lump of good butter.

CLEAR GRAVY SOUP.

Wash a piece of fresh beef; put in on the night before it is wanted; boil it several hours until perfectly tender; then take it off and strain it. In the morning separate every particle of fat from it and put it over the fire; season it with pepper and salt, and put in a spoonful of sage to color it; then prepare the vegetables nicely: carrots, celery, and turnips, cut small and boiled in the soup till tender.

CORN SOUP.

Take young corn, and cut the ears across; then grate them in water, 2 ears to a pint; about 6 quarts will make a good tureen of soup; to this quantity put a piece of pork and seasoning to your taste: vegetables if you like. It must boil 3 hours.

VEGETABLE SOUP.

Soak all night, in cold water, either two quarts of yellow split peas, or two quarts of dried white beans. In the morning drain them, and season them with a very little salt and cayenne, and a head of minced celery, or else a heaped tablespoonful of celery seed. Put them into a soup pot with four quarts of water, and boil them slowly till they are all dissolved. Stir them frequently. Have ready a quantity of fresh vegetables, such as turnips, carrots, parsnips, potatoes, onions, also salsify, and asparagus tops. Put in first the vegetables that require the longest boiling. They should all be cut into small pieces. Enrich the whole with some bits of fresh butter rolled in flour. Boil these vegetables in the soup till they are quite tender, put it in a tureen and serve it up.

POTATO SOUP.

Pare and slice thin half a dozen fine potatoes and a small onion. Boil them in three pints of water till so soft that you can pulp them through a cullender. When returned to the pot add a very little salt and cayenne pepper, and a quarter of a pound of fresh butter, divided into bits, and boil it 10 minutes longer. When you put it into the tureen, stir in 2 tablespoonfuls or more of sweet cream. This is a nice soup for Fridays, or for invalids.

COCOANUT SOUP.

Take eight calves' feet that have been scalded and scraped but not skinned, and put them into a soup kettle with 6 or 7 blades of mace, and the yellow rind of a lemon grated. Pour on a gallon of water, cover the kettle and let it boil very slowly (skimming it well) till the flesh is reduced to rags and has dropped entirely from the bones. Then strain it into a broad white-ware pan, and set it away to get cool. When it has congealed, scrape off the fat and sediment, cut up the cake of jelly (or stock) and put it into a clean porcelain kettle. Have ready half a pound of grated cocoanut (very fine), mix it with a pint of cream or rich milk, three ounces of the best fresh butter divided into three parts, each bit rolled in arrowroot or rice flour. Mix it gradually with the cocoanut, and add it to the calves' feet stock in the kettle, seasoned with a small nutmeg grated. Set it over the fire and boil it, slowly, about a quarter of an hour; stirring it well. Then put it into a tureen and serve it up. French rolls or light milk biscuits are very nice to eat with it; also powdered sugar, in case any of the company should wish to sweeten it.

GROUNDNUT SOUP.

To half a pint of shelled ground nuts, well beaten up, add two spoonfuls of flour, and mix well. Put to them a pint of oysters, and a pint and a half of water, while boiling. Throw in a red pepper, or two, if small.

CHESTNUT SOUP.

Make in the best manner, a soup of the lean of fresh beef, mutton or venison; season with cayenne pepper and a little salt, allowing rather less than a quart of water to each pound of meat; skimming and boiling it till the meat drops from the bone; strain it, and put it in a clean pot; have ready a quart or more of nice chestnuts, boiled and peeled; put them into the soup, with some small bits of fresh butter rolled in flour; boil the soup 10 minutes longer before it goes to the table.

CRAB SOUP.

Open and cleanse of the deadmen's fingers and sand, 18 young fat crabs, (raw), cut them into 4 parts and extract the meat from the crabs and the fat from the top of the shells; scald and skin 12 fine, ripe tomatoes; squeeze the pulp from the seeds and juice; chop fine; pour boiling water over seed and juice, and after straining it off, use to make the soup, adding more water, if required; stew in soup pot, one large onion and one clove of garlic in one spoonful of butter and two of lard; then put in tomatoes; after stewing a few minutes, add the meat from the claws, then the crabs, and lastly, the fat from the top shells; sift over it grated bread or crackers; season with salt, pepper, (black or cayenne) parsley, sweet marjoram, thyme, half teaspoonful of lemon juice and the peel of a lemon; pour in water in which seeds were scalded, and boil moderately for one hour. Firm and flaky fish prepared in the same way, make delicious soup. I use twelve good sized crabs, and think more lemon juice an improvement.

FRENCH SOUP.

Take the fleshy part of a rump of beef, put it on the fire early in the morning to boil; skim all the grease off; thyme, parsley and salt, put in with the rump; after the soup is sufficiently boiled and the grease carefully taken off, put in the small white onions and a few carrots cut round; then add cloves and allspice; just before you are ready to dish the soup, put two teaspoonfuls of brown sugar, to turn it dark. No flour is used.

OYSTER SOUP.

Take one hundred oysters, strain them through a cullender and set the liquor to boil; when the scum has all risen and been taken off, add two quarts of water, a tablespoonful of butter, one pint of rich milk or cream, mace, nutmeg, pepper and salt to the taste; boil these ingredients together, and just before serving up, throw in the oysters. If the soup be too thin, stir in a little wheat flour a few minutes before serving up.

OYSTER SOUP FOR SIX PERSONS.

Strain and drain two quarts of oysters; if you have less than a quart of liquor, make up that amount with water; add a handful of chopped ham, fat and lean, a few blades of mace, one-fourth of a large onion; salt and pepper to taste; boil one hour, then strain; make a tablespoonful of flour and a quarter pound of butter into a soft paste; set aside; put oysters into liquor, give them 8 or 10 minutes to plump up, then stir in the paste, and leave until dinner is ready; put the soup on again until it comes to a boil; add a pint each of milk and cream; stir all the time until it boils again, then dish and serve immediately.

OYSTER SOUP.

Take 2 quarts of oysters with the liquor; put 3 quarts of water, 3 slices of lean ham, and 2 onions; boil this down to half the quantity; then run it through a cullender, and put the liquor alone back into the pot and let it come just to a boil; while the oysters are boiling, beat up the yolks of 6 eggs with 4 tablepoonfuls of wheat flour and 1 pint of rich milk; stir this into the oyster liquor, after it has been strained and made boiling hot; add a quart of raw oysters and let the whole thicken a little on the fire; add then 1 teaspoonful of white pepper and a half of grated nutmeg.

OYSTER SOUP.

Three pints of large, fresh oysters, 2 tablespoonfuls of butter, rolled in flour, a bunch of sweet herbs, a saucer full of chopped celery, a quart of rich milk, pepper to your taste. As soon as the ingredients boil, take out the herbs and put in the oysters just before you send it to table. Boiling them a long time in the soup will shrivel them and destroy the flavor. The liquor must be taken from the 3 pints of oysters, strained, and set on the fire to make the soup.

MRS. COOLIDGE'S OYSTER SOUP.

Strain the liquor from 1½ pints of oysters, into a saucepan, with ½ pint of milk, 1 pint of water; add 3 soft crackers, pounded fine, a little pepper, mace, butter the size of an egg, small onion, and celery chopped fine, if you have it; boil all together a few minutes, add the oysters and let it boil up once. Serve immediately.

OKRA SOUP.

Take 1 gallon of water, let it boil; put into it 4 handfuls of cut okra, half an hour after, put in a handful of lima beans, 3 cymblins and a small piece of fresh meat or fowl, which is better than anything else, except beef or veal; then before you take up the soup, put in 5 tomatoes cut in slices; when all are well boiled and mixed together, take butter rolled in flour, but not to make the soup too thick; season with pepper and salt. Make it in a stone vessel and stir it with a wooden spoon. Put your soup on early, that it may simmer on the fire.

2

OKRA SOUP.

Cut up in small pieces a quarter of a peck of okra, skin one-half a peck of potatoes, and put them with a shin or leg of beef, into 10 quarts of cold water; boil it gently for 7 hours, skimming it well. Season with cayenne or black pepper and salt.

OKRA SOUP.

Cut up in fine slices two soup plates of okra, and put into a soup pot with 5 quarts of water and a little salt, at 10 o'clock; at 11 o'clock put your meat into the soup pot; at 12 o'clock peel a soup plate and a half of tomatoes, and after straining them through a cullender throw them into the soup pot; then season with pepper and salt. Allow all the ingredients to boil till 3 o'clock, when it is fit to be served up.

NEW ORLEANS GUMBO.

Take a turkey or fowl, cut it up with a piece of fresh beef; put them in a pot with a little lard, an onion, and water sufficient to cook the meat; after they have become soft, add 100 oysters with their liquor; season to your taste. Just before taking up the soup, warm it until it becomes mucilaginous, and add two spoonfuls of pulverized fillet.

CALF'S HEAD SOUP.

Clean thoroughly; remove the eyes, teeth, and nose bone, making the skin smooth and white as possible. Clean the liver, lights, feet and heart; put all these into an iron pot; cover with water and add salt enough to make the scum rise, about 2 tablespoonfuls; boil all until the meat cleaves from the scull bone, and the liver is tender to the touch of the fork; put the meat in a separate pot, cover with water and boil until the meat slips from the bone; the feet require so much more boiling than the head, that it is necessary to boil them separately. Fish out the head with a long skimmer, then pour out the liquor; wash the pot and strain the whole through a hair sieve into the pot; separate the head from the bone, cut it into pieces of proper size to give each person; divide the feet and liver also, and put into the strained liquor with 6 very small onions, minced very fine, $\frac{1}{2}$ coffee cup of very finely sifted sweet marjoram, $1\frac{1}{2}$ teaspoons black pepper, $1\frac{1}{2}$ ditto red, 2 tablespoons salt, small one of mace (powdered), 2 nutmegs, $\frac{1}{2}$ tablespoon of cloves, 3 ditto of butter mixed with 8 of flour, nicely browned, 4 pounds of crackers, 1 pint wine, and a bottle of claret for company. Let the whole simmer slowly till dinner time, 6 or 8 eggs, cut up, and put in as it goes to table, with small pieces of fresh lemon.—*Mrs. Ames.*

BALLS FOR MRS. AMES' CALF'S HEAD SOUP.

One-half pound beef or veal put in chopping tray with 2 slices of salt pork an inch thick; add some of the lights and liver, 6 small onions, $1\frac{1}{2}$ large tablespoonfuls of sweet marjoram, 1 nutmeg, 1 teaspoon black pepper, 1 desertspoon powdered mace, same of cloves, 3 eggs, 3 sifted crackers, $\frac{1}{2}$ gill of wine, butter the size of an egg, and 2 tablespoons salt; mix all well together, roll the balls in flour, and fry slowly in lard.

LAMB'S HEAD SOUP.

Prepare the head, and put to it 2 quarts of water; boil it until the head becomes so tender that the bones may be taken out. Then cut it into small pieces and put them back into the pot; cut up, also, into small pieces, half of the heart and liver, and add them; season with pepper, salt, a little onion (chopped), a few herbs, turnip, carrot and celery; boil all together over a slow fire for several hours, skimming well. If the water boils away too much add more, which must be boiling.

SHELL FISH.

TERRAPINS.

Select large, fat, thick bodies (females are best), put them whole into water that is boiling hard, add a little salt, and let them boil until done, then take off the shells, extract the meat, and carefully remove the sand-bags, gall and entrails, cut the meat into pieces, put in stew pan with eggs, and sufficient fresh butter to stew well; let it stew until quite hot, keeping the pan carefully covered and shaking it over the fire. Make a sauce of beaten yolks of eggs highly flavored with sherry or madeira, powdered nutmeg and mace, and a few lumps of butter. Stir this well over the fire until it comes almost to a boil, and serve separately if you prefer. A variation of this receipt says, simply add a small lump of liquorice about the size of a 5 cent piece. Serve very hot.

TERRAPIN PIES.

Take 1 large or 4 small terrapins, and after they have been opened, etc., have the meat well chopped, and add to it half a pound of butter, 6 eggs, allspice, mace, pepper, salt, and a small quantity of eschalot; also 2 or 3 slices of bread which have been soaked and mashed smooth; stir these well together. Have the shells washed, put the mixture into them and bake a light brown.

TO DRESS TURTLE STEAKS.

The steaks are taken from the thick part of the turtle fins; season them with pepper, salt and mace; flour them, and fry in butter and lard mixed together. When fried pour a little water over them and let them simmer for a quarter of an hour. Just before serving squeeze a lemon over the steaks.

CLAM PIE.

One full quart of clams after they are opened and the shells taken off, chop them quite fine, add 2 tablespoonfuls of butter and a coffee cup of cream; season with pepper and salt and bake it in a rich paste.

CLAM FRITTERS.

Strain the clams from the juice. Cut the clams fine, beat up 3 eggs very light, stir in the clams, cut up the parsley with a little salt and pepper, grate some nutmeg, and add these to the clams; then stir in 1 pint of cream, and slowly dredge in some flour until it is of the consistency of fritters; then have the pan hot and put in half butter and half lard, as in frying oysters, let it boil and drop in a spoonful of the fritter batter. Serve hot. They are very nice for breakfast.

CLAM CHOWDER.

Put into boiling water from 50 to 100 small clams, and when all their shells have opened, take them out and extract all the hard part and throw it away. Slice thin as much salt pork as will produce half a pint of liquid or gravy. Take out all the pork, leaving the liquid in the pot; add to it a layer of clams, then a layer of biscuits soaked in milk or warm water. Next another layer of clams, then another layer of soaked biscuits. Then more clams, seasoned with pepper and mace. If there is no objection to onions, add three or more, boiled and sliced. Also some nice potatoes, boiled, peeled and cut very fine. Cover the whole with a nice paste, and bake it in an iron oven.

TO PICKLE SHRIMPS.

Pick the shrimps and rinse them well in salt and water; take two parts of strong vinegar and one of water, add a few allspice, and boil this pickle; pour it hot over the shrimps. If the shrimps are to be sent to a distance, the pickle should be boiled again, adding a little more vinegar with a few tablespoonfuls of sweet oil; they must be entirely covered with the pickle; a paper wet with brandy should be placed over the top. They will thus keep a long time.

BAKED SHRIMPS.

Butter well a deep dish, upon which place a thick layer of pounded biscuits, having picked and boiled your shrimps; put a layer of stewed tomatoes, with a little butter, pepper and salt, then add a thinner layer of beat biscuits and another of shrimps, and so on till 3 or 4 layers of both are put in the dish; the last layer must be of biscuits; bake quite brown.

TO DRESS SHRIMPS IN TOMATO CATSUP.

Boil your shrimps, pick and put them into an a la braise dish; add two tablespoonfuls of catsup, and one of butter, to every half pint of shrimps; salt, red and black pepper to your taste.

TO DRESS SHRIMPS.

To every half pint of shrimps, put a tablespoonful of butter, adding a little salt, black and red pepper; when the gravy becomes of a pinkish hue, it is sufficiently cooked; stew over a slow fire till perfectly done.

A NICE WAY TO SERVE CRABS.

One dozen crabs, one pound bread crumbs, two tablespoons of butter, one full teaspoon of salt, half teaspoon black pepper, slice of onion, chopped very fine, half tablespoon chopped parsley, a pinch of thyme and one egg; boil the crabs five minutes, pick and chop them, adding all the ingredients, and shape in forms of mutton chops, and roll in the beaten egg; stick in a claw; put in a frying pan three tablespoons of lard; when boiling, put in the crabs to brown, which they will do in three minutes. Serve in a round dish with claws in the center.

STUFFED CRABS.

Boil two dozen; pick out all the meat, chop the yolks of two hard boiled eggs, some thyme, parsley and onion, (slightly fried in butter) lump of butter size of a hen's egg, and mix well. Before putting back in shell, add a little black pepper, (also cayenne) sprinkle over with bread crumbs; put a bit of butter on top. Bake them brown.

STUFFED CRABS.

Boil for a few moments one dozen crabs, crack and pick out all of the meat; to this meat, add one-third as much grated crackers, one onion chopped fine, a little parsley, pepper and salt, four tablespoons of butter; mix well; with them, add one egg; mix again, then add the juice of one lemon, with a good sized tomato; fill the shells with the mixture; bake about half hour before serving; grate over them some toasted bread crumbs.

STEWED CRABS.

Take 3 or 4 crabs, pick the meat out of the body and claws; take care that no spongy part be left among it, or any of the shell. Put this meat into a stew pan with a little white wine, some pepper and salt, and a little grated nutmeg; heat all this together and put in some crumbs of bread, the yolks of 2 eggs (beat up), and 1 spoonful of vinegar; stir all well together; make some toasted sippets, lay them on a plate and pour in the crabs. Serve it up hot.

PICKLED OYSTERS.

Boil the oysters till quite done, in their own liquor, with as much mace and pepper as will season them; pour off and strain the liquor and vinegar sufficient to cover the oysters; having first stirred in salt to your taste.

TO DRESS OYSTERS IN CREAM.

To 1 quart of oysters, after draining them, add ½ a pint of sweet cream, a tablespoonful of butter, salt and black and red pepper; place the whole in an a la braise dish; when nearly done, thicken it with wheat flour and serve it up hot.

FRIED OYSTERS.

Take 100 oysters, dry them in a coarse towel; beat very light the yolk of 4 eggs; add some bread crumbs or powdered biscuit, pepper, salt and a little mace; stir these well together, and dip your oysters into the mixture; fry them in boiling butter till they become a light brown. Corn meal may be substituted for the bread or biscuit.

TO STEW OYSTERS.

To 1 peck of oysters, put ½ pound of butter; let the oysters boil until they look plump: then add wine and thickening to your taste. When you put them in the tureen grate a little nutmeg on the top.

STEWED OYSTERS.

Put 1 quart of oysters with their liquor into a chopping dish or stew pan; crumble in a slice of stale bread, tablespoonful of butter, pepper and salt to your taste; stew from ten to fifteen minutes. The addition of a little celery cut up is a great improvement.

EPICUREAN OYSTERS.

Take 3 tablespoonfuls of butter, one of strong, dry mustard; put them in a chopping dish; add pepper and salt; when they commence boiling put in one-half pint of oysters without the liquor; have a hot dish in readiness. Take out the oysters with a fork when cooked, and continue to replace them until all are done.

SCOLLOPED OYSTERS.

Toast several slices of bread quite brown, and butter them on both sides; take a baking dish and put the toast around the sides; pour the oysters into the dish and season to your taste, with butter, pepper and salt; adding mace or cloves; crumb bread on the top of the oysters, and bake with quick heat for 15 minutes.

STEWED OYSTERS (VERY DELICATE).

Strain 3 pints of oysters through a cullender, and put in a clean saucepan 1 pint of rich cream; mix 1 teaspoonful of flour and 1 tablespoonful butter together; when mixed and the cream begins to heat, stir in the flour and butter slowly; let it simmer for a few minutes, then add the oysters; cook them ten minutes and dish hot for table.

OYSTER SAUSAGE.

Chop a pint of oysters with a quarter of a pound of veal and a quarter of a pound of suet, and some bread crumbs; add one egg and a little flour; season with salt and pepper; pound them in a mortar. Fry in small cakes.

COOKING CRABS.

Hard crabs should be cooked, immediately after they are caught, in an iron pot. To 2 dozen crabs add a pint of water, a pint of vinegar, 2 tablespoonfuls of salt; after the mixture boils, put the crabs in with a cloth over them, excluding the air. Let them boil from 12 to 15 minutes.

BAKED CLAMS.

Chop the clams fine, and mix with them 1 ounce of powdered mace and nutmeg; butter the sides and bottom of a large, deep dish, and cover the bottom with a layer of grated bread crumbs; over this scatter some very small bits of the best fresh butter; then add a thick layer of the chopped clams, next another layer of grated bread crumbs, and small bits of butter, then a layer of clams, and so on till the dish is full, finishing at the top with a layer of crumbs, butter and salt.

TO BATTER OYSTERS.

Make a light batter of 3 eggs, a dessertspoonful of butter, a little wheat flour, pepper and salt to the taste; drain the oysters from the liquor, and stir them into the batter; then drop the mixture from a ladle into boiling lard; and let the fritters cook until they are of a rich brown. This batter is sufficient for a quart of oysters.

PICKLED OYSTERS.

Be careful to save the liquor when opening the oysters, and scald them in it; take them out of the liquor, and to 1½ pints of it add 2 pints of vinegar, with allspice and mace; boil these ingredients together for ½ hour, and when cold pour it over the oysters.

STEWED OYSTERS (FRENCH).

Drain the juice from 100 first-rate oysters; pour the juice into a saucepan; let it slowly simmer; skim it very carefully; then rub the yolks of 3 hard boiled eggs and 1 large tablespoonful of flour well together, and stir this into the juice; add small pieces of butter, a teaspoonful of salt and 1 of allspice, a very little cayenne, and the juice of a large fresh lemon; let this simmer for 10 minutes, and just before dishing add the oysters.

SCALLOPED OYSTERS.

Scald 1 quart of oysters in their own liquor, and drain them; butter a pan, sprinkle powdered bread crumbs or crackers well over the bottom and sides; put a layer of oysters, then of bread crumbs; next, small pieces of butter, a few whole allspice and pepper corns, a very little mace; and so on, until the pan is full; cover last with crumbs; add small glass of cooking Maderia. Bake ½ hour.

OYSTER PIE.

Put a rich puff paste, and lay oysters over the bottom of the dish; boil some eggs hard, and put 2 or 3 pieces with butter, mace, salt and pepper; shake in a little flour; then more oysters and eggs, till the dish is full; cover with a crust and bake.

FRIED OYSTERS.

Wash them clean; beat up an egg; dip each oyster into the egg, and roll it in sifted cracker; and fry in butter.

FRIED OYSTERS.

Choose the largest and finest oysters; beat the yolks of 3 or 4 eggs; and mix with them grated bread and a small quantity of grated nutmeg, mace, and a little salt; having stirred this batter well, dip the oysters into it; and fry them in lard, till they are of a light brown color; take care not to do them too much. Serve them up hot.

SCALLOPED OYSTERS.

Take the oysters from their liquor; place them in the bottom of a dish or pan; cover them with bread crumbs, butter, pepper and salt; then add another layer of oysters, then the bread crumbs, etc; continue this till the dish is full; cover the top either with grated crackers or small champion biscuit. Bake about 30 minutes; and serve with slices of ham.

SHRIMP PIE.

Have a large plate of picked shrimp; then take 2 large slices of bread, cut off the crust, and make the crumb into a paste with 2 glasses of wine and 1 large spoonful of butter, add as much pepper, salt, nutmeg and mace, as you like; mix the shrimps with the bread, and bake in a dish or shells. The wine may be omitted and the bread grated instead.

FISH.

FRENCH FISH.

Have ready a boiled fish (you can use the remains of a fish); pick all from the bones, and have ready the following sauces: Put in stewpan 1 ounce of flour, to which add, by degrees, a quart of milk, mixing it very smoothly; then add 2 small peeled onions, a little parsley, a bay leaf, a sprig of thyme, tied together, a little grated nutmeg, teaspoonful of salt, ditto of pepper; place over fire; stir in ¼ pound fresh butter, and pass it through a sieve; lay a little on the bottom of your dish; then a layer of the fish; season lightly with white pepper and salt; then another layer of the sauce, until the fish is used up; finishing with sauce.

BAKED FISH.

Take a large fish, weighing 5 pounds, or more; scue the sides, and brown in a frying pan with a little sweet lard; pound fine 24 or 30 cloves, a little mace, a tablespoonful of salt, a small teaspoonful of cayenne, 2 ditto of black pepper, 12 balls of butter about the size of a walnut, each rolled in flour, 2 handfuls of chopped onion, 1 ditto of parsley, 1 of bread crumbs; fill the fish and sew up; rub over the outside with egg, and cover with remainder of dressing; put some slices of pork in the pan (if it has not been browned first); put the fish on, and set in the oven till brown; then add ½ pint of water, and bake 2 hours; basting it; 15 minutes before taking up, add ½ pint red wine. A few oysters with their liquor will improve it; also shrimps or tomatoes, mushrooms and truffles.

TO STEW RED FISH.

Have the scales well taken from the fish, well washed and wiped dry, put the fish into the pan and half fry it; put 1 teaspoonful of mace, 1 of allspice, and ¼ of a spoonful of cloves, 1 onion, a handful of parsley; chop them very fine together; 1 teacup of wine, and as much water as you think sufficient for the gravy; 1 large spoonful of butter, add 3 of flour to it; rub the butter and flour well together, then add warm water to thin it, then add all the ingredients. When ready to stew the fish, put it on the strainer, and then in the kettle, pour the gravy over it, stew it half an hour; then dish it for the table.

BOILED TROUT.

Buy large fresh spots, clean very nicely, wash them well, sprinkle well with salt, boil them for 15 minutes; when done, send in on a drainer, with boiled parsley over them. Use melted butter and catsup as a dressing.

BROILED MACKEREL.

Soak a No. 1 salted mackerel over night, and wipe it dry in the morning; have ready some clear, bright coals, heat and grease the gridiron, and lay the mackerel on it with the flesh side down; when cooked turn it, by placing a dish on it, then slip the skin side on the gridiron. Butter it and serve up hot.

FRIED COD FISH.

Cut the fresh cod into slices 1 inch in thickness, and dry it in a towel; have ready bread crumbs, and the yolk of an egg well beaten; salt and pepper the fish; dip each slice first in the egg and then in the bread crumbs; prepare boiling lard and lay them into it and fry till a nice brown; drain off all the fat from each slice and serve hot.

TO BOIL SALMON.

Put it in a cloth, and boil a piece of 8 lbs. 1 hour. Lobster, or parsley sauce, to eat with it, is very nice.

TO ROAST A FISH.

Clean very carefully, trim the tail and fins, but do not cut them off; stuff the fish with force meat, or only a piece of butter rolled in flour, with a little pepper, salt and marjoram. Tie a string around the fish, put some water in the pan, and raise the fish from it, put some pounded and sifted crackers over, salt it, and baste it often with butter; add a very little onion to the stuffing. For gravy, take what falls in the pan, add cloves and red wine. If it does not mix, put a little boiling water with it. If not rich enough, make it so by browning some flour and butter together and adding it to the gravy.

ROASTED SALMON.

Take a large piece of fine fresh salmon, cut from the middle of the fish, well cleaned and carefully scaled; wipe it dry in a clean coarse cloth; then dredge it with flour, put it on the spit, and place it before a clear bright fire. Baste it with fresh butter, and roast it well—seeing that it is thoroughly done to the bone. This mode of cooking salmon is very delightful. A salmon-trout may be roasted whole.

FRIED COD FISH.

Cut the fresh cod into slices about an inch in thickness; and dry it in a towel; have ready bread crumbs, and the yolk of an egg beaten; salt and pepper the dish; dip each slice first in the egg and then in the bread crumbs; have ready boiling lard; and lay them in to fry until a nice brown; drain off all the fat from each slice, and serve hot.

FLOUNDERS SAUTÉ.

Clean and trim the fish; dip them in a couple of eggs previously well beaten; put 6 tablespoonfuls of olive oil in a frying pan; place over the fire; when quite hot put in the fish; let it remain 5 minutes; turn over and fry the other side. This is a nice way to cook any flat fish.

COLD RED OR OTHER COLD FISH.

Set the cold fish away with some of the bones; put these bones on to stew, with onions and parsley cut up; make a thickening of milk, or cream, flour, the yolks of 1 or 2 eggs, pepper and salt; when the onions are done, take out the bones, and cut up the fish, as picked crabs; put it into the above gravy, and stew till quite hot; then add the above thickening; (very nice).

FISH CAKE.

Take any kind of fish, and cut off the flesh; put the heads, bones, fins, etc., on the fire, with a little water; season with herbs, a little pepper and salt, and stew for gravy; then mince the flesh of the fish fine, and mix it with a third of bread, parsley, pepper and salt; add the white of an egg, and a small quantity of melted butter. Form it into the shape of a cake, cover it with raspings of bread, and fry it a pale brown.

FISH AU GRATIN.

Cut off the fins, and make an incision in the back; then butter a saucepan, and put into it a teaspoonful of finely chopped onions and a wineglassful of white wine; then place the fish in the pan, pouring over it 6 tablespoonfuls of cullis (see sauces), and sprinkle fine bread crumbs over it, and stick a few small pieces of butter about it; put it now in a moderate oven for 20 minutes or $\frac{1}{2}$ hour; carefully lift it into the dish in which it is to be served (it should be a silver or plated dish), pouring over the following sauce: Put into the saucepan 4 tablespoonfuls of stock; let it boil 5 minutes, stirring all the time; add the juice of a lemon, a teaspoonful of chopped mushrooms, 1 of minced parsley, and 1 of Worcestershire or Sultana sauce, a little sugar, cayenne pepper, and salt; beat all together, and pour over the fish; around which put some whole mushrooms and sliced lemon. Put it into the oven for $\frac{1}{4}$ of an hour; pass the salamander over it and serve very hot.—*J. A. R.*

BAKED FISH A LA CRÊME.

Boil the fish with salt in the water; flake off from the bones; boil 1 quart of cream (or milk), and pour hot on the yolks of 4 well beaten eggs; add a bunch of parsley, 1 onion, and salt; let it boil up and then strain; put it on the fire again, and when boiling, throw in 3 tablespoonfuls of flour, perfectly smooth, and add ¼ pound of butter; butter a deep dish, and put a layer of fish, then a layer of sauce, putting in fish and sauce, until the dish is full; finish off with bread crumbs. Bake ½ hour.

TO STEW FISH.

Clean the fish well; and the best method is to put it in a dish and pour vinegar over it; this will take off the slime, and the scales come off easily; put some butter into a frying pan and make it hot; then put the fish into the pan and let it remain over the fire for 5 minutes more; then take it out and put it into the kettle in which it is to be stewed; sprinkle some flour into the pan; put it over the fire for 3 minutes and pour it over the fish; then take ¼ pound of good butter, and roll it well in flour, and put it to the fish, adding 2 blades of mace, 10 cloves, a little cinnamon, red pepper, and salt, with water sufficient to keep it from burning; put it over a slow fire to stew; when half done, add a pint of port wine; when done, put in a dish, pour the gravy over it, and garnish with lemon or horse radish.

TO DRESS SHEEPHEAD.

Take a sheephead 18 or 20 inches long; put it into a pan; place that in a dutch oven; add ½ pint of tomato catsup, a large spoonful of butter, ½ pint of water, salt, black and red pepper to suit the taste; cook it over the fire and serve it up with the dressing. Smaller fish may be dressed in the same manner; proportioning the quantity to the size of the fish, and using, instead of a dutch oven, an a la braise or chafing dish.

TO BAKE RED SNAPPER.

Take a large fish, clean it, cut off the head, and draw the entrails through that part, as it must not be cut open. Then take the crumbs of stale bread, some onions and parsley (chopped), pepper and salt; with this seasoning stuff the fish. Put small lumps of butter all over the dish, pour in water to the depth of 2 inches, sprinkle over it a little flour, put the pan in a well heated oven, and bake an hour and a half.

BAKED RED FISH.

After the fish is well cleaned, take off the fins and tail; cut it into 4 or 5 parts; lay in a deep dish some lumps of butter, parsley and onions; chop all very fine with a little allspice, then a layer of fish, well seasoned with pepper. and salt, flour it, and continue this until the dish is full. Bake 1 hour.

TURBOT, HALIBUT AND OTHER FISH,
A LA CRÈME.

Boil with salt and separate from bones; boil 1 quart of cream, or milk, with the yolks of 4 eggs beaten in; add 1 onion and a bunch of parsley, and when boiled, strain the cream, heat again, and when boiling stir in 3 tablespoonfuls of flour, perfectly smooth; add $\frac{1}{4}$ lb. clarified butter (and a little more; if not made with cream); butter a deep dish and place first a layer of fish, then of sauce, until it is full, having a layer of sauce on top; cover with bread crumbs, and bake $\frac{1}{2}$ hour.

COURTBOUILLON OF RED FISH.

Sliced red fish of from 2 to 3 or 4 lbs. is best. Rub the fish well with butter and roll in flour; pour over it a large wine-glass of boiling vinegar. Place the fish in a stewpan with wine enough to cover it; to which add salt, pepper, a laurel

4

leaf or two, 2 slices of lemon. Let all simmer gently, remove the fish, strain the liquor and pour it over the fish, and serve with dish garnished with slices of lemon. For simple courtbouillon, use water instead of wine.

COURTBOUILLON OF ANY SORT OF FISH.

One pint of water, 1 pint of white wine, 2 ounces of butter, a large bunch of parsley, 3 leeks, 1 clove of garlic, a bunch of thyme, 2 bay leaves, a little basil, all tied together; some slices of onion and carrots, salt and pepper. Boil the fish, or rather let it simmer in the courtbouillon until done; then remove the fish, strain the liquor, place fish in the dish and pour liquor over it. Garnish the sides of dish with slices of lemon.

COURTBOUILLON OF PERCH.

Perch, 1½ ounces of butter, a little flour, 2 or 3 small onions, a small bunch of sweet herbs, and a ½ pint of wine. Scale and clean the fish, place them in a stewpan, with the butter rolled in flour, the sweet herbs minced fine, and the small onions; pour over them the white wine and let them simmer until cooked enough. Garnish sides of dish with thin slices of lemon.

BROILED FISH.

Cut some slices (about 1 inch thick), season with pepper and salt; wrap each piece in half a sheet of white paper, well buttered; twist the ends of the paper and broil them over a fire of bright coals for 10 minutes. Serve in the butter, with drawn butter or anchovy sauce.

SOUR STEW.

Put into a saucepan a tablespoonful of butter and a sliced onion; let it simmer; then put in the fish, sliced about an inch thick, add boiling water enough to cover the fish. Make a sauce of six eggs, four lemons, and a teaspoonful of flour; add this mixture to the stew when cool.

TO POT FISH.

Take 1 tablespoonful of salt, 1 of black pepper, and 1 of allspice, mix them together and rub the fish, after being well cleaned. Put them in a deep dish of a size to suit the fish, as the bottom should be covered; butter the dish before putting the fish in, with a bit of butter on the top of each fish. Mix walnut pickle vinegar, and if it is very sharp, add a little water after the dish is filled. Bake it in a slow oven.

SAUCES.

RAGOUT SOUSE.

Fry the souse of a light brown; make in another vessel a gravy of a large lump of butter rolled in flour, with a little boiling water; add to it beaten cloves and allspice, with 1 glass of Madeira wine. A dozen or two of oysters dressed with the souse adds much to its excellence.

ONION SAUCE.

Take 1 dozen onions, boil them till quite tender, with a little salt in the water; take them out and chop them fine, then stew them in a small quantity of sweet cream.

CELERY SAUCE.

Mash a bunch of celery; boil it soft in water; cut the sticks into pieces 2 inches long; make a sauce with a pint of milk, a spoonful of butter, flour, and salt to the taste; put the celery in, let it boil up once, and serve.

EGG SAUCE.

Melt 3 tablespoonfuls of butter and stir into it the yolks of 4 or 5 eggs, hard boiled, mashed very smooth, with a little cayenne pepper and salt.

WHITE SAUCE FOR VEAL OR LAMB.

Take $\frac{1}{2}$ a pint of milk, thicken it with flour, a small piece of butter, a blade of mace, and grated nutmeg.

SAUCE PIQUANTE.

Mix in a stewpan $\frac{1}{4}$ of a pint of vinegar, a very little pepper and thyme; boil away to half the quantity; add 5 tablespoonfuls of broth or clear gravy; let that again boil away to half, and add a little salt.

TOMATO SAUCE.

Scald the tomatoes and rub them through the sieve; to 1 pint of juice, add a spoonful of butter, a little salt and pepper, 2 eggs, well beaten, a small handful of bread crumbs, soaked in a teacup of milk, and 1 onion thinly sliced; stew over a slow fire for 1 or 2 hours.

MAYONNAISE.

The yolk of 1 raw egg, a teaspoonful of made mustard, and $\frac{1}{2}$ a teaspoonful of salt; the mustard and salt to be well rubbed together; then add the egg; pour on very slowly the sweet oil, rubbing hard all the time, till as much is made as is wanted; then add a tablespoonful of vinegar; when these ingredients are mixed, they should look perfectly smooth; if it curdles, add a little more mustard or a little vinegar. With shrimps or oysters, a little red pepper rubbed in is an improvement.

FISH SAUCE.

Take 1 pound of anchovies, 1 pint of port wine, $\frac{1}{2}$ pint of strong vinegar, 1 onion, a few cloves, a little allspice and whole pepper, a few blades of mace, a handful of thyme, green or dried, 1 large lemon, sliced with the skin; put all these ingredients into a saucepan, cover close, and stew gently until the anchovies are dissolved; then strain and bottle for use.

WHITE SAUCE.

Take $\frac{1}{2}$ a pint of milk; thicken it with a little flour, a piece of butter, a blade of mace, and grated nutmeg.

WHITE SAUCE FOR FOWLS.

Melt, in a teacupful of milk, 1 large spoonful of butter kneaded in flour; beat up the yolk of an egg with a teaspoonful of cream; stir it into the butter and heat it over the fire, stirring it constantly. Chopped parsley improves the sauce.

OYSTER SAUCE FOR BOILED FOWL OR TURKEY.

Put into a stewpan, with their liquor, 2 dozen large oysters and a little water; when it boils, take out the oysters with a silver spoon, and drain them on a hair sieve; let the liquor settle, and pour it off from the sediment; put it into a stewpan with 1 or 2 spoonfuls of flour, and 2 ounces of fresh butter; let it stand until the flour is a little fried, and then add the liquor, which must be made quite hot.

EGG SAUCE.

Melt 3 tablespoonfuls of butter, and stir into it the yolks of 5 hard boiled eggs; mash very smooth; add, also, a little cayenne pepper and salt.

EGG SAUCE.

Just before serving the chickens, take ½ a pint of the chicken water; stew into it a dessertspoonful of butter, a tablespoonful of flour, and a little salt; set it on the fire and let it thicken; stirring all the time; then add 4 or 6 hard boiled eggs, chopped fine.

OYSTER SAUCE.

When the oysters are opened, take care of all the liquor, and boil them in it; then take the oysters out and put to the liquor 3 or 4 blades of mace; add to it some melted butter, with thick cream, or rich milk; put in the oysters and give them a boil; when that is done take them off the fire.

A CREAM SAUCE FOR FILLET.

Pour a can of mushrooms through a cullender, to drain them well; put them in a clean wooden bowl, and with a vegetable mincer, mince them as fine as you can; add a small box of truffles, well drained and minced; drain the juice of ½ of a small lemon over them; put 2 large tablespoonfuls of butter in a saucepan; when quite hot, stir in 1 large tablespoon of flour; have a small teaspoon of eschallot or onion, minced extremely fine, which stir in the butter and flour; stir it all the time to keep from burning, and let it remain long enough on the fire to take a golden color; then pour slowly in ¾ of a teacup of rich sweet milk; let this mix thoroughly, stirring all the time, for about 5 minutes, to prevent lumping; add to the sauce the minced mushrooms and truffles, and let all simmer together for a few minutes; season this highly with cayenne pepper and salt; the sauce should be quite pasty before the mushrooms are added. This sauce should be made quite thick, and can be made early in the day; and when wanted, place the vessel in one of boiling water, to get well heated. Last of all, add the juice of the other ½ of the lemon.—*Mrs. R. Pritchard.*

BROWN ROUX.

Melt some butter very slowly; stir into it browned flour till it is a fine, even brown; add as much to the butter as will make it the thickness of paste, stirring well with a wooden spoon for fifteen or twenty minutes, till it is of a yellowish brown color. Great care must be taken, for if the fire is too hot, it will become bitter and unfit for use. When cold it should be thick enough to cut with a knife.

WHITE ROUX.

Melt some good butter slowly, and stir into it sifted flour till it is like thin, firm paste; stir it well over a slow fire for a quarter of an hour, (but do not let it brown). Pour into a jar and keep for use.

CULLIS.

Put 6 lbs. of lean veal, cut in slices, and 2 lbs. of lean ham into a stewpan, with 2 ounces butter, a handful of chopped mushrooms, 3 onions, one carrot, a bunch of sweet herbs, the rind of a lemon, and ½ teaspoon of mixed allspice, mace and cloves. Let it just brown at the bottom and add

4 quarts of stock; and let it boil 3 or 4 hours; strain it off, thicken with brown roux, and boil it well for ten minutes, stirring all the time; then pass through a tamise.

TOMATO SAUCE.

Peel and slice 12 tomatoes, picking out the seed; add 3 pounded crackers, and pepper and salt to your taste; stew twenty minutes.

SAUCE FLAMANDE.

Put 4 yolks of eggs beaten, juice of ½ a lemon, a little grated nutmeg (to season, not enough to be detected), a tablespoonful of vinegar, and a good sized piece of butter, into a saucepan; set it on a gentle fire, stir well, but do not let it boil.

SAUCE TARTAR.

Mash the yolk of a hard boiled egg; add the yolks of 2 raw ones, with salt and pepper; mix with a wooden spoon, dropping slowly a pint of oil, and moisten with tarragon vinegar (to taste), but keep it thick; then add a tablespoonful of chopped gherkins, ½ ditto of chopped capers, ditto of eschallots and parsley, 2 of French mustard, a very little cayenne pepper, and sugar, and more salt, if required.

VENISON SAUCE.

The trimmings of the venison (½ lb. of meat) to ½ pint of water; boil, with a tablespoonful of whole cloves, down to 1 pint; strain, and add ½ tumbler of currant jelly, ditto of claret, ⅛ lb. of butter and flour rubbed together, ½ tablespoon of ground cinnamon, or mace, a little black pepper, and salt, if your taste requires.

SALMI OF DUCKS, VENISON OR BIRDS.

Put into the saucepan 1 tablespoonful of butter, stirring in 2 tablespoonfuls of flour, letting it melt without browning; add a cup of soup broth, 2 whole leeks, carrots, a little thyme and parsley, pepper and salt. Let it boil for half an hour; withdraw the vegetables, put in the pieces of game, and let simmer until done; then add a cup of claret wine, and juice of ½ a lemon. Have ready, some fried pieces of bread cut into diamonds, lay them around the dish, put in the game in the middle, pour the sauce over the whole. Garnish the dish with slices of lemon. This amount of sauce will answer for two ducks.

CREAM SAUCE.

Boil 1½ pints of rich cream with 4 tablespoonfuls of powdered sugar, some powdered nutmeg, and a dozen bitter almonds, slightly broken up, or a dozen peach leaves; when boiled, take it off the fire and strain it. If it is to be eaten with boiled pudding or with dumplings, send it to table hot. But let it get cold, if you intend it as an accompaniment to fruit pies or tarts.

APPLE SAUCE FOR ROASTED GOOSE.

Pare, core, and slice some fine apples; put them into a saucepan, with enough water to keep them from burning; stew them till quite soft and tender; mash them to a paste; make them very sweet, adding butter and nutmeg. Be careful not to have the sauce *thin* and *watery*.

HOW TO MAKE CURRY.

Take an onion of medium size, peel and slice it into a saucepan, in which some butter is boiling (just sufficient in which to fry the onion); let the onion fry till it is of a nice light brown color. Next, add a little more than a teaspoonful of curry powder, and let this fry with the onions about half a minute, stirring all the time. Have a breakfast cupful of gravy, or good stock, and mix upon a plate about a teaspoonful of flour, with a small piece of butter; when quite smooth, incorporate this with the gravy or stock. Add this to the onion and curry powder, stirring all the

5

time. Then add one clove, a little Harvy or Worcestershire sauce, a little lemon peel (chopped fine) and juice, about a teaspoonful of chutney and ½ teaspoonful of anchovy sauce, a pinch of ground mace, and salt to taste. Let this sauce simmer on the fire for about two hours or longer, and then add about a dessertspoonful of milk or cream (after this is added it must not boil, or it will curdle). Have the meat, chicken, or vegetable that is to be curried, ready cooked and cut into convenient pieces, put it into the curry sauce for about five minutes, heat thoroughly, but do not boil, and serve with rice, boiled, in a separate dish, and handed around before the curry. Chutney may be taken with the curry.

FOWL.

WILD DUCKS OR TEAL.

You must be particular in not roasting these birds too much; a duck, about 15 minutes with a good fire; baste them very frequently. A teal will, of course, take less time, but the fire and motion of the spit must be attended to; and when you dish it, draw the knife four times down the breast; have ready, a little hot butter, the juice of a lemon, cayenne pepper, a little dust of sugar, a glass of port wine; pour it hot over the ducks.

ROAST FOWLS.

If nicely trussed, make a stuffing of butter and some pepper; dry up the butter with a few bread crumbs; baste it well; add flour and salt before you take it from the fire. It is very nice to stuff the fowl with good sausage meat, truffles, or chestnuts.

ROAST FOWL.

Clean the fowl thoroughly; roast it 20 minutes, unless a very fine one; it will then take 3 quarters of an hour; serve with bread sauce, or parsley and butter; egg sauce is sometimes sent to table with it. If a small lump of butter, well covered with black pepper, is placed within the fowl previous to roasting, it will be found to improve the fowl, by removing the dryness which is met with in the back and side bones.

TO STEW PARTRIDGES.

After trussing the partridges, stuff them with force meat; then rub a lump of butter in pepper, salt, and powdered mace, and put it into the bodies; sew them up, and after dredging them with fine flour, fry them in butter, of a light brown; then put them in a stewpan with gravy sufficient to cover them; 2 spoonfuls of lemon pickle or anchovy, a quarter of a lemon sliced, and a sprig of sweet marjoram; cover them closely, and stew them for about ½ hour. If necessary, thicken the gravy.

BROWN FRICASEE.

The beef or veal is to be chopped very fine; take out all the stringy parts; season it with pepper, salt and a little ginger; beat up 4 eggs very light; a large plateful of stale bread; make them in balls; roll them in flour and fry them; then take 2 tablespoonfuls of flour, mixed with cold water; put some seasoning and hot water into the frying pan; after it has boiled throw it over the balls and let it stew about 15 minutes before dishing them in tomato or walnut catsup. To the 4 eggs, take 3 lbs. of veal and full ⅓ of bread.

STEWED DUCKS.

Truss the ducks and stuff them with bread, butter and onions; place then with lard in a frying pan; have prepared in an iron pot slips of bacon, giblets, water, pepper, salt, a little mace or cloves, if you like it; put in the ducks and let them stew gently, but constantly, for 2 hours; then add lemon juice or lemon pickle. Flour the ducks each time that you turn them in the pot. Thicken with butter rolled in flour. This receipt is for large ducks; those not grown require less time.

STEWED PIGEONS.

Season the pigeons with salt, pepper, cloves, mace and sweet herbs; wrap this seasoning up in a piece of butter and put in and stuff them; tie up the neck and vent, and half roast them; then put them in the saucepan, with 1 quart of good gravy, a little white wine, some picked mushrooms, pepper corns, a slice of onion, and some pickled oysters; stew all together till sufficiently done; then thicken it with butter and the yolk of 1 egg; garnish with lemons.

STEWED RABBITS OR DUCKS.

Take 2 rabbits, put 2 or 3 onions, 1 bunch of parsley, in with them, and half boil them and cut them in pieces, as for a fricasee; take the onions, parsley and the liver, cut it small; take 6 spoonfuls of claret wine, 3 of vinegar, and dissolve 2 or 3 anchovies into it; put all this in the stewpan with ¼ lb. of fresh butter worked up with flour; thicken it and serve it up. Ducks done in the same way are very nice.

DUCKS A LA MODE.

Take 2 fine ducks, cut them into quarters, fry them in butter a little brown; pour off all the fat and throw a little flour over them; add ½ pint of good gravy, ¼ of a pint of red wine, 2 eschallots, 1 anchovy and a few sweet herbs; cover them close; let them stew 15 minutes; take out the herbs; skim off the grease and let the sauce be as thick as cream; send it to table; garnish it with lemon.

ROAST DUCKS.

Ducks should be well plucked without tearing the skin, all the plugs being removed, clean the inside thoroughly with a little warm water, and stuff them with bread and butter, onion, sage, pepper and salt; roast them before a brisk fire, but not too close; baste very frequently; they will take from ½ hour to 1 hour, much depends on the age and size; when the breast plumps, they will be done; serve them with a rich brown gravy.

BOILED DUCKS.

Clean and pluck them, let the skin be preserved from rents; salt them for 30 hours previous to cooking; flour a clean white cloth and boil them in it. A moderate sized duck will take about 1 hour's boiling; make a rich onion sauce with milk, and send it to table with the duck. When the duck is boiled fresh it may be stuffed as for roasting and served with the same description of gravy.

TO HASH DUCKS.

The same receipt may be followed as for hashing fowl and game, with the exception that it will not require as much time to stew.

TO STEW DUCKS.

There is a difference between a stewed duck and stewed duck, and it is not the *a* alone; in the one case the duck is stewed whole, and in the other in pieces. To stew a duck, or ducks, they should be roasted for 20 minutes, and then placed in a stewpan with an onion, cut in slices, a little sage and mint and sweet herbs chopped fine, and about a pint of good beef gravy, seasoned with pepper and salt; let it stew gently for 20 minutes; take out the duck carefully and keep it warm; strain the gravy; pour it into a clean stewpan, and add to it, when well heated, the duck and a quart of green peas; let it simmer for a half hour; then add a little flour and butter, a glass of port wine, and send to table, with the peas in the same dish as the duck.

STEWED DUCK.

The ducks should be cut into joints and laid into a stewpan with a pint of good gravy; let it come to a boil; as the scum rises, remove it; season with salt and cayenne; let it stew gently three-quarters of an hour; mix smoothly 2 teaspoonfuls of fine ground rice with a glass of port wine; stir it into the gravy; let it have 7 or 8 minutes to amalgamate with the gravy; dish and send it to table very hot.

BATTERED CHICKEN.

Make a light batter with 3 eggs, a small tablespoonful of butter, a little wheat flour, and salt to the taste; joint the chicken, and put them into the batter; grease the frying pan, throw the mixture of chicken and batter into it and fry a good brown. This quantity of batter will suffice for one pair of chickens.

FRIED CHICKEN.

Having cut up a pair of young chickens, lay them in a pan of cold water to extract the blood; wipe them dry; season with pepper and salt, dredge them with flour, and fry them in lard; both sides should be of a rich brown; take them out of the pan and keep them near the fire; skim carefully the gravy in which the chickens have been fried, mix it with ½ pint of cream; season with a little mace, pepper and salt, adding some parsley.

TO MAKE A FRENCH PILAU.

Boil a pair of fowls; when done, take them out and put the rice in the same water, first taking out some of the liquor; when the rice is done, butter it well, cover the bottom of the dish with ½ of it, then put the fowls on it and add the remainder of the liquor; cover the fowls with the other ½ of the rice, make it smooth, and spread over it the yolks of 2 eggs, well beaten; bake in a moderate oven.

POULET A LA EUGENIE.

Prepare 1 or 2 chickens for boiling; cover well with water and put in a small piece of pork; boil until the chicken falls from the bone; select the white meat, and mince or mash in a mortar until it becomes paste; put in a skillet; place this where it will keep warm, and add nearly as much butter as you have chicken, a little salt, pepper, mace and celery seed, if you choose; boil a small, delicate onion, chopped fine; and mix through it when simmered; let it become quite firm and cold before pressing into jelly jars; it will keep some days in a cool place, and is a good relish for lunch or tea.

WHITE FRICASEE OF CHICKEN.

Cut a pair of chickens, wash the pieces through 2 or 3 waters; lay them in a large pan; sprinkle slightly with salt and fill the pan with boiling water; cover and let the chicken stand in it half an hour; then put them into a stew-pan; add a few blades of mace, and pepper corns (whole), a handful of celery, split thin and chopped fine, and a small onion sliced; pour on cold water and milk in equal quantities to cover the chicken; cover the pan and let them stew until quite done and tender; prepare gravy in a small saucepan by mixing 2 teaspoons of flour with enough cold water to make a batter, stir it quite smooth; add gradually ½ pint boiling milk, ¼ lb. fresh butter cut in pieces; set on the fire until it comes to a boil and the butter is perfectly mixed; then take off, and while hot, stir in a glass of madeira or sherry, a little nutmeg (very little), 4 tablespoons of rich cream; lastly, take chickens out of saucepan, pour off the liquor, return the chickens and pour the gravy over them; cover the pan closely and set it over a kettle of boiling water for 10 minutes; serve very hot.

BOILED FOWLS.

Flour a white cloth and put the fowls in cold water; let them simmer for ¾ of an hour; serve with parsley and butter, or oysters or celery sauce.

COLD FOWLS.

When cold fowl is cut up and served for the table, let it be done with a short knife, and with precision; the slices from the breast should be well cut and the whole arranged tastefully in the center of the dish, a layer of ham and tongue in alternate pieces may be laid around the dish, and handsome sprigs of parsley may garnish the dish.

POTTED PIGEONS.

First, wash them. For dressing, bread crumbs, plenty of sweet marjoram, a little salt, pepper, 1 egg, and either chopped pork, or piece of butter (very little); stuff and lay on their backs in a pan, put pork about an inch in size on breast of each; throw over them a very little salt, and powdered cloves; cover all thick with flour from dredging box; pour boiling water over the breasts, and cook about 2 hours, basting frequently.

TO DRESS A GOOSE.

Beat 2 eggs until very light; add a pint of cold water, and stir in flour until you have a stiff batter; when quite smooth add salt and pepper to taste, 2 good sized onions, sage, cloves, 2 tablespoons of thyme, chopped fine; put a large spoonful of lard and one of butter into pan, and when boiling stir in the batter, and continue to stir until it becomes dry and light. After stuffing, put the goose in oven with a slice of fat bacon, and pint of water; baste with flour as it cooks, adding some water (boiling is best) when necessary. If not a mere gosling, it should be first parboiled, more or less, as may be necessary.

BROILED CHICKENS.

Split a pair of chickens down the back; wipe the inside, season with pepper and salt; prepare some beaten yolks of eggs and bread crumbs; dip the outside of the chickens in the batter; put them on a gridiron (nicely washed) on a bed of bright coals. Lay the chickens on the gridiron, with the inside down, broiling them 20 minutes; just before taking them from the fire, add bits of butter. None but fine plump chickens are worth broiling.

COQUILLES DE VOLAILLE.

Have a good full grown chicken, which you boil until tender. Pull the meat from the chicken in flakes after skinning it; with a sharp knife cut the meat in square pieces about the size of the end of your thumb. Take one full cup of the liquor in which the chicken was boiled, mince a green onion or a piece of an old one very fine, enough to make about a teaspoonful, also a teaspoonful of parsley minced very fine. Put the broth on to boil, and put in the onion

6

and parsley.   When the broth comes to a boil, have a large
tablespoon of flour rubbed in 2 tablespoons of butter,   Put
a little of the boiling broth on the flour and butter and stir
in the broth, and gradually ½ pint of rich sweet milk, or
what is better, sweet cream.   To the chicken add a box of
mushrooms sliced thin; and, if you do not care for the ex-
pense, a small box of truffles cut up.   Season with cayenne
pepper and salt; stir this in the sauce long enough to heat
well.   Take from the fire, and when cold add a ½ cup of
sweet cream, another tablespoon of butter, and a claret glass
of best sherry wine.   This preparation of chicken should be
highly seasoned.   Fill the shells, and bake in a hot oven
15 or 20 minutes, and serve immediately.

COQUILLES DE VOLAILLE.

For one chicken, medium size (which makes a small
quantity).   Boil the chicken; cut in little pieces, hash up
with the chicken ½ can of mushrooms, ½ can of truffles (if
preferred, one or the other of these can be omitted), season
with salt, black and red pepper.   In a saucepan, throw a
tablespoonful of flour, and one of butter, and stir together
until they are thoroughly mixed.   Pour in one cupful of
milk, stirring all the while.   This sauce is then poured on
the chicken, and the water in which the chicken was boiled
added, until the whole is of the proper consistency.   It is
then put in the shells, brown bread crumbs grated over each,
and a small lump of butter the size of a pecan in the middle of each.   Put in the oven for a little while, and serve
while hot.

COQUILLES DE VOLAILLE.

Boil a large fowl till tender; when cold, cut into small
pieces.   Set that aside.   Mix well a heaping tablespoonful
of butter with 2 of flour.   When well mixed, put into a
stewpan.   Stir into it a tumblerful of the broth in which
the chicken has been boiled.   Season well with chopped

parsley, salt, cayenne pepper, a little eschallot, and a very little onion. Add a tumblerful of cream, a box of mushrooms, and a small can of truffles; then put in the chicken, and stir all well, and allow it to cook a little. Now add a wineglass of sherry. Put the mixture into shell, sprinkle bread crumbs over the top, and set in the oven to brown.

CROQUETTES—CHICKEN.

Boil a chicken tenderly; when cold, chop fine, put some of its liquor in pan with butter the size of a hen's egg, mix in a little flour, salt, red and black pepper, parsley, and small onion; add the minced chicken; and, when cold, shape, dip in egg with grated bread, and fry in lard.

CROQUETTES.

Of turkey, beef, chicken, or sweet bread, chop the meat very fine; add grated bread crumbs; season with a little grated lemon peel, salt, pepper, a very little nutmeg, and yolk of a hard boiled egg; moisten the whole with enough milk to make the ingredients adhere; form into cones, or pear-shaped balls; dip each into a batter of eggs, well beaten, and roll in bread crumbs, fry brown in butter, and serve with fried parsley. Croquettes are improved by adding chopped mushrooms or truffles.

SWEET BREADS.

Boil ten minutes to blanch, then throw them into cold water, skim and lard them; roll in grated bread crumbs, pepper and salt, and cook in boiling lard till quite tender; lay them in a dish and pour over the following gravy: a cup of hot water, a large wineglass of sherry, a little nutmeg and lemon juice, and thicken with a tablespoonful of flour.

TO ROAST A TURKEY.

Wash the turkey nicely; prepare the stuffing with bread crumbs, sweet herbs, lemon peel, nutmeg, pepper, salt, and beaten yolk of egg, with sufficient butter to moisten it, and a little old ham, cut very fine. Stuff the craw of the turkey with the force meat, of which there will be enough made to form into balls for frying, to garnish the dish, dredge it with flour, and roast it before a clear, brisk fire, basting it with cold lard; towards the last, put the turkey nearer the fire and dredge it lightly with flour, and baste it with butter. The time for roasting depends on the size of the turkey. Make the gravy of the giblets cut in pieces, seasoned and stewed for one hour, in very little water; thicken it with a spoonful of brown flour, and stir into it the native gravy, after having skimmed the grease from it.

MEATS.

BROILED VENISON.

Cut the slices medium size; thickly butter them, sprinkle with black pepper and a little salt, place the slices on a gridiron and broil them in a hurry. In this way you will preserve the flavor of the venison without drying, which is frequently done by allowing the meat to remain too long on the fire; send it to the table very hot, with a little melted butter over it. This is a palatable dish for breakfast or tea. Mutton or veal dressed in the same way is very nice.

STEWED VENISON.

Have the chafing dish ready; the slices of venison nicely cut, proper thickness, and between the slices, as you place them in the dish, put bits of good butter, pepper, mustard, salt, a little cayenne pepper and claret wine; let it stew 10 or 15 minutes. Mutton or cold roast beef cooked in this way is very nice. Put sufficient currant jelly to make it palatably sweet.

VENISON STEAK.

This is a delicious appetizer for breakfast. Cook it as beefsteak, washing it nicely, draining the water from it; butter it very thoroughly, sprinkle with pepper and salt, and cook it in a hurry; serve it very hot.

VENISON (THE HAUNCH).

Venison should always hang a considerable length of time; the delicacy of its flavor is obtained by hanging only. If it be cooked while fresh it will not equal, in any respect, a haunch of mutton. The haunch of venison when about to be roasted, should be washed in warm milk and water, and dried with a clean cloth; if it has hung very long, and the skin smells musty, it will be the safest plan to remove the skin and wrap the whole of the haunch in paper, well greased with fresh butter; during the time it is at the fire do not be afraid of basting it too much; it will require all the cook is likely to give it; if it be a buck haunch and large, it will take nearly 4 hours; if small, 3½ will answer; if a doe haunch, 3¼ hours will be enough. Remove the paper when it is done enough; sift flour over it to produce a froth; dish it, and serve; let there be nothing with it in the dish; but the gravy should be sent to the table in a dish with currant jelly.

COTELETTES EN CHEVIEUIL.
(CUTLETS, VENISON STYLE.)

Mutton chops, rather thick, should be soaked for 3 days in vinegar with slices of onions and eschallots; heat a glassful of this mixture with a glass of clear broth; add the cutlets and let them cook on a slow fire for ¼ hour; make a roux (brown butter); add the cutlets with their sauce, let them come to a boil; then serve with fresh toast.

BŒUF ROULÉ.
(ROLLED BEEF.)

A cut of beef, a cut of veal of same weight, ½ pound of sausage; add a piece of bread size of an egg steeped in milk; then a whole egg; sprinkle both cuts with pepper and salt, and spread on the sausage; roll each cut, leaving the ends thinner than the middle; then tie with a string; brown the cuts in butter till they have taken a good color; moisten with broth and let them cook for 1½ hours; thicken the sauce with corn starch; add juice of lemon, a few mushrooms and chopped parsley.

FOIE DE VEAU EN SAUTÉ.
(DAUBE OF VEAL LOIN.)

The livers to be well larded; place them in a stewpan with lard, onions, carrots, pepper, salt, a bunch of vegetables and a glass of white wine; cook for 3 hours. By adding a calf's foot the livers will, when cold, form jelly.

PATÉ DE VEAU.

(VEAL PIE.)

Take rouelle of veal and ½ pound of very fresh lard to 2 pounds of beef; add spices, bread crumbs, steeped in broth, 3 eggs, whites and yolks to be well beaten; with these fill in a fire-proof earthen pot, close well and let bake; make a jelly of calf's foot, scraps of meat and carrots, to garnish the paté when done.

TERRINE DE BŒUF.

(POTTED BEEF.)

Chop slices of beef with beef suet (gros de bœuf), add spices, mushroons, chopped, 4 yolks of eggs, and a glass of brandy; line the bottom of an earthen dish with strips of lard and cover top with same; bake for 3 hours.

STUFFED HAM.

Soak the ham in water for two days and nights; then begin at the back, and with a sharp knife cut down to the bone, cutting the meat from each side, until it is entirely loosened; then pull it out; have ready the stuffing, fill up the cavity with it, and sew the ham with a coarse needle and strong thread; take a strip of cotton about a yard in width, bind it tightly around the ham so as to preserve its shape, then boil it slowly for about 3 or 4 hours; when it is boiled let it remain in the bandage until perfectly cold; then cover it with sugar and bake; decorate to taste.

STUFFING FOR THE HAM.

One pound of pecans, 1 dozen eggs, 1 can of mushrooms, 5 or six truffles, some ham chopped very fine, 1 ounce of mustard seed, and six large cucumber pickles. This must all be minced very fine before putting into the ham. Roasted chestnuts can be substituted for pecans if preferred.

Season this mixture with pepper, a little allspice, cloves, parsley, a little onion, and very little salt.

BOUILLÉ.

Put a rump of beef in cold water, take off the scum as it rises, and when it begins to boil, pour in a little cold water to clear it; when the scum is all taken off, put it to stew gently; season with salt, cloves, pepper, 4 onions, the same number of carrots and turnips, with 1 head of celery; when they are done, take all out to enrich the soup; make the glazing while the bouillé is doing, as follows: stew a piece of veal with a little bacon, and the same kinds of vegetables that were put in the bouillé; when it is sufficiently done, strain off the broth and reduce it to the consistency of glazing and put it over the bouillé at the moment it is served up; for the gravy, a piece of butter the size of an egg, worked up in flour, 3 pickled cucumbers cut up with capers and anchovies; the whole put in the pan in which the glazing is made, with a little water, stir it up, and the moment it boils, take it off and put it in a sauce-boat.

STEWED RUMP OF BEEF.

Put it on the fire, first rubbing with black and cayenne pepper, salt and orange peel, 2 bay leaves, 18 cloves; let it stew until the water is exhausted and the beef brown; put to it boiling water sufficient for the gravy; take off the fat clean, and before dishing it, put in two wineglasses of Madeira wine, and 1 glass of walnut catsup; turn the beef in the gravy and take off the fat a second time before you dish.

BEEFSTEAK PIE.

To 3 pounds of beefsteak put 1 gill of water, 1 gill of catsup, 5 eggs boiled hard and cut in pieces; 1 quart of fine oysters should be added, with salt, nutmeg, and pepper to taste.

POTTED BEEF.

Cut up the head (the tongue being taken out to salt) and after washing, put it in soak for about 1 hour; then put it in a middle-sized pot filled with water, and let it stew till perfectly soft; take out the bones and let it stew again till sufficiently soft to beat in a mortar to a perfect jelly; taking out the gristly part; season it to your taste with pepper and salt; when cold, cover it all over with melted butter to exclude the air. The brains must not be taken out, as they serve to enrich the dish very much.

BEEF A LA DAUB.

Get a fat steak, wash, salt, and pepper it, and lard it all over; pierce it through with a knife and slip in thin pieces of raw middling; flour it and brown it well in a spider; put 1 pint of water, after the meat is well browned, with some parsley, thyme, bay leaves, and 1 dozen onions, peeled, and a little flour to thicken the gravy, a dessertspoonful of allspice; stew the whole together for about 4 hours. You may add a little garlic to the gravy if you please.

BEEF STEAKS.

Cut steaks from the rump, not more than ½ an inch in thickness; pepper and salt them; broil them slightly both sides. Take them off the gridiron and lay them in a spider or small oven; put a layer of onions between each steak; cover them close, and let them stew very gently till the meat is sufficiently done; then take out the steaks and cover them close; tilt the gravy to the side of the vessel, take off the fat, and stir in a lump of butter rolled in a very little flour. Add as much brown sugar as will make the gravy a proper color.

BEEF STEWED WITH OYSTERS.

Prepare 2 or 3 lbs. of the best beef, by trimming off the fat and removing the bone. Lay in the bottom of the stew-

7

pan a few bits of fresh butter, rolled in flour. Then put in the meat, and sprinkle a little pepper over each piece. Have ready a quart of large, fresh oysters; strain the liquor to clear it from bits of the shell, and pour it over the meat in the stewpan. Stew the meat in the oyster liquor till it is thoroughly cooked, skimming it well, and keeping it covered, except when skimming. Then add grated nutmeg and a few blades of mace. Lastly, put in the oysters and let them remain in just long enough to plump, which will be in a few minutes. When all is done, serve up the whole in one dish, and send very hot to the table.

IRISH STEW.

Cut a square, thick piece of beef from the round or sirloin, and trim off the fat. Put it into a stewpan with water enough to cover it, and season it slightly with salt and pepper; let it stew slowly till tender all through; then add potatoes, being first pared and cut into quarters.

STEWED SMOKED BEEF.

Chip it very thin; put it into a skillet, with fresh butter, pepper, and 2 or 3 beaten yolks of eggs. Let it stew till the beef is crisp and curled up.

BEEF PATTIES.

A nice way of disposing of underdone roast beef is to mince all the lean, and a very little of the fat; season it with cayenne and powdered nutmeg, or mace, or else chopped sweet herbs; if you have a fancy for mushroom gravy, moisten the meat with that; make a nice paste and cut it into small circular sheets, rolled out not very thin; cover $\frac{1}{2}$ of each sheet of paste with the minced beef (not too near the edge), and fold over the other $\frac{1}{2}$ so as to form a half-moon; then crimp them with a sharp knife; lay the patties in square baking pans, prick them with a fork and bake them brown. Cold veal minced with cold ham or tongue, makes very nice patties, also cold chicken or turkey made in balls, and fried in lard.

POTATO BEEF.

Boil some potatoes till well done all through; peel them, put them into a large pan, and mash them smoothly, adding, as you proceed, some milk and 1 or more beaten eggs, well mixed, to the potatoes; rub the bottom of a white pudding dish with nice butter, or some drippings of cold beef, and cover it with a thick layer of mashed potatoes; next, put in thin slices of beef (without the fat), enough to cover the potatoes; then a layer of mashed potatoes, then beef, then potatoes, till the dish is full, heaping them up in the centre; bake it in an oven.

COLD BRISKET OF BEEF.

Cut brisket from the bones, wash and lay in a large dish; cover well with salt, pepper and a little saltpetre; then cover to stand several days, as the weather will permit; next, wipe off the dressing, place on a clean dish, powder mace and cloves, and allspice together, and spread thickly over the beef; then roll it over and over and tie up well; lastly, sew up tightly in a cloth and boil slowly all day; serve cold.

SPICED BEEF.

A round of beef of 10 pounds, 1 teaspoonful of saltpetre, 1 tablespoonful of brown sugar to stand in it about 2 days; then rub in a slop-bowl full of salt, and let stand 10 days, turning it every day; sprinkle over about a spoonful of all-spice; cut salt pork in strips size of your finger, and have them well dipped in ground allspice; gash the beef with a knife and stuff in thick as you please on both sides; put in a large kettle, cover well with water and the juices from the meat; boil slowly about 6 hours, when cold turn and trim.

VEAL PATÉ, TO SERVE COLD.

3 pounds of veal cutlets, chopped fine, with a good slice of salt pork, 2 eggs, broken in, after meat is well mixed, 6

crackers, (powdered fine), butter to size of a hen's egg, rubbed in a tablespoonful of salt, cayenne pepper, and sweet herbs to your taste; mix the whole thoroughly; make up like a loaf of bread; smooth over the top with butter melted in water, and bake in a moderate oven; when cold, cut in thin slices and serve.

PRESSED BEEF.

Salt a brisket of beef with salt and saltpetre, 5 days, then boil it gently till extremely tender; put it under a large weight, or in a cheese press, till perfectly cold. It is very nice for sandwiches.

COLD JELLY DAUBE.

Four lbs. round of beef; season well with salt, pepper, a little garlic, 1 bay leaf, and 1 clove. Lard well through and through; sprinkle with a tablespoonful of vinegar, and let it stand for 24 hours. Put the daube in a pot with a small piece of lard; cover with heavy cover on a slow fire, and let it smother for about 4 hours, until thoroughly done; then take off the cover, let it fry a light brown, then remove from the fire. In a separate pot, have 3 pigs feet and 3 calves feet boiling steadily till they leave the bone; (to be skimmed well at the first boil); add one carrot to boil about ½ hour, then slice in length and place at bottom of bowl when the daube is to be served. Break 2 eggs, whites and shells to be beaten together and boiled with jelly briskly, then strain through thick flannel or cloth. Mix the daube gravy with jelly; let it rest about ½ an hour, then pour slowly over the daube. Set it in a cold place, and when cold, take the lard from the top with a spoon, and with a round edge knife detach carefully the daube and turn into a round plate. To avoid breaking the jelly, place the plate on top of the bowl and turn it over.

RAVIOLÉ A LA AVEGNO.

Four lbs. round of beef to be larded, put in a pot with a

tablespoonful of lard; smother on a slow fire; when ready
to fry, sprinkle with a little flour; fry brown; add onions,
salt, and pepper to taste, and water enough to cook thoroughly; about ½ an hour before done, put in ¼ pound of dry
mushrooms. This daube is made for its gravy to the
raviolés.

FARE OR STUFFING.

Boil 2 bunches of spinach, chop fine with the white meat
of a roast or boiled chicken; add 1 calf's brain, previously
boiled and cleaned; stir the whole well in a bowl with 6
raw eggs, ¼ bottle of sweet oil, and season with salt and
pepper to taste; now take a pint of flour, add 2 eggs, with a
little water, making the paste as stiff as possible; roll out
flat and thin, put in a layer of the stuffing all the length of
the paste; double the paste over and cut lengthways with
a paste wheel, and also cut crossways, making small squares;
put squares of paste in a pot of boiling water, and boil
steadily for ½ hour; strain and put 1 layer of squares in
bottom of deep dish; sprinkle grated parmesan cheese; pour
some of the daube gravy with mushrooms, previously made
thin, another layer of squares, cheese and gravy, and so on;
serve hot.

CROQUETS OF COLD MEAT.

You may take any kind of boiled or roasted meat and
mix them together, so that it is clear of bones; make a hash
of it, and mix it with a piquante sauce; the mixture must
be very thick; if it be too thin, put a little bread with it;
add capers, mushrooms, salt, spices and fine herbs, boiled
together; let it get cold on a chopping board or dish; make
balls of it and press them flat; roll them in egg and grated
bread, and fry them in butter, brown on both sides.

TO MAKE SWEET BREADS.

Take 1 lb. of raw veal, and shred it very fine; add ½
lb. of marrow or beef suet, and season it with pepper and

salt; beat it very fine in a marble mortar, and make it the shape of sweet breads; beat well the yolk of an egg and dip these into it; fry them in a good deal of butter, and lay crumbs of bread between them; pour a little melted butter on them. Some put in the white of an egg, also, which makes them lighter. They must not be fried of a dark color.

FRIED LAMB.

Cut a loin of lamb into thin slices, beat them and lay them in water to take out the blood; then fry them in butter; make the sauce with butter, anchovies and lemon.

VEAL OLIVES.

Slice pieces of the fillet of veal ½ an inch thick and 8 or 10 inches wide and long; put them in a dish; sprinkle over them on 1 side, a little pepper, salt and mace, all finely pounded; roll tightly and tie them up separately; put them into a stewpan with a little water and butter, and simmer down to a brown gravy; when they are to be served, have ready some pounded biscuit or bread crumbs, which sprinkle over them after they are put into the dish; stew them 1 hour. Beef may be prepared in the same way.

SPICED BEEF.

Rub well on both sides of the round with 1 ounce of saltpetre, then rub in one pound of brown sugar, after which, rub all with salt, into which you will mix a tablespoonful of allspice, 2 of black pepper, 2 teaspoonfuls of cloves and 1 of mace; let it stand 30 days, turning it every other day, and bathing it with the liquor that runs from it.

CORN BEEF.

For rounds it is only necessary to rub them first with saltpetre and then with common salt; they will make their own brine, in which they should be turned every day; this will answer for all beef that is to be quickly used; a round of small beef only requires ten days in winter; it grows hard if kept longer; in warm weather less time suffices.

TO PICKLE TONGUES.

Take a beef's tongue, rub it with 1 pound of white salt, 1 ounce of saltpetre, ½ pound of coarse salt; rub it well and turn it every day in the pickle for 2 weeks; this pickle will do several tongues, only adding a little more white salt.

BOILED BEEF.

To have it very tender it should be boiled slowly, and the pot well skimmed; the meat should be well covered with water, so that the skim may be removed easily; when beef is very salt it should boil ¾ of an hour; then take it up, throw away the water it has boiled in, fill up the pot with fresh water, replace the beef and let it boil gently for 3 hours; the round is the most choice piece to boil, next, the H bone. Observe to take off all the scum as it rises.

A LA MODE BEEF.

A round of fresh beef weighing from 18 to 20 lbs., 1 lb. of the fat of bacon or corned pork, the marrow from the bone of the beef, a ¼ lb. of beef suet, chopped together, 2 bundles of herbs, parsley, thyme, small onions, etc., chopped fine, 2 large bunches of sweet marjoram, 2 bunches of sweet basil, 2 large nutmegs, ½ ounce of cloves beaten to a powder, ½ ounce of mace, 1 tablespoonful of salt, 2 glasses of Madeira wine. If the a la mode beef is to be eaten cold, prepare it 3 days before it is wanted. Take out the bone, fasten up the opening with skewers, and tie the meat all round with tape; rub it all over on both sides with salt; (a large round of beef will be more tender than a small one); chop the marrow and suet together; pound the spice; chop the herbs very fine; pick the pot marjoram and sweet basil clean from the stalks, and rub the leaves to a powder, making 4 tablespoonfuls of each; add the pepper and salt, and mix all together—all the ingredients that compose the seasoning; cut the fat of the bacon into pieces 2 inches long, with a sharp knife make deep incisions all over the round of beef and very near each other, put a little of the seasoning into each hole and a slip of bacon pressed down hard, covered with more seasoning, with a little wine in each hole; stuff both sides alike, put it in a deep baking dish, pour over it some wine, cover it, and let it stand till next morning; next day put a little water in the dish, set it in a covered oven, and bake or stew it for 12 hours, at least; let it remain all night in the oven, and it must be eaten hot at dinner the next day; when cold, ornament with parsley.

A COLD DISH FOR LUNCH.

Cut a hard boiled egg in thin slices, and place it in the middle of a bowl; put a layer of raw veal cut in thin slices, and sprinkled with a mixture of pepper, salt and herbs (such as parsley, thyme and sage). Place next very thin slices of bacon, and continue to put alternate layers of veal, seasoned with a little mace and of bacon, until the bowl is filled. Mash it down and tie a floured cloth over it very tight. Turn it down in a pot of hot water, and let it boil 2 hours. It is eaten cold.

HAM TOAST.

Grate some lean ham; mix with it the yolk of an egg, pepper it, and fry it in butter; pour on square bits of toast, and brown it with a salamander.

BOUILLÉ.

After boiling the bouillé in the soup, take it out, and make a sauce of flour and butter, and add either capers or parsley, as you prefer.

BEEF BALLS.

Mince very fine a piece of tender beef, fat and lean; mince also an onion, with some boiled parsley; add grated crumbs of bread, and season with pepper, salt, and nutmeg; mix the whole together; moisten with a beaten egg, roll it into balls, flour, and fry them.

BEEFSTEAK PIE.

Butter a deep dish, spread a thin paste over the bottom, sides and edges. Cut away from the beef all the bone, fat and gristle; cut the beef in thin pieces the size of the palm of your hand; beat it well with a rollingpin; put a layer of the beef, seasoned with pepper, salt, nutmeg, allspice, a little catsup and onion. Slice boiled Irish potatoes, and put a layer on the meat until the dish is filled; pour in a little water and butter. Bake 1 hour.

SPICED, OR SMOKED BEEF.

The most choice part for this purpose is the round. Wash the meat and dry well with a cloth. Grind to powder an equal quantity of cloves and mace, and having mixed them together, rub them well into the beef with your hand. The spice will be found a great improvement, both to the taste and smell of the meat. To 50 lbs. of meat allow 3 lbs. of fine salt, 1½ ounces of saltpetre, 2 lbs. of good brown sugar, and 2 quarts of molasses; mix these well together, boil and skim it for 20 minutes, and when no more scum rises, take it from the fire. Have the beef ready in a tub or barrel; pour the brine upon it; cover well with a thick cloth, looking at it frequently, and skimming off whatever may be floating on the top. Keep the beef in this pickle about 2 weeks, when it may be used as spiced beef. Take the meat from the pickle at the expiration of the above mentioned time; hang in a hogshead or smokehouse, and with a constant smoking for 6 days, you will have something nice.

TO STEW BEEF.

Wash the beef, rub salt over it, and put it in a pot, and just cover it with water, set it over a slow fire, and after it has stewed an hour, put in some potatoes, pared and cut in half, and some parsnips, scraped and split; let them stew with the beef till quite tender. Turn the meat several times in the pot. When all is done, serve up the meat and vegetables together, and the gravy in a boat, having first skimmed it.

TO PICKLE BEEF.

Salt the beef with the usual quantity of saltpetre and salt, and let it remain 2 days in the tub to drain off the bloody brine. Then put a brine made as follows: To 20 quarts of cold water, made salty enough to bear an egg, with common salt, put 3 lbs. of brown sugar, $\frac{1}{2}$ to 1 lb. of saltpetre, and 2 lbs. alum salt; spice them well together, and put in the beef; let it remain 4 or 5 weeks, according to size. Then hang it up to dry in a cool place, frequently rubbing it with wheat bran. It is then ready to smoke. Or you may head it in small barrels, where it will keep any length of time, if covered with brine, and kept close from the air. The latter way is preferable, as the meat is more juicy, and not exposed to the bug or worm, to which it is always liable if the fly can approach it. To guard it, a tub in which beef is salted, should always be covered with a coarse cloth tied closely around it.

BEEF HAM.

Rub a little common salt over a piece of beef of 20 lbs. weight; take out the bone, and in 1 or 2 days, rub well into the beef the following ingredients: 2 ounces of saltpetre, 4 ounces of brown sugar, 6 ounces of bag salt, 1 ounce of white pepper, 1 of cloves and nutmeg; strew over it $\frac{1}{2}$ lb. of common salt; let it remain 15 days, turning it daily; it is then hung up, or boiled, and allowed to stand till cold in the water in which it was boiled.

RONFOLK CURED HAMS.

To each ham, or piece of meat, use 1 tablespoonful of

saltpetre; rub it in thoroughly. Then rub with the common salt, in which pack it away; letting it remain for 6 weeks. Then take it out and wipe it very dry with a coarse towel, and rub the thick part and bone with black pepper; and smoke it for 6 or 8 weeks.

TO CURE BACON.

To every bushel of salt add 1 lb. of saltpetre, 1 lb. of brown sugar, and 2 ounces of common red pepper, coarsely beaten; this is a sufficient quantity for every 100 lbs. of meat, and in rubbing over the hams and shoulders, have mixed an additional quantity of saltpetre and pepper (say a handful of each), to stuff around the hocks. The meat must be very well rubbed with something harder than the hand; and in packing it away, must be completely covered with the former preparation. Let the hams remain in salt 4 weeks, the jowls and shoulders 3, and the middlings a fortnight. When they are ready to hang up, have them washed, and the hams and shoulders hung by the large end; the next day begin to smoke them, and make 1 good smoke every day, until the weather becomes mild, or about the last of March; afterwards it must be occasionally examined, and the most indifferent used first.

TO CURE BEEF.

To 10 gallons of water, add 10 quarts of salt, 1 lb. of brown sugar, and 1 of saltpetre; boil it until the froth is done rising, then take it off, and let it remain to get quite cold; pack the beef down close in a barrel, and cover it with brine, weight it down with rocks, but it must not be covered. This quantity of brine is sufficient for 1 quarter of beef.

FILLET DE BŒUF.

Remove, with a sharp bladed knife, every particle of the sinewy skin which covers the fillet, then lard it if you choose, (a thing the French never omit, though others generally dislike the mixture of pork and beef); place in an oblong tin pan, well buttered, lay the trimmings all around, with 2 bay leaves, 3 carrots, a little celery, faggot of parsley, a little thyme, 2 blades of mace, a couple of onions, with 2 cloves stuck in each, and 2 green ones, or eschallots; moisten with a ½ pint of broth, and a ½ bottle of wine (white), cover the whole with a piece of buttered paper, set in oven, and let it braize gently, moistening frequently with its own liquor, for about ¾ of an hour, then strain the gravy; have ready a nice brown sauce, into which you have cut some truffles and mushrooms, and put a wineglass of madeira; add the strained gravy, place the fillet on a dish, pour the sauce nicely all around, and serve.—N. B: A pound and a half of nice fillet makes a very nice family dish, if cut into small steaks, simply broiled, and placed in straight lines on dish, with this same sauce, made of the trimmings, poured around.

MINCED MEAT.

Take cold boiled beef, removing all bones and gristle, with a good proportion of cold boiled potatoes; chop them middling fine; fry 3 slices of salt pork in a spider; when the pork is brown, take it up, and put in the minced meat and potatoes. Let it cook 20 minutes. Take it up in a covered dish, with the slices of pork placed on the top of the dish.

CURING HAMS.

To each green ham of 18 lbs. 1 dessertspoonful of saltpetre and ¼ pound of brown sugar, applied to the fleshy side of the ham and about the hock; cover the fleshy side with fine salt ½ inch thick and pack away in tubs, to remain from 3 to 6 weeks, according to size; before smoking, rub off all the salt from the ham, and cover well with ground black pepper, particularly about the bone and hock; hang up and drain for 2 weeks; smoke with green wood 8 weeks, till the rind is brown.

APPLE PORK.

This preparation of apples for fresh pork is a great improvement. Take a fillet of pork, rub it over with a little salt and pepper; score the outside skin; take out the bone, and fill it with nice stewed apples, free of paring and cores, nicely seasoned with nutmeg and sugar, with bits of the rind of a lemon; then have ready some 2 dozen apples, pared, cored and cut in slices or quarters, sweetened well with sugar, and flavored with lemon (a little of the juice added will be an improvement); put the pork into a large pot or iron bake oven; fill up with the cut apples the space all around, adding just sufficient water to keep it from burning; stew or bake it for 3 hours; when done, serve it on a clean dish and send it very hot to the table.

HOW TO BOIL HAM.

A ham, if dry, should be soaked 12 hours in warm water; then put it on in cold water, and let it simmer and boil 5 or 6 hours, according to size.

PICKLED BEEF.

Sprinkle the beef with salt and let it steam 24 hours, where the bloody brine can run off; then pack into a barrel and cover with a pickle made as follows: to 16 gallons water, add 24 lbs. salt, 6 lbs. brown sugar, and 8 ounces saltpetre; let it stand till cold, then pour over; every 4 or 5 minutes boil over again and add a little of each ingredient.

PICKLED CHINE.

One gallon water, 1 quart salt, $\frac{1}{2}$ lb. sugar and $\frac{1}{4}$ lb. saltpetre. Also good for beef.

VEAL LOAF.

Three pounds of veal, 2 slices of salt pork, both chopped fine, 2 eggs, well beaten, 2 Boston crackers, rolled fine, 1 teaspoonful of salt, 2 teaspoonfuls of pepper, $\frac{1}{4}$ nutmeg; mix well; bake from $2\frac{1}{2}$ to 3 hours; bake well and serve cold sliced.

SPICED TONGUE.

Corn a fresh tongue 2 days, with salt and a little saltpetre mixed; then lay it on one side and bore holes with a steel used for knives, and stuff these with the following mixture: 1 tablespoonful each of allspice, cloves and nutmeg, 1 lemon peel, grated, 1 teaspoonful ginger, ditto of thyme, ditto of summer savory, a piece of lemon, 1 ounce of suet, chopped fine, salt and pepper to taste; place in a dish and under a heavy press for 24 hours; then add water to its own brine, and boil until it will skin; cut off its roots even, or nicely; begin at the small end to roll; bandage very tightly; stuff the paste into the middle, then boil 3 hours, and when done put under heavy press again.

BEWITCHED BEEF OR VEAL.

Three lbs. of lean beef or veal, ½ lb. of salt pork, ¼ teaspoon of cayenne pepper, ¼ teaspoon of black pepper, ½ teaspoon of cloves, allspice and mace, teacupful of bread crumbs, tablespoonful of butter, 3 eggs, ½ teaspoon of salt; chop the meat very fine; mix all of the ingredients thoroughly and steam in a mould for 3 hours.

POT AU FEU.

To each 1 lb. of beef, a cup of water; put in at the same time a carrot, a turnip and other greens; let simmer slowly; add salt to suit taste. This is for invalids.

ROLY POLY.

One lb. veal, 1 lb. lean beef, ½ lb. pork, ½ loaf bread, chopped fine, wet it and squeeze the water out; 1 chopped onion; then spice to taste; beat well into the mixture, 3 eggs; form into a roll, and bake 1½ hours, basting all the while with beef stock, the shin of veal, or calves' feet; set it away to cool, then cut in slices and serve.

DAUB.

You will require about 8 lbs. of a round of beef. Make

incisions in it; put strips of pork, a small piece of onion and garlic, salt and pepper; put'it away for several hours; then pour over it 1 pint of vinegar, and let it remain all night; in the morning let it brown a little; fill the saucepan full of water and cook it slowly 4 or 5 hours before taking it up; then add 1 ounce of gelatine dissolved in a little cold water; pour all in a mould; in the morning skim off the grease.

COLD HASH.

Boil a chicken until it is tender; take out all the bones; chop the meat fine; season with butter, pepper and salt; pour in enough of the liquid, the chicken was boiled in, to make it moist; simmer for a few moments; then put it in a mould to cool. It is excellent when sliced nicely.

VEGETABLES.

As a general rule, add a little salt to the water in which you cook the vegetables, with the exception of dried beans and peas.

BOILED POTATOES.

The easiest way to cook potatoes is to put them in just water enough to cover them, with the skins on, and to boil them constantly till done, then squeeze them in a dry cloth and send them to the table very hot. Potatoes should not remain soaking in the water without boiling, if you wish them mealy. (Irish.)

IRISH POTATO SNOW BALLS.

After boiled tender, drain off the water, and let the potatoes steam till they break to pieces; then mix them with the yolk of an egg, a small piece of butter, bread crumbs, with salt to the taste; fry them in good lard, (after forming them into balls) or brown them in an oven.

ROAST POTATOES.

Take potatoes of the same size, wash and dry them, put them in the oven of the stove or some convenient toaster; do not burn the outside before they are warmed through; roast large ones about 2 hours. They will roast quicker, if first parboiled.

BAKED IRISH POTATOES.

Boil soft 8 good sized Irish potatoes; mash them, and add 2 tablespoonfuls of butter, while hot; mix with it 1 pint of milk, add salt; put in a dish and bake ½ hour.

POTATOES IN CREAM.

Put into a stewpan a good sized piece of butter, a dessert-spoonful of flour, some salt, pepper and parsley, (chopped) to which add ½ pint of cream; put this sauce on the fire, stir it till it boils, slice the potatoes and throw into the sauce.

POTATO SNOW.

Use potatoes that are white, mealy and smooth; boil them carefully, and when done, peel them, pour off the water and set them on a trivet before the fire until they are quite dry and powdery; then rub them through a coarse wire sieve into the dish on which they are to go to table.

BOILED POTATOES.

Wash them, but do not pare them; put them in a pot with water enough to cover them an inch, and do not put on the lid; when the water is near boiling, pour it off and replace it with cold water, with a good portion of salt. The cold water sends the heat from the surface to the heart, and makes the potato mealy. Potatoes of a moderate size require ½ hour's boiling; large ones 1 hour; try them with a fork. When done pour off the water, cover the pot with a folded napkin and let them stand by the fire about ¼ hour to dry. Potatoes served with the skins on have a negligée appearance for the table.

FRIED POTATOES.

Use cold potatoes that have been boiled, mash them, make them into flat cakes, and fry them in butter. Very nice for breakfast.

POTATO BALLS.

Mix mashed potatoes with the yolk of an egg, roll them into balls in a little flour, with egg and bread crumbs; fry them in very nice lard, or brown them in a hot oven.

POTATOES WITH THICK BATTER.

Three ozs. butter, ½ oz. of flour and ½ pint of water; stir over the fire until it is melted into a sauce; put the boiled potatoes into the sauce; dish it very hot, seasoning it with

9

salt, nutmeg and pepper. (You may also mix fine chopped parsley with it). German receipt.

FRIED IRISH POTATOES.

Boil the potatoes, peel and mash them into small cakes, fry them in lard, of a rich brown on both sides.

IRISH POTATOES MASHED.

Boil the potatoes and mash them in a mortar with butter; to a tablespoonful of butter use 8 or 10 common sized potatoes; salt to the taste.

POTATO BALLS FOR BREAKFAST.

Pare and boil dry the potatoes as directed, then put them into a hot pan and mash with a lump of butter and a little salt; beat this well and make it into little cakes or roll it into balls and dip them into egg, and sprinkle with bread crumbs; fry a nice brown.

SWEET POTATOES.

Among the various ways of dressing sweet potatoes, that which appears most popular is to bake them twice. You may put 2 or 3 platefuls at once into the oven; bake them till soft; peel and put them on a tin sheet, and bake them again for $\frac{1}{2}$ an hour; serve them up hot.

FRIED SWEET POTATOES.

Sweet potatoes may be dressed, either cut in long slices and fried in lard, or half boiled, peeled, cut round, and fried quickly. In the latter case they must be drained, and served up as dry as possible.

GREEN PEAS.

Put the peas in a covered vessel with a little salt; place this in another vessel filled with water, which must be boiled until the peas are tender.

GREEN PEAS A LA BOURGEOISE.

Wash 1½ pints of green peas, put them into a stewpan, with fresh butter, parsley, lettuce cut in fours, and a little sugar. Let these boil in their own juice over a slow fire. When all the liquid is boiled away, add a thickening made of the yolk of 2 eggs and a little cream; let the whole remain a few minutes on the fire.

GREEN PEAS.

Green peas should be young and freshly shelled; wash them clean; put them in a bag and the bag into plenty of boiling water, with a little salt and a teaspoonful of pounded loaf sugar; boil them till tender. It takes from ½ to 1 hour to boil them. Never let them stand in the water after they are done. Season them with butter, salt and pepper.

POTATO SALAD.

Boil good Irish potatoes very dry; let them cool thoroughly; slice and pour a dressing over them, made of the yolks of 3 eggs, oil, vinegar, pepper, salt and parsley.

JUMBALLAYA.

A SPANISH CREOLE DISH.

Wash 1 lb. of rice, and soak it an hour; cut up a cold roast chicken or the remnants of a turkey and a slice of ham, which fry in a tablespoonful of lard; stir in the rice, and add slowly, while stirring in a pint of hot water; cover your pot, and set where it can cook slowly. Jumballaya is very nice made with oysters or shrimp.

ON COOKING TOMATOES.

The art of cooking tomatoes lies mostly in cooking them enough; in whatever way prepared, they should be put on some hours before dinner. This vegetable is good in all soups and stews, where such a decided flavoring is wanted.

TO KEEP TOMATOES

THE WHOLE YEAR.

Take the tomatoes, when perfectly ripe, and scald them in hot water, in order to take off the skin easily. When skinned, boil them well in a little sugar or salt, but no water. Then spread them in cakes about an inch thick, and place the cakes in the sun; they will be ready in 3 or 4 days to pack away in bags, which should be hung in a dry place.

TOMATO OMELETTE.

Parboil 2 onions; while this is doing, peel a sufficient quantity of tomatoes to make 3 pints when cooked (this is easily done when hot water has been poured over them); cut them up, and add the onions, also 1½ teaspoonfuls of crumbs of bread, 1 tablespoonful of salt, 1 heaping teaspoonful of black pepper, and 4 tablespoonfuls of butter; beat these thoroughly together and set them over a slow fire, gradually to stew; they should cook never less than 3 hours, but the longer the better; about 15 minutes before they are to be served up, beat 6 eggs, and stir them in; put them on a hot fire, and let them boil, stirring them all the time.

STEWED TOMATOES.

Peel the tomatoes, cut them in half, and squeeze out the seeds; then put them into a stewpan, without any water; add to them salt and cayenne pepper to your taste, 1 teaspoonful of brown sugar, some grated bread, or cracker, butter and mace (powdered); stew them slowly, till perfectly done; send them to table very hot.—A very nice appendage to beefsteak, and other tasteless dishes.

STUFFED TOMATOES.

Take 12 large tomatoes and take out as much of the pulp and seed as you can with convenience scoop out, without injuring the form; chop up the pulp, and add to it salt, pepper, thyme, to the taste, with 1 tablespoonful of butter;

form this into a stuffing with crumbs of bread, and put back into the skins, bake them in a pan very nicely in a moderate oven.

TOMATO OMELET.

Select 1 quart of fine, ripe tomatoes, pour over them boiling water to remove the skin, then chop them finely, put them into a saucepan without any water; chop 2 onions very finely, cover closely, and let them simmer slowly, an hour; then add a little salt and cayenne pepper, a large spoonful of bread crumbs, and cover tightly; beat up 5 eggs to a stiff froth; have ready a heated pan, and a small piece of butter and grease it; stir the eggs into the tomatoes; mix all together, and pour it into the pan; brown it on one side, fold it over, and serve up on a hot dish.

TO BAKE TOMATOES.

Scald and peel about a dozen or more fine, ripe tomatoes, butter a shallow baking dish, and put in the finest, without breaking them, and not quite touching; fill up the space between with stale bread, buttered; the rest of the tomatoes mash, and strain out all the hard parts; then mix with a spoonful of butter, pepper and salt; pour it over the dish; strew bread crumbs on the top; bake about ½ hour; sprinkle sugar between each layer of tomatoes.

TOMATO SOUP.

Boil 1 quart milk; thicken with 1 tablespoonful flour; season with salt, pepper and a little butter; stew 1 dozen fine tomatoes; drain partially, strain through cullender, pour the boiling milk to it; boil up once, and serve.

FRIED TOMATOES.

Peel 1 dozen ripe tomatoes, and fry them in a little fresh butter, together with 2 or 3 sliced green peppers; sprinkle on them a little salt, then add 1 or 2 onions sliced, and let the whole cook thoroughly. (Spanish.)

BAKED TOMATOES.

Scald and peel 1 dozen or more fine, ripe tomatoes; butter a shallow baking dish, and put in the finest without breaking them; fill up the space between with small pieces of bread well buttered; the rest of the tomatoes mash, and strain out all the hard parts; then mix with a spoonful of butter, pepper and salt; pour it over the dish, and strew bread crumbs on the top; bake about ½ an hour.

STUFFED TOMATOES.

Scald and peel them; stuff with bread, parsley, salt, pepper and butter, well mixed together; place in pan and bake.

TO PREPARE AND BOIL RICE.

Wash and pick 1 pint of rice; add to it 3 pints of water, and 1 tablespoonful of salt; boil over a quick fire for 10 minutes, stirring occasionally; then pour off all, or nearly all the water (as the rice will be soft or grainy, according to the quantity of water left on it when put to steam, and the length of time allowed in the steaming; the larger the quantity of water, and the shorter the steaming, the softer will be the rice). Cover the vessel for 15 minutes on a very slow fire, stirring it occasionally.

HOW TO WASH RICE.

Pour upon it water enough to cover it; stir it round briskly with the hand for several seconds; pour off the water, and add fresh; stir as before, and repeat this several times. The whiteness of the rice depends, in a great degree, upon the washing being thorough.

PREPARING RICE OR HOMINY.

Boil the rice or hominy in the ordinary way, in a pot lined with china. After being well soaked, dip the pot into cold water, and it will come out in a cake.

EGG PLANTS.

Parboil them, after splitting them in half, scrape out the middle, which you chop up with little slips of bacon, onion cut up small, and crumbs of bread mixed with a raw egg; then fill the skins with this stuffing and bake them nicely. The bread is also grated on the surface of them.

STUFFED EGG PLANT.

Cut in half, take out the centre, boil the inside; when soft, chop fine, and season with fried onions, parsley, egg, salt, butter, pepper and bread, then stuff the outsides; cover with bread crumbs, and add the insides of fresh tomatoes, if you choose.

TURKISH EGG PLANT.

Slice 1, and just brown it in a frying pan, chop 2 lbs. cold beef, mutton or veal, very fine, season with one fine chopped onion, 6 whole peppers, $\frac{1}{2}$ teaspoon cloves, ditto allspice, celery seed, white pepper and salt, put in baking dish a layer of egg plant, then of beef, and so on until it is filled, having layer of egg plant on top; pour cold gravy or water on the whole; cover with another dish when set in oven, but remove it in time to let the top brown a little before done.

TO COOK SALSIFY.

Boil salsify, or vegetable oysters, till the skin comes off easily; when taken off, cut the roots in pieces, about the size of an oyster; put into a deep vegetable dish a layer of crumbs of bread or crackers, a little salt, pepper and nutmeg, and a covering of butter as thin as you can cut it, then a layer of salsify; these layers must be put alternately, until the dish is filled, having crumbs of bread on the top; pour in them as much water as the dish will hold, and bake brown.

SALSIFY OYSTERS.

Scrape and boil the salsify, then beat fine in a mortar;

season with salt and red pepper; mix them in a batter of eggs, and a very little flour, drop the size of an oyster and fry a light brown.

SALSIFY FRITTERS.

Scrape the salsify and lay it in water to prevent its becoming black; boil it quick, and mash it fine, mix it in a batter prepared with 5 eggs, beaten very light, yolk and white separate; add 1 pint of milk, a large spoonful of butter, and thicken the whole with flour, to the consistency of fritter batter; then stir in the salsify and fry them nicely; season with pepper and salt to the taste. It requires a very large bunch of salsify for this batter.

CAROLINA BOILED RICE.

Pick your rice clean, and wash it in two cold waters, not draining off the last water, till you are ready to put the rice on the fire. Prepare a saucepan with water and a little salt in it, and when it boils, sprinkle in the rice; boil it hard twenty minutes, keeping it covered; then take it from the fire and pour off the water, afterwards set the saucepan on the back of the stove, with the lid off, to allow the rice to dry and the grains to separate.

Rice, when properly boiled, should be soft and white, every grain separate and alone. It is a nice embellishment to either roasted or boiled chickens.

RICE, AS COOKED IN JAPAN.

Pour on just enough cold water to prevent the rice from burning to the pot, (which has a close fitting cover), and set it on a moderate fire; the rice is steamed rather than boiled, until it is nearly done, then take off the cover of the pot, and allow the surplus steam and water to escape; do not forget to add the necessary salt before boiling.

CORN BAKED IN A DISH.

Cut sweet corn from the ear, add plenty of milk, season

with salt, pepper and butter, turn into a baking dish; beat an egg and spread over the top; bake 20 minutes.

CORN FRITTERS.

Grate from uncooked ears. For batter, 1 cup flour, 1 egg, milk enough to soften the whole sufficiently, add salt and pepper; fry brown in thin cakes. Salsify boiled, mashed, and prepared in the same way, is an excellent substitute for oyster fritters.

CORN OYSTERS.

Twelve ears of corn, 1 cup of flour, a teaspoonful of salt, ditto of pepper, 1 egg; stir well and fry in butter.

CORN OYSTERS.

Grate the corn while green and tender, with a coarse grater, into a deep dish. To 2 ears of corn allow 1 egg; beat the whites and yolks separately, and add them to the corn, with 1 tablespoonful of wheat flour, and 1 of butter, salt and pepper to the taste; lay them in hot butter with a spoon and fry them on both sides.

VERY HEALTHY SLAW.

Take a nice, fresh, white cabbage, wash and drain it, and cut off the stalk; shave it in small and very even shreds, with a cabbage cutter, or a sharp knife; put it into a deep china dish, and prepare the following dressing for it: take ½ pint of best cider vinegar, and mix it with ¼ lb. of fresh butter, divided into 4 bits, and rolled in flour; a small saltspoon of salt, and the same quantity of cayenne; stir this all well together, and boil it in a saucepan. Have ready the yolks of 4 eggs nicely beaten; as soon as the mixture has boiled, take it off the fire, and stir in the beaten egg; then pour it boiling hot over the shred cabbage, and mix it well all through with a spoon; set it to cool on ice, or in the open air. It must be perfectly cold before it is placed on the table.

10

WARM SLAW.

Take a large, red cabbage, wash, drain, and shred it finely ; put it in a deep dish, cover it closely and set it on the top of a stove, or in a bake oven, till it is warm all through, then make a dressing as for cold slaw ; pour it boiling over the cabbage ; cover the dish, and send it to the table warm as possible.

TO BOIL A CAULIFLOWER.

Let it lie a short time in salt and water, then put it into boiling water, with a handful of salt ; keep the pot uncovered, and skim the water well. A small cauliflower will require 15 minutes, a large one 20, to boil ; dress with drawn butter.

STEWED SPINACH.

When the spinach is nicely picked and boiled, press it well in a cullender ; then add some pepper and salt, a spoonful of fresh butter, and put it back in the skillet, and let it stew gently a little longer, adding a small cup of sweet cream.

TO BOIL ARTICHOKES.

Wash and scrape the artichokes ; parboil them in the water, then boil in milk, salt to the taste ; 15 minutes will boil them sufficiently long in the water, and in the milk, until they are so soft that a straw may be passed through them.

STUFFED MACARONI.

Boil a chicken until the meat separates from the bones, pound the meat, and add 1 egg whole, and the yolks of 2 others, a little cinnamon, pepper, salt, and a cupful of Parmesan cheese, finely grated. After the ingredients are well mixed, stuff the macaroni and put it to boil in the broth or water in which the chicken was boiled.

BAKED MACARONI.

Boil as much macaroni as will fill the dish, in milk and water, till quite tender, drain it on a sieve, sprinkle a little salt over it, put a layer in the dish, and one of grated cheese, with butter, pepper and mustard, until you fill the dish; bake it in a quick oven, some 20 or 30 minutes.

CAULIFLOWER OMELET.

Take the white part of a boiled cauliflower after it is cold; chop it very small and mix with it a sufficient quantity of well-beaten egg, to make a very thick batter; then fry it in fresh butter in a small pan, and send it hot to table.

STEWED CARROTS.

Half boil the carrots, scrape them nicely, and cut them into thick slices; put them into a stewpan with as much milk as will barely cover them, a very little salt and pepper, and a sprig or two of chopped parsley; simmer them till perfectly tender; when nearly done, add a piece of fresh butter rolled in flour. Send them to table hot.

PARSNIP FRITTERS.

Boil and peel ½ dozen large parsnips, then split and cut them in pieces. Make a nice batter, allowing 4 beaten eggs to 1 pint of milk and 4 tablespoonfuls of flour. Have ready over the fire a frying pan with boiling lard; put in a large spoonful of batter upon every piece of parsnip, and cover with another spoonful of batter. Proceed thus till you have used up the parsnips; when done, drain them from the lard, and serve them hot at breakfast or dinner.

DRIED OKRA.

Take fine, large, fresh okra; cut them into thin round slices; string them on threads, and hang them up in festoons in the storeroom to dry. Before using them, they must be soaked in water during 24 hours; they will then be good (with the addition of tomato paste) to use as a vegetable, or in gumbo, or soup.

BOILED OKRA.

For boiling, the okra should be small and tender. Wash them, and cut off a small piece from each end; boil them till very tender throughout; then drain well, and transfer them to a deep dish. Lay among them some bits of fresh butter, and season with pepper; cover the dish, that the butter may melt the sooner; or you may make a sauce of ½ pint of milk boiled, then add ¼ lb. of good fresh butter, divided into 4 pieces, each piece rolled in a little flour; the butter to be stirred in gradually and smoothly as the milk is taken off the fire; pour this sauce over the dish of okra, and keep it covered till it has gone to table.

FRIED CUCUMBERS.

Slice 8 middle sized cucumbers, flour them slightly and fry a light brown in a little lard; pour off the lard and add to the cucumbers 4 tablespoonfuls of hot water, 2 of wine, 2 of walnut catsup, pepper, salt, and sliced onion, (if you like it) a lump of butter dipped in flour; stew about 15 minutes. A teaspoonful of mustard is better than the onion.

FRIED PLANTAINS.

The plantains should be perfectly ripe and yellow all over. Peel them, split them in long slips, and dredge slightly with flour. Have ready a frying pan filled with boiling lard; put in the plantains and fry them well; when done, take them up on a perforated skimmer and drain back the lard into the frying pan; dish, and send them to table with powdered sugar to eat with them.

ONION CUSTARD.

Peel and slice 10 or 12 mild onions, and fry them in fresh butter, draining them well when you take them up; then mince them as fine as possible; beat 4 eggs until very thick and light, and stir them gradually into 1 pint of milk in turn with the minced onions; season the whole with plenty of grated nutmeg, and stir it very hard; then put into a deep white dish, and bake it about $\frac{1}{4}$ hour; send it to table as a side dish, to be eaten with poultry. It is a French preparation, and will be found very nice by those who have no dislike to onions.

ASPARAGUS—ITALIAN FASHION.

Take some asparagus, break them in pieces, and then boil them soft and drain the water off; take a little sweet oil, water and vinegar; let it boil, season it with pepper and salt, and pour it over the asparagus.

TOASTED CHEESE.

Mix with 3 ounces of cheese, finely grated, 4 ounces of grated bread crumbs, $2\frac{1}{4}$ ounces of fresh butter, the yolks of 2 eggs well beaten, 1 tablespoonful of cream, 1 teaspoonful of mustard, and a little salt and pepper; put it into a saucepan, and stir it over the fire till heated; then lay it thick upon toasted bread, and brown it, or put it covered with a dish into a Dutch oven, till thoroughly heated; let the cheese be just brown.

STEWED BEETS.

Boil them first; then scrape and slice them; put them into a stewpan, with a piece of butter, rolled in flour, with finely chopped parsley, a little vinegar, salt and pepper; set the pan on hot coals and let the beets stew for $\frac{1}{4}$ hour.

COLD SLAW.

Shave cabbage into shreds; mix 1 well beaten raw egg in $\frac{1}{2}$ teacup condensed milk, 1 cup vinegar; boil till it thickens; pour this over the cabbage; sprinkle with salt.

FONDS L'ARTICHAUX, STUFFED.

Get the very best French artichokes in cans; then prepare a stuffing as follows: Boil a chicken in very little water; when done, chop it as fine as possible; beat the yolks of 3 eggs and stir them into the chicken water; put $\frac{1}{2}$ spoonful of butter in a frying pan; thicken it with a little flour; fry some onion minced very fine in it; then pour in some of the chicken broth; stir it until it is like a rich cream; then stir in the chicken; chop some mushrooms very fine, also 2 or 3 truffles, and add to it; season with salt, pepper, and parsley, a little lemon juice; let it get cold; then put it in the artichokes in pyramid shape; cover each one with very finely sifted bread crumbs; put them in a pan; pour over them the balance of the chicken broth, and let them simmer slowly, taking great care to preserve their shape; put a few mushrooms or truffles sliced into the gravy; serve them upon a dish dressed with sprigs of parsley or sliced lemons, and the sauce in a boat.

BREAD, ETC.

FAMILY BREAD.

Take 2½ quarts of flour, 2 eggs, 2 or 3 tablespoonfuls of sugar, 1 pint of water, 1 gill of yeast, salt; beat the eggs with the sugar, and 4 tablespoonfuls of the flour; stir the yeast and water with the salt well together, and add gradually to the egg; sprinkle some of the flour in the bottom of the breadpan; pour in the batter; sprinkle some of the flour on the top, and set it in a cool place to rise; when risen enough, work in the remainder of the flour; make the batter at 12 o'clock in winter, and 4 in summer.

LIGHTENED LOAF.

Two lbs. of flour, 1 pint of sugar, 1 pint of raisins, ½ lb. of butter, 5 eggs, ½ pint of yeast, ½ pint of milk, 1 nutmeg; mix a part of the flour, milk and yeast at night to rise, and work in the other materials in the morning.

TEA ROLLS.

Sift 1 lb. of flour into a pan, with a teaspoonful of salt, warm together a gill of water and one of milk, 1 gill of good yeast; mix into the liquid enough flour to make a thin batter; stirring it till quite smooth and free from lumps; then put a handful of flour over the top, and set it in a warm place to rise, for 2 hours or more; when it is quite light, make it into a dough, with some more milk and water; knead it well for 10 minutes; then mould it into rolls, or round balls, and bake it.

SPANISH ROLLS.

Sift 1 quart of good flour, a pinch of salt, 1 spoonful of yeast, 2 eggs well beaten, ½ pint of milk; knead it and set it to rise; next morning work in 1 ounce of butter; make the dough into small rolls, and bake them; the top crust should not be hard.

FRENCH ROLLS.

One quart of lukewarm milk to 1 quart of flour; melt 2 ounces of butter; add to it 2 eggs and a teaspoonful of salt; when cool, stir in 6 spoonfuls of yeast, and flour sufficient to mould it; set it in a warm place; when light, mould it into small rolls, lay them on flat buttered tins, and let them remain 20 minutes before baking.

SPONGE BREAD.

Take 4 loaves of bread, 3 quarts of wheat flour, 3 quarts of boiling water, mix them thoroughly and let the mixture remain until lukewarm, then add 12 spoonfuls of family yeast (or six of brewers), put it in a warm place to rise; when light, knead in flour to make it sufficiently stiff, to mould off, let it stand for a minute rising, and then bake it.

FAMILY BREAD.

Take 1 peck of sifted flour, $\frac{1}{2}$ pint of family yeast, and wet with new or skim milk, adding a little shortening and a teaspoonful of salt; knead it well. Be particular to have the dough soft, if wheat flour, and stiff, if made of rye.

BROWN BREAD.

Take equal quantities of Indian meal and rye flour, scald the meal; when lukewarm, mix in the flour, adding yeast and salt, kneading as for other bread; bake from 2 to 3 hours.

ROLLS WITH MILK.

One quart of flour, 1 tablespoonful of yeast, as much new milk as will make a slack dough, add a little salt and set it to rise. In the morning work it up with very little flour. Bake in a brisk oven.

DIET BREAD.

Nine eggs, 1 pound of sugar and 14 ozs. of flour; beat the

yolks with a whisk till quite thick, then mix the sugar with them, and beat till light; beat the whites well, and add them by degrees; put the flour in gradually; bake in a quick oven.

DIET BREAD.

Sift 1 lb. of flour, 1 lb. of sugar, a little mace, grated nutmeg and a little rose water; stir this well together; beat 6 eggs very light, add a pinch of salt; after all the ingredients are well mixed, bake it slowly in a pan.

ECONOMICAL MUFFINS.

Put to an unbaked loaf of bread as much new milk as will make a batter; beat it well; let it stand one hour, and bake it in small ones on the hoe, thick enough to split.

HAMPTON MUFFINS.

Beat 2 eggs well, 2 spoonfuls of yeast, 1 pint of flour, as much cold water as will make a stiff batter; when light, bake them in hoops for breakfast.

INDIAN MUFFINS.

Stir into 1 quart of boiling water as much cornmeal as will make a nice batter; when warm, put in as much flour as will make a stiff batter; add $\frac{1}{2}$ a teaspoonful of salt, and $\frac{1}{2}$ a wine glass of yeast; set it to rise, and when risen, pour into the muffin rings, and bake slowly in an oven; serve them with nice fresh butter.

WATER MUFFINS.

Put 4 tablespoonfuls of good yeast into 1 pint of lukewarm water, add a little salt, stir in gradually as much sifted flour, as will make a thick batter, cover the pan, and set it in a warm place to rise. When it is quite light, and the middle is hot, grease and set your muffin rings on it, having first buttered them round the inside; put a ladleful of the batter for each ring; bake them over a quick fire.

11

When sent to table do not cut them; split them by pulling them open with the hands.

CORNMEAL MUFFINS.

Three cups of cornmeal, ½ cup of sifted wheat flour, 3 eggs, well beaten, 2 large spoonfuls of butter, and 1 teaspoonful of soda, dissolved in 1 pint of buttermilk, a large pinch of salt, pour into rings and bake a nice brown in the oven.

EGG MUFFINS.

One pint of wheat flour, 1 pint of milk, 1 dessertspoonful of butter, 2 eggs and a little salt; beat the eggs light, and add the other ingredients, stirring them well together; put into patties and bake in rather a quick oven. The muffins are equally good without the butter.

PLAIN MUFFINS.

Make a stiff batter with flour, yeast and warm water, at night; in the morning, have a little warm milk and 4 eggs, and flour to make it sufficiently stiff to bake.

RISEN MUFFINS.

Half a pint of milk and the same of water, 1 egg, 1 teacupful of yeast, 2 large lumps of loaf sugar; mix with flour to the consistency of pound cake; make the milk lukewarm, and rise over night. Very nice.

CORN BREAD.

Take 1 cup of cornmeal, 1 cup of breakfast hominy, (boiled) 1 egg, a pinch of salt, 1 teaspoonful of yeast powder, and sufficient sweet milk to make a soft batter; bake quickly in a slightly larded hot pan, and serve instantly.

MOLASSES TOAST.

Make a thick slice of very nice toast, evenly browned on both sides, but not the least burnt; lay it in a pint bowl, and pour over it a small ½ pint of the best West India molasses, having stirred into the molasses a heaped table-spoonful of ground ginger; mix the molasses with ½ pint of hot water, and pour the whole over the toast; cover it with a plate for a few minutes, and eat it while warm, previous to going to bed.

SWEET JOURNEY CAKE.

Stir together 2 large spoonfuls of brown sugar, and 2 large spoonfuls of good butter; beat the yolks of 3 eggs and add it to the sugar and butter; then grate ½ nutmeg; add an equal proportion of cornmeal and flour to knead it; then spread it on a board, and glaize it with the white of an egg; bake before the fire as other journey cake.

BREAD CAKE.

Two teacups of risen dough, ½ teacup of sugar, ½ cup of butter, 2 eggs and a few raisins, stoned and cut; mix these; adding a mite of soda and cream of tartar; mix the cream of tartar with the dough, and dissolve the soda in a little milk and add lastly. (Very nice.)

CORN BREAD RUSK.

Take six cupfuls of cornmeal, 4 of wheat flour, 2 of molasses, 2 teaspoonfuls of soda, and a little salt; mix this well together; knead it into dough;' then make 2 cakes of it, and pour into tin or iron pans, and bake 1 hour.

CORN BREAD.

Thicken 1½ pints of rich buttermilk with cornmeal to the consistency of batter; dissolve 1 teaspoonful of soda in a cup of new milk, add a little salt and beat very light; pour this into buttered pans, and bake two hours; serve hot.

CORN CAKE.

Thicken 1 quart of sour milk with sifted cornmeal, 1 teaspoonful of salt, ½ teaspoonful of soda dissolved in a cup of milk, 1 teacup of good molasses, 1 large spoonful of lard, or butter; beat these ingredients well together; pour it into a well greased iron baking pan, with an iron cover; put it in the fire-place when the fire is raked for the night, and put fire and hot ashes over and around it. In the morning you will have a nice brown loaf for breakfast.

VIRGINIA EGG BREAD.

One quart of meal, ½ pint of wheat flour, 1½ pints of milk, 2 eggs, and a tablespoonful of butter, or lard; mix all well together, and bake either in cups or a tinpan.

POTATO CORN BREAD.

One quart of fine cornmeal, ½ pint of milk, ½ lb. of sweet potatoes, ½ lb. of butter, 1 lb. of brown sugar, and 8 eggs; boil, and mash smooth the potatoes; beat the eggs, and stir them into the butter; then add the milk, and lastly the meal; beat the whole well together, and bake in a pan.

SWEET CORN BREAD.

A pint of cornmeal, ½ pint of milk, ½ pint of molasses, 1 tablespoonful of butter, 1 tablespoonful of powdered ginger, and 2 eggs; beat the eggs light, and add the other ingredients—the meal last; bake in a pan.

CORN WAFERS.

One pint of meal, 1 gill of milk, 1 gill of water, 1 dessert-spoonful of butter and a pinch of salt; bake a light brown.

HOE CAKE.

Three spoonfuls of hominy, 2 of rice flour, a little butter, and milk sufficient to make it soft; bake on a griddle or on a hoe.

SODA BREAD.

Rub into 1 lb. of flour perfectly dry a teaspoonful of tartaric acid, dry; then make a batter of milk or buttermilk, as you please; add a little saleratus or soda.

POTATO BREAD.

Half a pint of warm water, the same of yeast, 6 moderate sized potatoes, 1 dessertspoonful of salt, and 3 pints of flour stirred in lightly.

BATTER BREAD.

Take 6 spoonfuls of flour and 3 of cornmeal, with a little salt, sift them, and make a thin batter with flour, eggs, and a sufficient quantity of rich milk; bake it in little tin moulds in a quick oven—the yolks and whites of the eggs to be beaten separately.

CORNMEAL RUSK.

Take 6 cups of cornmeal, 4 of flour, 2 cups of molasses, 2 teaspoonfuls of saleratus; mix all well together, knead it into dough; then make into 2 cakes; bake them as you would pone, for ¾ hour. Very nice.

RISEN CORN CAKE.

Pour 1 pint of scalding milk on 1 quart of sifted cornmeal and when cool stir in a spoonful of good lard, 3 well beaten eggs, 1 teaspoonful of salt; stir this with 2 tablespoonfuls of yeast; beat all together, and set it to rise; when risen, bake in tins.

DRIED BREAD CRUMBS.

Save all the pieces of bread, put them into an oven; then roll them on the paste board; put them in a jar in a dry place; use for cooking purposes.

CORNMEAL BREAD.

Take a piece of butter the size of a hen's egg; rub it into 1 pint of cornmeal; make it a batter, with 2 eggs and some new milk; add a spoonful of yeast, and set it by the fire 1 hour to rise; butter little pans, and bake it.

CORN BREAD.

One quart of thick, sour cream, 1 spoonful of fresh butter, 1 teaspoonful of soda dissolved in hot water, 1 tablespoonful of sifted flour; white cornmeal to form a soft dough; work well with the hands and bake in a buttered pan; serve very hot.

CORNMEAL BREAD.

Rub a piece of butter the size of an egg into a pint of cornmeal; make a batter with 2 eggs and some new milk, 1 spoonful of yeast; set it by the fire 1 hour to rise; butter small pans and bake it.

MUFFIN BREAD.

Three pints of flour, $\frac{1}{2}$ lb. of butter, 5 eggs (whites and yolks beaten separately); work the butter well in the flour; put in the eggs; beat all very light; add 3 tablespoonfuls of good yeast; bake it in a pan; oven rather quick at the bottom, and clear at the top, until it begins to bake; then quicken the fire by degrees.

HOMINY CAKES.

Take warm hominy, seasoned with salt, butter, cream and 1 or 2 eggs; add a little flour to stiffen it; fry on a griddle; serve hot.

GRUEL BATTER CAKES.

One quart of thick gruel, 1 large tablespoonful of butter, 9 eggs, a little salt, 2 spoonfuls of flour and cornmeal, to form a batter; cook the butter in the gruel, remove from the fire, pour into a wooden bowl and stir until almost cool; then add the eggs and meal, and lastly one small teaspoonful of soda dissolved in warm water; the cornmeal should be white and fresh.

VIRGINIA CORN CAKE.

Dissolve 1 tablespoonful of butter in $1\frac{1}{2}$ pints of boiling milk; into this scald 1 quart of Indian meal; when cool, add $\frac{1}{2}$ pint of wheat flour, a tablespoonful of sugar, a little salt, 2 eggs well beaten; bake in 2 cakes. Very nice.

VIRGINIA CAKES.

Equal quantities of flour and meal, well sifted together; 4 eggs to a quart, 1 teacup of good yeast; make it up with water and salt.

LAPLAND CAKES.

Beat 5 eggs very light with 1 pint of new cream; then beat in well 1½ pints of flour; bake in tins or cups on a quick fire.

FLANNEL CAKES WITHOUT YEAST.

Thicken 1 quart of buttermilk with wheat flour, a large tablespoonful of butter, add a little salt, and 2 teaspoonfuls of carbonate of soda; pour on a griddle iron or in rings. This is beautifully light and spongy, and much nicer without the butter.

SWEET FLANNEL CAKES.

Half a pint of soft-boiled rice, a teacup of cream, a teacup of sugar, 3 eggs, 1 tablespoonful of yeast, or 1 teaspoonful of pearl ash; let the rice cool, and add the other ingredients, rubbing them well together; bake on a griddle. Very nice for tea.

FLANNEL CAKES.

One quart of new milk, thicken with flour to the consistency of fritter batter, 2 eggs well beaten, 1 large spoonful of yeast, and a little salt; mix this all well together, set it to rise at night for breakfast; it must not be stirred in the morning; bake on the griddle as buckwheat cakes.

BERMUDA JOHNNY CAKE.

To each pint of flour allow 2 ounces of butter; work in a small part of the butter with flour; mix it up with a little salt and milk to consistency of paste; roll it out and spread on the butter as for paste, (twice dividing the butter); put the paste into as many pieces as you wish cakes, and roll them out round; 1 pint of flour will make 2 cakes the size of large plate; bake them on a griddle, and let each cake remain on the griddle a short time off the fire after being done, to make them crisp; then tear open each, and butter quickly.

BUCKWHEAT CAKES.

Take as much warm water as you will require for the size of the family; thicken this with good buckwheat to a fritter batter, add a teaspoonful of salt, if 2 quarts is made, 2 handfuls of cornmeal, and 1 wineglassful of good yeast. Warm milk in the place of warm water is a great improvement, but be particular not to scald the yeast, or the cakes will be heavy.

CREAM CAKE.

Beat very lightly 2 eggs; stir them into 1 pint of sour cream; sift in as much flour as will make a stiff batter; dissolve 1 teaspoonful of soda in a cup of new milk; add this, and a little salt, mix them well, and pour into rather a shallow pan; bake quickly a nice brown; serve hot.

STEEVEN CAKES.

Pick and wash ½ pint of rice; boil it very soft; then drain it and let it get cold; sift 1½ pints of flour over the pan of rice, and mix in ¼ lb. of butter that has been warmed by the fire, and a salt spoonful of salt; add 5 eggs, beat very light, and stir them gradually into a quart of milk; beat all together very light, and bake it in muffin rings, or waffle irons; send them to the table very hot, and eat them with butter, honey or molasses.

WHIGS.

Cream, ½ lb. of butter, and the same of sugar; when well mixed, stir in 6 well beaten eggs; sift in 2 lbs. of flour, 1 pint of new milk, a little salt; mix this well together, then add 1 gill of good yeast; bake in small tins, or muffin rings; for breakfast or tea.

GERMAN WAFFLES.

Warm a quart of milk, and cut up in it ¼ lb. of the best fresh butter, and stir it about to soften in the warm milk; beat 8 eggs till very thick and smooth, and stir them gradually into the milk and butter, in turn with ½ lb. of sifted flour; then add 2 tablespoonfuls of strong, fresh yeast; cover the pan with a clean cloth and set it in a warm place to rise; when the batter has risen nearly to the top, and is covered with bubbles, it is time to bake, first stirring in a wineglass of rose water. Having heated your waffle iron in a good fire, grease its inside with the fresh butter used for the waffle mixture; fill it and shut the iron closely; turn it on the fire, so that both sides of the cakes may be equally well done; take them out of the iron by slipping a knife underneath; then grease and prepare the iron for another waffle; butter them and send them to the tea table very hot; and you should have a glass dish of sugar, flavored with powdered cinnamon, to eat with them.

SWEET POTATO WAFFLES.

Two tablespoonfuls of mashed sweet potato, 1 of butter, 1 of sugar, 1 pint of milk, 4 tablespoonfuls of wheat flour; mix all well together, and bake in a waffle iron.

RICE WAFFLES.

Boil 2 cups of rice till quite soft; make it into a thick batter with 2 eggs, 1 spoonful of butter, ½ pint of milk; beat it till quite light, and bake in a waffle iron.

RICE WAFFLES.

Stir into 2 pints of well boiled rice, 1 large spoonful of butter and a pinch of salt; when cool, add 2 eggs well beaten, 1 pint of milk, 1 pint of sifted flour, 1 teaspoonful of yeast; let it stand 2 hours before baking.

12

WAFFLES.

One quart of flour, 1 egg, and a spoonful of good yeast; make these into a thin batter with milk; then put in 2 ounces of butter. In summer this should be done early in the morning; in winter, the night before.

POTATO WAFFLES.

One lb. of potatoes, 1 lb. of flour, 4 eggs, and as much milk as will make it the consistency of fritters; add 1 cup of yeast.

BREAD CAKE.

Make up a loaf of bread with milk and yeast; next morning add to it 5 eggs, 1 lb. of sugar, ½ lb. of butter and 1 nutmeg; beat it well, set it in a mould to rise until evening. Very nice for tea.

RICE BREAD.

One pint of rice, 1 pint of flour, 2 spoonfuls of the butter, the yolks of 3 eggs, whites of 2; make up with milk, not too stiff.

FLANNEL CAKES.

Two lbs. of flour sifted, 4 eggs, 3 tablespoonfuls of yeast, 1 pint of milk; mix a teaspoonful of salt with the flour, and set the pan before the fire to rise; then warm the milk and stir it into the flour, so as to make a stiff batter; beat the eggs very light and stir them into the yeast; add the eggs and yeast to the batter, and beat all well together; if it is too stiff, add a little more warm milk; cover the pan closely and set it to rise near the fire; bake it when quite light; have the baking irons hot, grease them, pour on a ladleful of batter, let it slowly bake, and when done on one side, turn it to the other; butter them and send them to the table hot.

MILK BISCUITS.

Take 1 lb. of sifted flour, ¼ lb. of good butter, cut in small pieces, ½ pint of new milk, warmed, and a little salt;

stir this into the flour, mix well, and add a wineglass of good yeast, 3 eggs beaten, and grated nutmeg; set it to rise, and when risen, sift on the board ½ lb. of flour; mix all together, make it into cakes, and bake quickly.

TO MAKE ROLLS.

Two quarts of flour, ¼ lb. of butter rubbed in, 5 eggs beat up and mixed with it, ½ pint of yeast, well mixed together as other bread and covered up to lighten; then bake in rolls.

CRUMPETS.

Three eggs to 1 quart of milk, made into stiff batter, as for pancakes; add yeast; make over night in cool weather, and set to rise.

PANCAKES.

Break 5 yolks of eggs in ½ lb. of flour well sifted; mix it well with cream until the batter is very thin; beat up the whites of 3 eggs very light and mix it with the batter; have ready fresh butter creamed, and to each pancake put 2 tablespoonfuls in the pan, which must be made hot; fry them a light brown; turn a plate up in the dish, and lay them on one another, powdering each with white sugar.

SWEET WAFERS.

Take 6 spoonfuls of white sugar, 6 of flour, 3 of butter, 6 eggs, and milk enough to make it into a thin batter.

TAVERN BISCUITS.

Three lbs. of flour, ½ lb. of brown sugar, 4 glasses of wine, 8 of sweet cream, 1 lb. of butter, 2 ounces of allspice, or ½ ounce of cinnamon, nutmeg or mace, is still better; cut out the biscuits and bake on tin sheets; the above quantity makes 146 biscuits.

BREAKFAST CAKES.

Take dough early in the morning and make it into a thin batter with cream or new milk; set it to rise; put it thin on a hoe and bake it quickly; have ready melted butter to put over it.

BUTTERMILK BREAD.

One quart of wheat flour, 1 dessertspoonful (not heaped) of super-carbonate of soda, 1 tablespoonful of butter, ½ lb. of powdered sugar, 1½ tumblers of buttermilk; mix these ingredients, and knead them into soft dough, which place in a greased pan, and set it to rise in a slightly warm oven; when risen, bake. This bread keeps a long time, and makes excellent toast.

RICE BREAD.

Boil 6 ounces of rice in a quart of water till dry and soft; put it into 2 lbs. of flour; mix it well, add 2 teaspoonfuls of salt, 2 of yeast, and enough milk or water to make it a proper consistency; bake it in moulds, when well risen.

POTATO BREAD.

Boil thoroughly and mash fine, mealy potatoes; add salt and a very little butter; rub them with twice their quantity of flour; stir in the yeast, moisten with lukewarm water or milk, till stiff enough to mould; it will rise quicker than common wheat bread, and should be baked as soon as risen, as it quickly sours.

YANKEE BISCUITS.

Mix 2 teaspoonfuls of cream of tartar into 1 quart of flour, (add lard or butter, if you wish, but it is very good without); dissolve 1 teaspoonful of soda in water or milk; mix all together, roll it out, cut it into cakes, and bake it as soon as you please.

SUFFOLK CAKES.

One pint of flour, 3 eggs, cream enough to make a batter, and a little salt; bake in cups for breakfast.

BUTTER BISCUITS.

Two lbs. of sifted flour, ½ lb. of butter, ½ pint of milk, 2 wineglasses of the best brewers' yeast, 2 eggs; mix all well together; set it to rise; bake in a moderate oven.

CLAREVILLE BISCUITS.

Two lbs. of sifted flour, ½ lb. of butter, ½ pint of milk or cold water, a pinch of salt, put the batter in buttered pans, and bake a light brown in a slow oven.

THIN BISCUITS.

Warm 2 ounces of butter in as much skimmed milk as will make 1 lb. of flour into a stiff paste; beat it with a rolling pin, and work it smooth; roll it thin, and cut it into round biscuits, prick them full of holes with a fork; about 6 minutes will bake them.

SWEET POTATO BUNS.

Boil and mash 2 nice potatoes; rub in as much flour as will make it like bread; add nutmeg and sugar to your taste, with 1 tablespoonful of good yeast; when it has risen, work in 2 tablespoonfuls of butter, cut finely, then form it into small rolls, and bake on tins a nice brown; serve hot; break open and butter; either good for tea or breakfast.

VIRGINIA BUNS.

Sift into a pan 2 lbs. of flour; warm 1 pint of new milk, ¾ lb. of butter; stir this, if not too warm, into the flour; 8 eggs beaten very light, separating the yolks from the whites, 1½ grated nutmegs, 1 teaspoonful of cinnamon; beat these well together, adding the whites of the eggs lastly, 1½ wineglassfuls of yeast; set it to rise; when risen, stir in 1 lb. of white sugar, to be sifted in and mixed through; set to rise in the pans in which they are to be baked.

RICHMOND MUFFINS.

Sift 2 lbs. of flour; warm 1½ pints of new milk and 2 large spoonfuls of butter; stir into the flour, beat 3 eggs very lightly, a little salt; beat all well together till thoroughly mixed; then add 3 spoonfuls of good yeast; set it to rise, and when risen, bake in muffin rings in an oven.

MARYLAND BISCUIT.

Take any quantity of flour the family may require, put in salt and lump of butter, or lard, rub it well in the flour; then moisten it with new milk, work it well, and beat it with a rolling pin until perfectly light; bake rather slowly a light brown. On the lightness depends the goodness of the biscuits.

SALLY LUNN.

Eight eggs, 2 cups of butter, 2 of sugar, 1 pint of milk, $\frac{1}{2}$ pint of yeast, the juice and rind of 1 lemon, with flour to make it as stiff as pound cake; make it early in the morning in winter, and about 12 o'clock in the summer; bake it for tea, and eat it with fresh butter.

WASHINGTON LOAF.

One tumblerful of good rice flour, 1 teacupful of wheat flour, 1 teaspoonful of cream of tartar stirred in, 1 large spoonful of butter, cut up very finely, 1 egg well beaten, a pinch of salt, 1 teaspoonful of soda, dissolved in a cup of new milk; mix these well together, and bake in a pan like pound cake; serve hot for tea or breakfast.

BACHELOR'S LOAF.

Pour on $\frac{3}{4}$ lb. of sifted cornmeal 1 pint of boiling hot new milk, stir well together; then beat the whites and yolks of 3 eggs separately, reserving the whites for the last ingredient added, a pinch of salt, and 1 spoonful of lard; the whole to be beaten quite light; grease the pan, pour in the above, and bake 1 hour.

WARSAW BREAKFAST CAKE.

Cut up in warm milk 1 spoonful of good butter; when cool, stir in $1\frac{1}{4}$ lbs. of sifted flour, 2 eggs well beaten, a pinch of salt, and a large spoonful of good yeast; mix these well together, put it into buttered tins to rise; when risen, bake ¾ hour.

BUTTERMILK ROLLS.

Mix 1 teaspoonful of cream of tartar into 1 quart of flour, 1 quart of buttermilk, with 1 large spoonful of soda dissolved in it; stir it well and quickly, a little salt added lastly; pour into tins, or make into rolls; bake quickly.

LIGHT CAKES.

One pint of milk, 4 potatoes, a piece of butter the size of an egg, a little salt; pass the potatoes through a cullender with the milk, and then mix enough flour in it to make it the thickness of muffins, 1 small teacup of home made yeast; let it stand 4 hours; then add sufficient flour to make it as stiff as bread dough; mould it off, put it in pans, let it remain for 3 hours; bake in a quick oven 20 minutes.

CREAM CAKES.

Melt as much butter in a pint of milk as will make it as rich as cream; make the flour into a paste with this; knead it well, roll it out frequently, cut in squares, and bake on a griddle.

SALLY LUNN OR TEA BUNS.

To 1 quart of milk add ¼ quart of good yeast; put in as much flour as will make a stiff batter; let it stand 6 or 8 hours; then add ½ lb. of butter melted in sweet milk, 4 eggs to ¾ lb. of loaf sugar; work in sufficient flour to make it the consistency of dough; let it stand 1 hour, then work it off, forming it into buns, or else in a large mould; let it stand ½ hour, then bake it in a quick oven.

NAPLES BISCUIT.

One lb. of flour, 1 lb. of sugar, 12 whites and 10 yolks of

eggs, 2 glasses of wine; these should gradually harden in the oven till quite crisp, though frequently turned in the tins.

NEW YORK RUSK.

Three lbs. of flour, 8 ounces of sugar, 6 ounces of butter, 5 spoonfuls of yeast, 1 pint of milk tepid heat; the butter must be rubbed into the flour, then the sugar, then the yeast; if the milk is not sufficient, add a little warm water; the dough must be made stiff; make them after breakfast, and bake for tea on tin sheets.

SPONGE BISCUIT.

The weight of 10 eggs in sugar, and of 6 in flour; beat the whites and yolks separately; when the whites are sufficiently light to adhere to the side of the dish, add the yolks and the sugar; add the flour and the juice and rind of 1 lemon; bake in cups, or deep tins half full; the bottom of the oven should be warmer than the top.

ZOUAVE RUSKS.

A pint and a half of good flour, ½ pint of white sugar, a heaped tablespoon of butter, a teacup of milk, 2 teaspoonfuls of yeast, mixed with the dry flour; rub the sugar, butter, and yolks of 4 eggs (as in pound cake); beat the whites to a stiff froth; add the milk just before you put in the beaten whites; the flour should be added last; bake immediately.

RAISED WAFFLES.

Make a thick batter of milk and wheat flour, add 4 eggs, beat light, a gill of yeast, and a spoonful of butter; let it rise some hours; as you take them out of the iron, butter and sprinkle them.

INDIAN BREAD.

Mix (as for a thick gruel) Indian meal and cold water; stir the mixture into boiling water, let it boil ½ hour; stir in a little salt; take it from the fire; let it remain until lukewarm, then stir in yeast and Indian meal, making it the consistency of common dough; when light, take it out and put into buttered pans; let it remain a few minutes, then bake it about 2½ hours.

INDIAN MEAL GRIDDLE CAKES.

One pint bowl of Indian meal, 1 of flour, 1 quart of milk, a little salt, a good sized cup of yeast.

DYSPEPSIA BREAD.

One heaping quart of dyspepsia flour, and one handful over 2 teaspoonfuls of yeast, 1 teacupful of molasses, 1½ teaspoonfuls of saleratus, salt; mix this with 1 pint of water; the saleratus must be dissolved in a part of the pint, as no more than that quantity must be used; beat well together and put immediately into the oven; the yeast must be put into the flour dry, and it must be made up with cold water.

DYSPEPSIA BREAD.

Put 1 gill of molasses and 1 gill of yeast into 1 quart of lukewarm water, a teaspoonful of saleratus or not, as you please, and a little salt; then stir in dyspepsia flour, until two-thirds as stiff as flour bread. Excellent.

TANCREDI CAKE.

Six ounces of butter, the same quantity of sugar, ¾ lb. of flour, a couple of eggs, and a teaspoonful of rose water; stir to a cream the butter and sugar, then add the eggs, flour and spice; roll it out thin, and cut it into small cakes.

EGG TOAST.

Take a glass of thick cream, a cup of white sugar, 3 macaroons pounded, with a few almonds, a little grated lemon; let it boil; then add the yolks of 8, and whites of 3 eggs;

13

beat the whole up over a slow fire, and lay on very thin slices of fried bread and butter; sprinkle sugar, and serve for tea.

TONGUE TOAST.

Make some slices of nice toast, not very thick, but browned evenly all over, on both sides; take off the crust; butter the toast slightly; grate with a large grater plenty of cold tongue, and spread it thickly over the toast; lay the slices side by side, on a large dish—not one slice on the top of the other. It is very nice for breakfast or tea.

HAM TOAST.

Is prepared in the same way, of grated ham (cold) spread on slices of buttered toast.

HOME MADE CRACKERS.

Take a lump of light bread dough; roll it out; spread it with butter; dredge a little flour over it; roll it up and pound it well; roll out very thin; cut in small cakes and bake quickly.

BANNOCK.

One pint of meal, stirred into 1 pint of boiling water, 1 pint of milk; then added with 3 eggs well beaten, add salt to taste, also sugar; when in the oven 10 minutes, stir it up, and clear well the sides; return it to the oven; in 10 more minutes stir it again; then put it in the oven, and bake until done; eat with butter. Excellent for breakfast.

RUSK.

Two eggs, 1 cup white sugar, $\frac{1}{2}$ cup butter, 1 teaspoonful salt, 1 pint milk, warm, $\frac{1}{2}$ yeast cake dissolved in $\frac{1}{4}$ cup water; beat hard; add flour thoroughly until thick; set in warm place; cover close to rise; knead well; add flour to keep from sticking only; roll out and cut like biscuit; when risen light, bake.

CORN BREAD.

Two cups cornmeal, 1 cup flour, 1½ pints milk, 2 egg, 2 tablespoonfuls of butter and molasses, 1 tablespoonful yeast powder, little salt; bake in pans, in a not very hot oven.

BROWN BREAD.

One and a half pints corn meal, 1½ pints graham flour, 1½ cups molasses, 2 teaspoons soda dissolved in a little boiling water and mixed with the molasses; 1 pint of milk, 1 pint of water, a little salt; pour into a well greased 3-quart tinpail; steam 3 hours and bake one hour.

MRS. MEYER'S MUFFINS.

One quart flour, 3 eggs, ¼ lb. butter, 2 spoonfuls of yeast, about ½ pint of water; beat light at night, and bake in rings.

MRS. L. WAYNE'S BREAD RECEIPT.

One-half yeast cake dissolved in ½ cup cold water (whole cake in cold weather), 1 quart lukewarm water, 1 tablespoon white sugar, ½ cup lard; 1 tablespoon salt; beat hard with hand; add flour to make thick dough; (use gallon tin bucket, with tight fitting cover) when risen to top, add flour to make dough stiff, in bucket; knead on board 15 minutes, use as little flour as possible, keeping dough soft; make in loaves; cover to rise; when to the top of pans, bake in moderately hot oven.

PASTE.

This requires care and good materials; the flour must be dried and sifted before using it; the butter which is employed washed, and all the water worked out; the best paste is made with beef suet. Render 6 lbs. of beef suet; strain it through a hair sieve into a clean pan; to this add a bottle of the best olive oil; stir it well and then put into jars, each containing about 3 lbs.; cover tightly, and keep in a very cool place. Not more than 2 jars should be prepared at a time for family use, as the suet is liable to become musty and will not keep long.   In making the pastry for pies, when you require it flaky and particularly good, sift 1 lb. of best flour into a pan, then ¾ lb. of the prepared suet; be careful to use the hands as little as possible, and the less worked the better; when all the required suet is cut up, add salt to the taste; moisten it with cold water (in summer, ice water) then flour paste board, which must be very clean and never used twice without scouring; roll it as little as possible, and add another ¼ lb. of the suet in thin slices; between each rolling, add the slices of suet, and dust it with flour; the thinner it is rolled, the lighter the paste.   Have ready the pie plates or pudding; be careful in rolling that you always roll from you, and make it as quickly as possible. For meat pies, the nicest paste is made by sifting into a pan 1 lb. of flour; make a hole in the centre of the dry flour and put into it ¾ lb. of suet (not prepared) but strip off all the skin; then pour over this suet ½ pint of boiling water, sprinkle some flour over it, and let it stand for 1 hour to become cold; add a little salt; stir the whole with a knife; turn it out on the board; dust it well with flour.

PYRAMID OF PASTE.

Roll out some nicely prepared puff paste, an inch in thickness, and cut the paste into any shape you may fancy; make each smaller until the top one is not larger than a cent; between each piece of paste spread some nice preserve or jam; then turn up the edges of the paste, and brush the sides and top with the yolk of an egg well beaten; lay the pyramid on a baking tin, and bake a nice brown; serve hot.

PASTE FOR CROQUANTS.

Sift ½ lb. of flour and ¼ lb. of loaf sugar together; mix them well with a knife; then stir in as many yolks of eggs as will make it into a stiff paste; this must be well stirred; then roll it on a flour board, and cut into shape of leaves with a cutter; they are a very pretty ornament for tarts or puddings; bake a light brown, as other paste.

BREAD DOUGH PASTE.

This is best for apple, peach or berry dumplings; and a very good pudding is made by rolling out, and spreading it very thickly with any kind of jam or preserves; then roll it over carefully, and tie up in a nicely floured square stout cloth; have ready a pot of boiling water, and drop in the pudding; keep it boiling briskly ¾ hour; keep a kettle of water on the fire, to renew the water as it evaporates, as the lightness of the pudding depends much on the pot being kept full and boiling, until served.

PATENT FLOUR.

Pulverize 6 lbs. of flour; mix 5 teaspoonfuls of dry soda all through it, then 6 teaspoonfuls of cream of tartar, and 6 of salt; incorporate all these, and you have risen cakes at hand to which add milk and flour, a little shortening; make into a soft dough; bake in tins.

VERY LIGHT PASTE.

To 3 lbs. of flour, add 2¾ lbs. of butter and ¼ lb. of lard; add to the flour 2 well beaten eggs; wash the butter nicely, and then salt the crust; this makes it flaky. Paste must be rolled lightly, as much depends on it. Wet it with water enough to make it roll easily; after having rolled it out once, divide the paste and put rather more butter in 1 part for the top; if possible, get it all in 3 times rolling it. Paste requires a moderate heat; if the oven is too slow, it will be solid; if too hot, it will not rise; therefore, great care is necessary.

POTATO PASTE.

Boil mealy potatoes soft; rub them through a sieve while hot; put them in a stewpan over the fire with as much water as will make them the consistency of mush;

sift 1 quart of flour in, and make into a paste; knead it till very light.

POOR MAN'S PASTE.

To 1 quart of flour add ¼ lb. of butter, 2 eggs, a pinch of salt; mix with water.

RICE PASTE.

Rub 3 ounces of butter well into ½ lb. of ground rice; moisten it with water, and roll it out with a little flour.

PUFF PASTE.

One lb. of butter, 1 lb. 2 ounces of flour; divide the flour in half and put one half into a tin pan; divide the butter into 4 parts, and put 1 part into the pan with the flour; mix it all with water, then roll it out and flour it, adding another part of the butter, fold it up, roll it out again, and add another part of the butter; and so on, until it is all used; in mixing it, use only a knife.

HOP YEAST.

To a handful of hops, take 3 pints of water, and boil strong; also 3 or 4 potatoes, put them in a crock and mash very fine; put the flour on top, then pour the hop water on boiling hot, mixing well with the potatoes and flour; let it stand until milkwarm, and add some yeast to make it rise; when it gets light, add 1 teacup of warm water, 1 of brown sugar, 1 teaspoon of ginger, 1 tablespoon of salt; stir it down well, when you put in the ingredients; let it rise and fall several times, and put away for use.

PATENT YEAST.

To 1 pint of potatoes put ½ pint of water, and boil it until reduced to 1 teaspoonful of water; then peel the potatoes and mash them into a light teacupful of flour with the boiling water in which they were boiled; after mixing well, add 1 pint of cold water in small quantity at a time, also ½ pint of hop tea, and set it to rise.

POTATO YEAST.

Peel and boil soft a large Irish potato; rub it through a sieve, add an equal quantity of flour; make it liquid with hop tea; when a little warmer than new milk, add a gill of good yeast; stir it well, and keep it closely covered in a small pitcher.

BAKER'S YEAST.

Boil 2 ounces or more of hops into a vessel with 3 pints of water; as it decreases, carefully stir all the time; strain the liquor and mix it with well with 2 lbs. of malt; cover, and let it stand for 8 hours, or until it is milkwarm; then stir in ½ pint of good yeast; when mixed well together, let it work for 10 hours; strain it through a sieve, or it may be strained before it is set aside to ferment.

COUNTRY YEAST.

Put a large handful of hops into a vessel with 3 pints of water, and boil half an hour, or until the strength is extracted; and then strain it through a sieve on to 8 or 10 spoonfuls of flour, and stir until all the dry flour is moistened, or as thick as griddle cakes; add a heaping teaspoonful of salt, and when about blood-warm, stir in a large teacupful of lively yeast.

NORFOLK YEAST.

Have ready 2 quarts of boiling water; put into it a large handful of hops and let them boil 20 minutes; sift into a pan 1½ lbs. of flour, strain the liquor from the hops, and pour half of it over the hops; let the other half of the liquid stand till it is cool, and then pour it gradually into the pan of flour, mixing it well; stir into it a large teacupful of good yeast (brewers' yeast, if you can get it); put it in bottles, and cork tightly; in each bottle put a teaspoonful of pearl ash.

MILK YEAST.

It is very nice for biscuits. Take half the milk needed

for the biscuits, put it in a warm place adding a little flour and salt; when light, mix it with the rest of the milk, and use it directly for the biscuits; 1 pint of this yeast is sufficient for 5 or 6 loaves of bread; it makes sweeter bread than any other yeast, but it will not keep.

WILLIAMSBURG YEAST.

Put into sufficient water 2 quarts of wheat bran, 1 pint of Indian bran, a handful of hops, and a teacup of parched corn; boil all together; strain it when all but cold; stir in a teacup of molasses, and add sufficient old yeast to make it ferment; then turn off the white scum, and bottle it. Mix some of the yeast, with a little flour, in a teacup, adding a little sugar, and set it near the fire, about 1 hour before wanted for use. Take off from the dough a piece for use, any time during the day.

CAKES.

CREAM PUFFS.

Put 1 cup of water on the fire, and when hot, melt in ½ cup of the best butter; when it boils, beat in 1 cup of sifted flour; if lumpy, stir till perfectly smooth; set it aside to cool; when cold, stir in, one at a time, three eggs without first beating them; drop the batter on tins in small spoonfuls, and bake ½ hour in a quick oven. For the cream : put ½ cup of milk to boil; beat the yolks of 2 eggs very stiff, add 4 tablespoonfuls of powdered sugar; when the milk boils, pour it on the eggs, stirring all the time; wet 2 tablespoonfuls of cornstarch, or fine flour, with a little cold milk, add it to the custard, and return it to the fire; stir until quite thick; when cold, flavor with vanilla. The cream is put in the puff by lifting the top with a knife and dropping in the cream with a spoon.

NEW YORK CUP CAKE.

Four eggs, 4 cups of sifted flour, 3 cups of powdered white sugar, 1 cup of butter, 1 cup of rich milk, 1 glass of wine, 1 grated nutmeg, 1 teaspoonful of cinnamon, beaten, a small teaspoonful of pearl ash; the cups should hold ½ pint; warm the milk, and cut up the butter in it; beat the eggs very light, and stir them into the milk, in turn with the flour; add the spice and wine, and lastly the pearl ash dissolved in a little vinegar; stir all very hard.

INDIAN POUND CAKE.

Eight eggs, 1 pint of powdered sugar, 1 pint of Indian meal sifted, ½ pint of wheat flour, ½ lb. of butter, 1 nutmeg grated, 1 teaspoonful of cinnamon, ¼ glass of wine and brandy mixed; stir the butter and sugar to a cream, beat

14

the eggs very light, stir the meal and eggs alternately
into the butter and sugar, add the spice and liquor;
stir all well; butter a tin pan, put in the mixture, and bake
it in a moderate oven.

MARBLED CAKE.

Take 3 or 4 cochineals, and soak in a wineglass of water,
adding a small pinch of soda; pour the cake into the pan
for baking, and at the same time pour with it this water,
mixing it well with the cake; this will marble a sponge
cake made with 10 eggs; any white cake will do.

SAVOY BISCUITS.

Take 12 eggs and their weight of good crushed sugar, also
the weight of 7 eggs of flour; beat the yolks and whites
separate; add the flour and sugar, stir them lightly with
the juice of 2 nice lemons, and the rind of 1, or 4 spoonfuls
of rose water; stir all well together, and bake on tins in a
moderately hot oven.

ABERDEEN CRULLA CAKE.

Beat to a cream $\frac{1}{4}$ lb. of fresh butter, and mix it with the
same quantity of pounded and sifted loaf sugar, 4 well
beaten eggs; add flour till thick enough to roll out; cut
the paste into oblong pieces, 4 or 5 inches in length, with a
paste cutter; divide the centre into 3 or 4 strips, wet the
edges, and plait one bar over the other, so as to meet in the
centre; throw them into boiling lard, or clarified suet;
when fried a light brown, drain them before the fire, and
cover them with pounded sugar. Very nice for tea.

SONTAG CAKE.

To 1 lb. of sifted flour, allow $\frac{1}{2}$ lb. of fresh butter washed
in rose water, 1 lb. of treacle, 1 nutmeg grated, a little
pounded mace and cinnamon, 1 ounce of pounded ginger,
$\frac{1}{2}$ ounce of blanched sweet almonds, 2 well beaten eggs;
melt the butter with the treacle, and when nearly cold, stir

in the eggs and the rest of the ingredients; mix all well together, make it into round cakes, and bake them upon tins.

FAMILY CAKE.

Take rice and flour, 6 ounces of each, the yolks and whites of 9 eggs, ½ lb. of lump sugar pounded and sifted, ¼ ounce of carraway seeds; beat this 1 hour, and bake it for the the same length of time in a quick oven. This is a very light cake; for delicate persons.

COCOANUT CAKE.

A moderate sized cup of grated cocoanut, an equal quantity of pounded sugar, the whites of 2 eggs well beaten; to each cup of the grated nut, add a little of the cocoanut milk.

COTTAGE CAKE.

Take 3 eggs, separately beaten, 1 common sized teacup of brown sugar, 2 of molasses, 1 of beaten ginger, 2 of butter, 1 of cream or milk, with a small piece of soda dissolved in it, 3 cups of flour; make it the consistency of pound cake, and flavor with orange or lemon peel; bake it either in a large size or small tins.

CARRAWAY CAKES.

Mix ½ lb. of sifted loaf sugar with 1 lb. of flour and ¼ lb. of butter; add some carraway seeds; make it into a stiff paste with 3 well beaten eggs and a little rose water; roll it out thin, cut it into round cakes, prick them with a fork, and bake them upon floured tins in a quick oven.

HAMPTON CAKES.

Beat the yolks of 8 eggs and the whites of 5, add ½ lb. of pounded loaf sugar, ¼ lb. of sifted flour, and the grated peel of a small lemon; beat all well together, and bake it in a floured tin.

CREAM CAKES.

Put 1 lb. of flour upon a pie-board; make a hole in the middle, put in ½ pint of clotted cream, and a little salt; mix the paste lightly, let it stand for ½ hour, then add ½ lb. of butter, roll it out 5 times, the same as puff paste, form it into small cakes, gild them with the yolk of egg, and bake in an oven.

CAKE WITHOUT BUTTER.

Take the weight of 3 eggs in sugar, and the weight of 2 in flour; when the 5 are well beaten, gradually add the sugar, and then the flour, with a little orange flower water; beat all well together, and bake it in a floured tin.

FRENCH CAKE.

Six ounces of sweet almonds, 3 ounces of bitter almonds, 3 ounces of sifted flour, dried near the fire, 14 eggs, 1 lb. of powdered sugar; flavor it with vanilla or orange flower water.

COMMON CAKE.

One lb. of sugar, 2 lbs. of flour, 1 lb. of butter, the yolks of 5 eggs, 8 spoonfuls of cream; 1 wineglass of brandy; spice to the taste.

OAK HILL CAKES.

To 4 quarts of flour, add 1 lb. of brown sugar, 2 ounces of beaten ginger, a little allspice, 1 lb. of butter rubbed in very fine, 4 eggs beaten up light, 1 quart of molasses is necessary to make it up; then roll it in thin cakes, and bake them.

BLACK CAKE.

PLAIN.

Ten cups of flour to 10 eggs, 4 cups of sugar, 4 of molasses, 4 of butter, 3 of lard, 2 cups of seasoning, such as ginger, cinnamon and mace, 1 spoonful of soda to a tablespoonful of milk; mix all well together, and bake in a regular oven.

BLACK CAKE.

To 1 lb. of butter and 1 lb. of crushed sugar, beaten to a cream, stir in 12 eggs whipped to a froth; sift in 1 lb. of flour, and add 3 lbs. of stoned raisins, 3 lbs. of cleaned currants, 5 grated nutmegs, $\frac{1}{2}$ ounce of pounded cinnamon, 1 teaspoonful of ground cloves, sifted; 1 lb. of citron cut into thin slices; mix all well together; bake in a buttered pan, in rather a moderate oven.

SWEET BISCUITS.

Two quarts of flour, 1 quart of sugar, 8 spoonfuls of milk, butter sufficient to knead them; season with the rind of 3 lemons and the juice of 1.

SPRING CAKE.

Fifteen eggs, the weight of 14 in sugar, and 7 in flour, the rind and juice of 2 lemons.

LOVE KNOTS.

Take 3 eggs, 5 spoonfuls of white sugar, $\frac{1}{2}$ teaspoonful of soda dissolved in 2 teaspoonfuls of cold water, 1 tablespoonful of butter, and flour enough to roll; cut the sheet in slips, tie them in love knots, and fry in pure white lard.

SPANISH CAKE.

Rub, till quite fine and smooth, 1 lb. of butter with 2 lbs. of flour; add 1 lb. of good brown sugar; roll fine; mix all together with 4 well beaten eggs; break the paste into small bits, and bake upon floured tins.

SUGAR CAKES.

Take $\frac{1}{2}$ lb. of dry sifted flour, the same quantity of fresh butter washed in rose water, and $\frac{1}{4}$ lb. of sifted loaf sugar; then mix together the flour and sugar; rub in the butter, and add the yolk of an egg beaten with a tablespoonful of cream; make it into a paste roll, and cut it into small round cakes; bake upon a floured tin.

SHREWSBURY CAKE.

One quart of flour, 2 large or 3 small eggs, ½ lb. of butter, 1 quart of good brown sugar, 2 nutmegs, and orange peel to the taste.

SPONGE CAKE, WITH BUTTER.

The weight of 14 eggs in sugar, 8 in flour and 6 or 7 in butter; cream the butter and flour together; then beat the eggs and sugar light; then add the rind and juice of a lemon; bake in cups.

SPONGE CAKE.

The weight of 10 eggs in very fine sugar, 6 in flour; beat the yolks with the flour, and the whites alone; then, by degrees, mix the whites and flour with the other ingredients; bake in a quick oven.

COMMENCEMENT CAKE.

Six lbs. of flour, 3 lbs. of sugar, 3 lbs of butter, 6 eggs, 1 quart of milk, 1 pint of wine, 1 pint of yeast, 4 lbs. of fruit, 1 ounce of citron, 1 ounce of nutmeg, mace to the taste; this quantity must be divided, and baked in moulds, which hold about 2 lbs.

CUMBERLAND CAKE.

One and a half lbs. of flour, 1 lb. of sugar, 12 ounces of butter, 10 eggs, 1 glass of orange or lemon brandy, a few cloves, mace, or nutmeg; beat as pound cake; bake in small tins.

BENTON TEA CAKES.

Rub into 1 lb. of flour 6 ounces of butter and 3 spoonfuls of yeast; make into a paste with new milk; make into biscuits, and prick them with a clean fork.

ORANGE CAKE.

Take 4 ripe oranges; roll them under your hand on the table till quite soft; break up 1 lb. of the best loaf sugar, and on some of the pieces, rub off the yellow rind of the oranges;

then cut the oranges, and squeeze the juice through a strainer; powder the sugar and mix the orange juice with it; wash and squeeze in a pan of cold water, 1 lb. of good butter, till you have extracted all the salt and milk. Cut up the butter in the pan of sugar and orange, and stir it hard till perfectly light; sift into a pan 14 ounces of flour; beat 10 eggs very light and thick; then stir them by degrees, into the butter and sugar, alternately with the flour, a little of each at a time; beat the whole very hard for some time, after all the ingredients are in; have a large, shallow, square pan, well buttered; put in the mixture, and set immediately into a brisk oven; when properly baked, it is delicious.

REDDIE CAKE.

Rub ¾ lb. of butter into 1 lb. of sifted flour; mix in 1 lb. of powdered sugar, 1 tablespoonful of powdered cinnamon, 3 well beaten eggs; mix all into a dough; roll it out; cut it into round cakes, and bake in a quick oven.

DROP BISCUITS.

One lb. of flour, ½ lb. sugar, ¼ lb. butter, 5 eggs, mace and nutmeg to the taste, drop them on tin sheets and bake them in a quick oven.

LEMON POUND CAKE.

Twenty ounce of sugar, 14 of flour, 14 of butter, 15 eggs, leaving out the whites of 3, rind and juice of fresh lemons.

BROWN CAKES.

Half a lb. of butter, 1 lb. of flour, ½ lb. of sugar, 3 eggs, leaving out the yolk of one; mix all together in a stiff paste; roll it out and cut it into strips; mix the yolk of 1 egg with rose water, and spread it on the top of the cakes, with mace, pounded almonds and fine sugar; bake them on tin sheets. Delicious.

SILVER CAKE.

Stir to a cream, 1 cup of butter with 2 of white sugar, and

the whites of 6 eggs beaten stiff, 1 cup of sweet milk, with ½ teaspoonful of soda dissolved in it; stir 1 teaspoonful cream of tartar into 4 cups of flour, and add to the cake; flavor with vanilla, bitter almond or rose water.

GOLD CAKE.

Stir to a cream ½ cup of butter with 2 of sugar; add the yolks of 6 eggs beaten very stiff; then add ½ cup of milk with ½ teaspoonful of soda in it; mix 1 teaspoonful of cream of tartar with flour enough to make it as thick as cup cake; flavor as for silver cake, or with 1 teaspoonful of cinnamon, ½ nutmeg; currants and raisins are considered an improvement by some.

FRENCH CAKE.

Twelve eggs, the yolks and whites beaten well and separately, 1 lb. of pounded and sifted loaf sugar, the grated peel of a lemon, ½ lb. of sifted flour, the same weight of sifted, dried-ground rice, 4 ounces of sweet, and 1 of bitter almonds, pounded in a mortar together with a tablespoonful of orange flower water; mix all these ingredients gradually, and beat them well; paper the pan, and bake the cake for one hour.

ALMOND CAKES.

One lb. of butter beaten to a cream, ½ lb. of finely pounded white sugar, ½ lb. dried and sifted flour, and the same quantity of blanched sweet almonds cut into small thin pieces, one well beaten egg, and a little rose water; mix all well together, and with a spoon drop the batter upon wafer paper, or tins, and then bake.

BROWN CAKES.

Half lb. of butter, 1 lb. of flour, ¼ lb. of sugar, 3 eggs, leaving out the yolk of one; mix all together in a stiff paste; roll it out; cut it in strips; mix the yolk of 1 egg with rose water, and spread it on the top of the cakes; strew mace with pounded sugar and almonds on the top of the cakes also, and bake them on tin sheets.

COCOANUT CAKE.

Whip the whites of 10 eggs; grate 2 nuts and add them; 1 lb. of white sugar, ½ lb. of sifted flour; stir this well, flavor with rose water; pour into pans, and bake ¾ of an hour.

MERINGUES.

Beat the whites of 10 eggs to a stiff froth, adding slowly 10 tablespoonfuls of sifted crushed sugar, very finely powdered; when well beaten, and quite stiff, put it in the form of a large egg on paper; then ornament with the glaizing sugar and lay the paper on a tin, in a moderate oven; when of a light brown, take them out, and remove from beneath all that which is not cooked with a spoon; this must be done with care, placing them when cold in the oven to dry; then put any kind of delicate preserve in each, and flavor with anything fancied.

DERBY CAKE.

In 2 lbs. of sifted flour, put 1 lb. of butter, 1 lb. of raisins, 1 lb. of good brown sugar; beat 1 egg very lightly, 1 pint of new milk; mix all well together; roll it out thin and cut it into round cakes; lay them on baking tins in a moderately heated oven for 10 minutes.

ROSA CAKE.

Two lbs. of flour, 2 lbs. of butter, 2 lbs of sugar, the yolks of 4 eggs, with the whites of 8, a glass of wine, and 1 of rose water; mix all well together; lay them on tin sheets in small lumps and bake in a quick oven.

SHREWSBURY BISCUIT.

Two lbs. of flour, 1 lb. of butter, 3 ounces of ginger, 5 eggs, 1½ lbs. of white sugar; season with nutmeg or orange peel; mix all well together and bake them in a slow oven.

15

CHARLOTTE CAKE.

Take 6 eggs, ½ lb. of white sugar, ½ lb. of butter creamed with ¾ lb. of yeast dough; flavor with lemon or bitter almond to suit the taste; bake as you would light bread.

VICTORIA BUNS.

Take 2½ lbs. of flour, ¾ lb. of butter, 1 lb. of sugar, 8 eggs, 1 glass of wine, 1 nutmeg, 1 pint of milk; put in as much yeast as will rise them.

NORFOLK BLACK CAKE.

Take 1 lb. of flour, 1 lb. of butter, 1 lb. of white sugar, 12 eggs, 2 lbs. of raisins, 2 lbs. of currants, 1 lb. of citron, 2 tablespoonfuls of mixed spice (mace and cinnamon), 2 nutmegs powdered, a large glass of wine, 1 of brandy, ½ glass of rose water; this cake will require 4 or 5 hours to bake. Ice it next day.

ALMOND CAKE.

Two ounces of blanched bitter almonds, beat very fine, 7 ounces of finely sifted flour, well dried, 10 eggs, 1 lb. of loaf sugar, pounded and sifted, 2 tablespoonfuls of rose water; iced with the whites of eggs and 24 teaspoonfuls of loaf sugar; season with lemon, rose water, or vanilla.

INDIAN POUND CAKE.

The weight of 8 eggs in pounded sugar, weight of 6 in sifted Indian meal, ½ lb. of butter, 1 grated nutmeg, or a teaspoonful of cinnamon.

SUGAR BISCUITS.

Take 3 lbs. of sifted flour, 1 lb, of butter, 1½ lbs. of powdered sugar, ½ pint of milk, 2 tablespoonfuls of brandy, 1 small teaspoonful of soda dissolved in water, 4 tablespoonfuls of carraway seed.

DOUGHNUTS.

Three lbs. of sifted flour, 1 lb. of powdered sugar, 3 lbs. of butter, 4 eggs, ½ cup of the best brewers' yeast, 1½ pints of milk, 1 teaspoonful of powdered cinnamon, 1 grated nutmeg, a tablespoonful of rose water; fry them in lard, and grate fine loaf sugar over them.

BROWN CAKES.

Two cups of sugar, 1 of butter, 3 eggs, 1 pint of milk, 1 teaspoonful of soda, a pinch of salt, mace to the taste, flour enough to make a soft dough; roll and cut into small cakes; then throw them into boiling lard, turn them over, and take them out with a fork, dripping all the lard from them; sift sugar over each one whilst hot.

ORANGE CAKES.

To 2 quarts of flour, add 2 tablespoonfuls of butter, 1 large cup of brown sugar; mix it with molasses enough to roll thin, after seasoning with a great deal of orange peel, well powdered; these cakes being made without eggs, are very nice and very economical.

SUGAR CAKES.

To 2 quarts of flour, add 6 eggs, 2 tablespoonfuls of brown sugar to each egg, 1 of butter, and 2 of lard; dissolve 1 teaspoonful of soda in $\frac{1}{2}$ wineglass of wine; season it with orange peel or cinnamon, to the taste, and after rolling thin, bake in a quick oven.

HOLIDAY CAKE.

Three lbs. of flour, 6 ounces of butter, 1 ounce of the best powdered ginger, 1 ounce of carraway seeds ground, $\frac{1}{2}$ ounce of sweet pepper, 2 lbs. of treacle, $\frac{1}{4}$ lb. of sugar, a large teaspoonful of soda, mixed in boiling water; butter and treacle both melted; bake in a slow oven for $2\frac{1}{2}$ hours.

SCOTCH BREAD.

One lb. and a quarter of flour, $\frac{3}{4}$ lb. of sugar, $\frac{3}{4}$ lb. of butter, lemon to taste; bake 20 minutes in rather a slow oven·

EXPRESS PUDDING.

Beat up 8 eggs, put them into a stewpan with ½ lb. of sugar, the same of butter, and some grated nutmeg; put it on the fire, stirring it till it thickens; then pour it into a bowl to cool; set a rich paste around the edge of the dish, pour in the pudding, and bake it in a moderate oven.

PREMIUM CAKE.

Three cups of loaf sugar, 1 of butter; rub the butter and sugar to a cream; then stir in the yolks of 5 eggs well beaten; dissolve a teaspoonful of soda in a cup of milk, add the milk, beat the whites of the eggs to a froth, add them; sift in 4 cups of flour as light as possible; lastly, add the juice and peel of one lemon—the peel grated.

SPICE CAKE.

One lb. of flour, 1 lb. of sugar, ¾ lb. of butter, 6 eggs, 1 small spoonful of cinnamon, the same of cloves, and 1 wine-glass of brandy; beat the butter and sugar together until smooth, add the flour and eggs by degrees, the brandy and spice alternately, and immediately before cooking, dissolve a teaspoonful of soda in a cup of sour cream; stir it all well, and put in the mould to bake.

SILVER CAKE.

One lb. of pulverized sugar, ¾ lb. of flour, 7 ounces of butter, the whites of 14 eggs, ¼ teaspoonful of baking powder; put the powder in the flour before sifting; cream the butter and sugar, then add the eggs; lastly, add the flour; put 2 or 3 thicknesses of paper around the pan, and an iron lid over the top until the cake is pretty well cooked through, so as not to have it cook too rapidly on the outside.

WAFERS.

To 6 eggs add 1 lb. of sugar, ¾ lb. of flour, ½ lb. of butter, 2 winglasses of wine, and a grated nutmeg; bake in wafer irons.

KENDALL CAKES.

To 1¼ lbs. of white sugar add 2 eggs, 1 teaspoonful of soda, ½ pint of milk, ¼ lb. of butter, some mace, a little wine; these ingredients to be well beaten with a sufficient quantity of flour to roll out; makes very nice small cakes; cut into pretty shapes.

TEA CAKES.

Three cups of sugar, 3 eggs, 1 cup of milk, 1 cup of butter, 2 cups of flour, a teaspoonful of soda; roll out, and bake in small cakes.

OATLAND CAKES.

The yolks of 8 eggs, 8 spoonfuls of sugar, flour enough to roll out, a small lump of butter (melted), 1 spoonful of powdered ginger and mace; roll in sugar, and bake in shapes.

PLAIN CAKE.

Take 12 eggs, leave out the whites of 2, 1 lb. of sugar, a good lb. of butter, 1 lb. of flour, with 2 tablespoonfuls taken out, a glass of wine, and mace to your taste.

CUP CAKE.

Two and one-half cups of unsifted flour, 2 cups of sugar, 1 cup of butter, whites of 8 eggs, ½ cup of sweet milk, 2 teaspoonfuls of yeast powder, sifted in the flour, cream butter and sugar together; add to this the whites of the eggs well beaten, then the flour, and lastly the milk.

JELLY CAKE.

The above baked in jelly pans, or whole and sliced, makes a delicious cake spread with the following: to 1 pint of fresh milk, boiling hot, add 2 tablespoons of cornstarch dissolved in a little cold milk; stir continually until as thick as blanc mange; put on a layer of this and grated cocoanut.

LEMON JELLY CAKE.

Lemon jelly cake is made by using this same cake, and a jelly made by the following receipt: the juice and rind of 3 lemons, ¾ lb. of butter, 1 lb. of white sugar, yolks of 6 eggs; beat the eggs and sugar very light; melt the butter and pour it on the eggs and sugar; pour boiling water over the lemons, then grate the outside, first pressing out the juice; add rind and juice; boil slowly and stir constantly, until of the consistency of blanc mange.

ANGEL'S FOOD.

The whites of 11 eggs, 1½ tumblers of sifted powdered sugar, 1 tumbler of sifted flour, 1 teaspoonful of cream of tartar; sift the flour 4 times, leaving the tumbler even full; then add the cream of tartar and sift again; beat the eggs to a stiff froth on a dish, and on the same dish add sugar lightly, then flour gently, then vanilla, and do not stop beating until you put it in the oven to bake; bake 40 minutes in a moderately heated oven, and if then too soft, let it remain a few minutes longer; do not open the oven until it has been in 15 minutes; turn the pan upside down to cool, and when cold, take out the cake by loosening it with a knife; then ice; the pan must never have been used, that is to say, greased. The tumbler must be of dimensions of 2½ gills.

NAPLES BISCUIT.

One lb. flour, 1 lb. sugar, 12 whites and 10 yolks of eggs, 2 glasses of Madeira wine, 1 teaspoonful of mace; drop on pans, and let them harden gradually in the stove until quite crisp, turning frequently.

CAKE FOR SAUCE.

Two eggs, 1 cup of sugar, ½ cup of butter, 1 cup of milk or water, 2½ cups of flour, 1 spoon of yeast powder; flavor to taste. For sauce: 2 eggs, 1 cup of sugar, 1 tablespoon of butter; stir in 1 pint of boiling water, a little salt, and season; let it thicken, but not turn.

COFFEE CAKE.

One cup of sugar, 1 cup of butter, 1 cup of molasses, 1 egg, well mixed together; then add 1 cup of warm coffee, with 1 teaspoonful of soda, 4 cups of flour, 1 lb. of raisins or currants, 1 tablespoonful, each, of cloves, cinnamon and nutmeg.

SPICE CAKE.

Four cups of sifted flour, 1 of butter, 1 of sugar, 1 of molasses, ½ cup of sour milk, 1 teaspoon of soda, 3 eggs, 1 teaspoon of ginger, 1 of spice, 1 of cinnamon, 1 of cloves, 1 of mace. Very nice fruit cake can be made by doubling above quantities, and adding all kinds of fruit; it also makes excellent Christmas cake.

SNOW BALLS.

One lb. of butter, 1 of flour, 1 of sugar, 10 eggs, 2 teaspoonfuls of mace, 2 of nutmeg, 1 large wineglass of brandy, 1 of wine, 1 lb. of citron, 1 lb. of almonds, blanch them and beat fine with rose water; separate the whites of the eggs from the yolks; mix the yolks and sugar together; the whites should be beaten to a very light froth, then added to the yolks and sugar; cream the butter light and mix in by degrees; beat all together very light, then mix in the flour, beat it till quite smooth, add the mace and nutmeg, then the wine and brandy, and lastly the raisins; then the citron and almonds; stir all well together, butter the cups, fill them nearly full, and bake in a quick oven.

CUP CAKE.

Three cups of flour, 2 of sugar, 1 of butter, 1 of cream, 4 eggs, a teaspoonful of soda and cream of tartar; mix all well together, beat light, and bake in a moderate oven.

PEARL CAKE.

Take 1 pint of milk and boil it; melt ¾ lb. of butter in the same quantity of sugar, 4 eggs, 1 teaspoonful of soda, spice to the taste, and sufficient flour to make it as stiff as pound cake.

PORTSMOUTH CAKES.

Three cups of sugar, 1 cup of butter, 3 eggs, 1 cup of milk, 1 teaspoonful of soda dissolved, 4 cups of flour well beaten; if it is too stiff, add a little more milk; season with nutmeg and mace; roll out thin, and bake in a moderate oven.

JENNY LINDS.

Two lbs. of sugar, 3 lbs. of flour, 1 lb. of butter, 7 eggs, nutmeg and orange peel to the taste.

THOMPSON CAKE.

Stir together till very light and white, ½ lb. of butter, ¾ lb. of sugar; beat the yolks and whites of 7 eggs, separately, to a froth; stir them into the cake, and put in a wineglass of brandy, a grated nutmeg, and 1½ lbs. of sifted flour; just before it is baked, add ½ pint of thick cream and 1 lb. of seeded raisins.

CRULLERS.

Four eggs, 3 cups brown sugar, 1 nutmeg, 1 tablespoonful butter, 1 cup water, 1 teaspoonful yeast powder, and flour to roll; cut out with a biscuit cutter, then cut from the centre with an apple corer; twist into fanciful shapes, and fry in a potato fryer in plenty of boiling lard.

WHITE CAKE.

One lb. powdered sugar, ¾ lb. butter, ¾ lb. of flour, ¼ lb. corn starch, whites of 15 eggs; wash the butter free of salt; cream it well, and add the sugar, using a porcelain potato masher instead of a spoon; add gradually the flour and cornstarch, and lastly the well beaten whites; flavor with almond to taste, and bake as pound cake.

ALMOND BALLS.

Half a pound of almonds blanched and pounded very fine, with as much rose or orange flower water as will prevent their oiling, the yolks of 8 and the whites of 4 eggs, beaten until very light, and added to the almonds; then beat in ¾ lb. of loaf sugar; continue to beat while the oven is heating; when ready, add 3 ounces of wheat flour, which must be stirred in and not beaten; butter the pans and fill them half full; sprinkle a little sugar over them, as you put them in the oven, which must be a moderate one.

NUT CAKES.

One lb. of nut kernels, 1 lb. of sugar, the whites of 6 eggs beaten to a stiff froth, 2 tablespoonfuls of flour.

POUND CAKE.

Sixteen whites of eggs, 1 lb. of white sugar, ¾ lb. of butter, 1 lb. of flour, cream butter; then mix the sugar, and put in flour and eggs alternately; bake 2 hours.

MRS. CLAY'S PREMIUM CAKE.

Fourteen eggs, whites only, 1 lb. of sugar, ¾ lb. of flour, ½ lb. of butter, whisky and lemon to taste.

COCOANUT CAKE.

Grate 1 cocoanut, and set aside, the whites of 7 eggs, beat very light, 3 teacups of sifted flour, 2 teacups of sifted white sugar, ½ cup of butter, and ½ cup of milk or water; beat well together, and add 2 teaspoons yeast powder; bake in 4 jelly cake pans; make an icing of 3 whites of eggs and 1 lb. of sugar beaten together until stiff enough to stand as you drop it from the beater; flavor to taste; spread the icing on one of the cakes, then sprinkle cocoanut over, and lightly

16

press with palm of the hand; place another cake upon the first, and continue the process until all are used. I think it is prettier to use icing only on the top of the last cake, but some prefer to reserve enough of the grated cocoanut to spread of it as over the others; the yellows can be well made into gold cake or custard.

BERWICK SPONGE CAKE.

Beat 6 eggs, yolks and whites together, 2 minutes; add 3 cups of sugar and beat 5 minutes; 2 cups of flour with 2 teaspoons cream of tartar and beat 2 minutes; 1 cup of cold water with 1 teaspoon of soda dissolved in it, and beat 1 minute; flavor; add a little salt, and 3 more cups of flour (without cream of tartar) and beat 1 minute. Observe time exactly.

TEA CAKES,

To 3 pints of flour add 3 eggs, 1 pint of sugar, ½ teaspoonful of soda to a teacup of milk, and a large spoonful of butter.

CHARLOTTE RUSSE, WITHOUT CREAM.

One box of gelatine, 1 quart of milk, 1 lb. of powdered sugar, 10 eggs; pour over the gelatine 1 pint of cold water, allow it to soak at least 10 minutes; then pour over a pint of boiling water; beat the yolks of the eggs with the sugar, boil the milk in a porcelain or brass kettle; when it comes to a boil, pour in the gelatine, and let the mixture come to a boil again, stirring all the time; as soon as it boils, pour over the beaten eggs and sugar, stirring briskly to mix it well; have the kettle thoroughly scraped at the bottom; then pour the whole back into it, and put it over a moderate fire to thicken; be careful not to let it curdle; the moment it begins to simmer, take it off and pour out, stirring occasionally until it cools; when cool, add the beaten whites, and flavor with vanilla; line a pan with lady fingers or sponge cake, and pour in the mixture; then set it in the coolest place possible to congeal; to prevent the lady fingers floating out of their places, pour a little of the mixture in and let it congeal so as to fix them at the bottom and sides of the pan; when that is done, pour in the rest of the mixture and it will congeal, as it should, within the cake.

GINGER BREAD NUTS.

One lb. of flour; rub into it ¼ lb. of butter, ¼ lb. of white powdered sugar, 1 ounce of grated ginger, and the peel of a lemon; bake in a slow oven.

WINTER GINGER CAKES.

Break 3 eggs in a bowl, beat them well, add ½ pint of sweet cream, which must be beaten with them, and the whole put into a saucepan over the fire; stir till it gets warm; then add 1 lb. of butter, and ½ lb. of loaf sugar, and 2½ ounces of ginger, both powdered; stir the whole carefully over the fire, just to melt the butter; then pour it on to 2 lbs. of flour, and form it all into a paste; roll it or break it into pieces, as you think proper, and bake it.

ROYAL GINGER CAKES.

Three lbs. of flour, 1 lb. of sugar, 1 lb. of butter, mixed well together with ½ pint of molasses, 1 gill of cream, 1 cup of ginger; roll out, and bake in a slack oven.

SOFT GINGER BREAD.

Five cups of flour, 2 of molasses, 1 of sugar, 1 of butter, 8 eggs, 1 teacup of allspice and ginger mixed; bake in a pan or small cups.

JELLY SPONGE CAKE.

One cup of flour, 1 of sugar, 4 eggs, the whites beaten separately, ½ teaspoonful of soda, ½ a lemon; bake it thin in square pans; spread the bottom with jelly, and roll in as soon as taken from the oven.

LIGHT GINGER BREAD.

Two lbs. of flour, 1 lb. of butter, ½ lb. of sugar, 1 pint of molasses, 6 eggs; dissolve a teaspoonful of soda in the juice of a lemon, add the rind, and bake it in cake pans; raisins and citron are a great improvement.

GINGER CAKES.

Take 6 cups of flour, 3 cups of molasses, 1 cup of sour milk, 1 cup of butter, 1 tablespoonful of soda dissolved in water, 1 tablespoonful of ginger, a little salt and 4 eggs.

GINGER NUTS.

Two lbs. of sifted flour, 2 quarts of molasses, ¾ lb. of sugar, ½ lb. of candied orange peel, cut small, 1 ounce of strong ginger (ground), 1 ounce of allspice, ¾ lb. of butter oiled; mix all well together, and set it by for some time; then roll it out in pieces the size of a walnut, put them in rows on a baking plate, press them flat with the hand, and bake them in a slow oven for 10 minutes. Very nice.

LIGHT GINGER BREAD.

Take 2 lbs. of flour, 1 lb. of butter, ½ lb. of sugar, 1 pint of molasses, 6 eggs, dissolve 1 teaspoonful of soda in the juice of a lemon, add the rind, and bake in cake pans; citron and raisins are a great improvement.

DICKSON GINGER BREAD.

To 4 eggs add 2 cups of brown sugar, 4 cups of flour, 2 of butter, 1 of cream, 2 of molasses, 1 teaspoonful of soda, ½ cup of ginger; beat very light, and bake in cups or a pan.

LIGHT GINGER CAKES.

Take 6 eggs, 1 lb. of flour, ¾ lb. of brown sugar, ½ lb. of butter, ginger and mace to the taste; put in small cups or tins, and bake in a slow oven.

NIAGARA GINGER BREAD.

Take 4 eggs, 2 teacups of brown sugar, 4 cups of flour, 2 cups of butter, 1 cup of cream, 2 cups of molasses, 1 teaspoonful of soda, ½ cup of ginger; beat very light, and bake very light.

GINGER CUP CAKE.

Three cups of flour, 1 of sugar, 1 of molasses, 1 of butter, 1 tablespoonful of ginger, 1 teaspoonful of soda, 3 eggs, 1 lb. of stoned and chopped raisins; bake in small pans.

SOFT GINGER BREAD.

Five cups of flour, 2 cups of molasses, 1 cup of sugar, 1 cup of butter, 8 eggs, 1 teacup of allspice and ginger, mixed; bake quickly.

GINGER BREAD.

Four lbs. of flour, 1 lb. of brown sugar, 1 lb. butter, 2 ounces of ginger, 1 gill of cream, warmed, 1 quart of molasses; knead them well together, roll them out and bake quickly.

SPONGE GINGER CAKE.

Warm 1 pint of molasses; stir in while warm a piece of butter the size of an egg, 1 tablespoonful of white ginger, 1 teaspoonful of soda dissolved in milk; strain this into the mixture; when cool, sift in as much flour as will make it stiff; roll it out in cake, and bake on tins.

SUGAR GINGER BREAD.

Two lbs. of flour, 1½ lbs. of brown sugar, 1 lb. of butter, 9 eggs, 1 cup of powdered ginger, 1 cup of wine; rub the butter and sugar to a cream, beat the eggs and add them, stir in the flour, ginger and wine; bake in a quick oven.

JUMBLES.

Six eggs, well beaten separately, to 1 lb. of flour, good weight, ¾ lb. of sugar, ½ lb. of butter; mix them as you would beaten cake, except that the batter must be stiff enough to roll in cakes; have ½ lb. of white sugar beaten to roll them in; mace and orange peel to the taste; 2 grains of soda

JUMBLES.

One egg, 1 lb. of flour, ½ lb. of sugar, ½ lb. of butter, 1 tablespoonful of cream, the rind of 3 lemons, and the juice of 1, all made into a paste, and rolled in the form of rings, before baking.

COCOANUT JUMBLES.

Grate a large cocoanut, rub ½ lb. of butter into 1 lb. of flour, 3 eggs; add the nut to form a stiff dough; make the jumbles with the hands, grate cocoanut and sugar over them, and then bake them.

JUMBLES.

Three eggs, ½ lb. flour sifted, ½ lb. butter, ½ lb. pounded loaf sugar, a tablespoonful of rose water, a grated nutmeg, mixed mace and cinnamon; stir the sugar and butter to a cream, beat the eggs very light, put them all at once into the pan of flour, butter and sugar; then add the spice and rose water; stir the whole with a knife; when this is done, take a portion of the dough and lay it on the board; roll it lightly with the hands into long thin rolls, which must be cut into equal lengths, curled up into rings, and laid into an iron or tin pan, buttered; bake them in a quick oven for 5 minutes; grate loaf sugar over them.

FEDERAL CAKE.

One coffee cup of butter, 1½ of sugar, 1 of milk, 3 of flour, 4 eggs, 1 teaspoonful of soda, all well mixed together.

FRENCH JUMBLES.

Take 1¼ lbs. of flour; ¾ lb. of sugar, a very large spoonful of butter, ½ lb. of almonds, 1 nutmeg and 4 eggs.

TEA CAKE.

One lb. of flour, 1 lb. of sugar, ½ lb. of butter, 6 eggs, 2 teaspoonfuls of cream of tartar, and 1 teaspoonful of soda, mixed with the flour; seasoned with mace; salt to the taste.

HARRISON CAKE.

Eight eggs, 6 cups of flour, 4 cups of sugar, 2 cups of butter, 1 cup of cream, 1 teaspoonful of soda, and 1 nutmeg; it is very nice eaten with fresh butter.

WHIGS.

One pint of milk, 2 lbs. of flour, ½ lb. of butter, 4 tablespoonfuls of white sugar, 6 eggs, 1 teacup of yeast, 2 teaspoonfuls of salt; season with mace or nutmeg; make it up in the morning, and set it to rise; bake it in a pan for tea; eat it hot with fresh butter and pounded sugar, sifted over it; if it should not rise sufficient, add a small teaspoonful of yeast powder, dissolved in a little milk, just before it is baked. Genuine.

COMMON CAKE.

One lb. and a half of flour, 1 lb. of good brown sugar, 8 well beaten eggs, and 1 ounce of carraway seeds are to be mixed together; then add of fresh yeast, milk, and of water, 1 tablespoonful each, let it stand a short time, and bake it in a floured tin. Very good.

CURD CAKES.

One quart of curds, 8 eggs, leaving out 4 whites, 4 tablespoonfuls of sugar, grated nutmeg, and a little flour; mix all well together; heat butter in a frying-pan; drop them in and fry like fritters.

JAPAN CAKE.

Stir together ¾ lb. of sugar, ½ lb. of butter; when white, add 5 beaten eggs, 1 teaspoonful of rose water, or a nutmeg, and 1 lb. of flour; drop it with a large spoon on flat tins that have been buttered; sift sugar over them.

CAKE WITHOUT EGGS.

One cup of butter, 3 cups of sugar, 1 pint of sour cream, 1½ pints of flour, 1 lb. of chopped raisins, 1 spoonful of soda, spice to the taste; bake about 1 hour.

LANCERS CAKE.

Take 1 lb. of fresh butter, 1 lb. of powdered white sugar, and 2 lbs. of sifted flour, and rub the butter into it, crumbled fine; add a heaping tablespoonful of mixed nutmeg and cinnamon; put no water, but moisten it entirely with butter; a small glass of brandy is an improvement; roll it out into a large, thick sheet, and cut it into round cakes about the size of saucers; bake them on flat tins, slightly buttered. This cake is very crumbly, but very good, and keeps very well; it may be taken to camp packed in boxes.

CHOCOLATE MACAROONS.

Scrape down, very fine, ½ lb. of the best prepared cocoa; beat to a stiff froth the whites of 4 eggs, and beat into the white of egg 1 lb. of powdered sugar, in turn with the chocolate, adding a little sifted flour, if the mixture appears too thin; grease the bottom of some oblong tin pans, very slightly, with sweet oil or good butter; having formed the mixture into small, thick cakes, lay them (not close) in the pan, and bake them a few minutes; sift sugar over them while warm.

ORANGE CAKES.

Make a mixture precisely as for queen cake, only omit the wine, brandy and rose water, and substitute the grated yellow rind and the juice of 4 large, ripe oranges, stirred into the batter in turn with the eggs and flour; flavor the icing with orange juice.

JUMBLES.

One egg, 1 lb. of flour, ½ lb. of sugar, ½ lb. of butter, 1 tablespoonful of cream, the rind of 3 lemons and juice of 1; mix all well together in a thick paste; roll out, and bake quickly.

SPONGE CAKE.

Four cups of flour, 1 cup of sugar, 1 cup of cold water, 8 eggs and a little soda dissolved in vinegar.

PEACH LEATHERS.

Take ripe peaches and add sugar to taste; boil until they will spread smoothly over a dish; dry chiefly in the stove and then in the sun, covering with a net; when sufficiently dry, warm slightly; cut in strips; roll in sugar and eat, say, Christmas.

GINGER COOKIES.

One teacup of sugar, 1 egg, 1 spoonful soda, 1 spoonful ginger, 1 spoonful vinegar; mix all with 7 cups of flour.

FILLING FOR CHOCOLATE CAKE.

Five tablespoonfuls of grated chocolate with enough cream or milk to wet it, 1 cupful sugar, and 1 egg well beaten; stir the ingredients over the fire until thoroughly mixed; then flavor with vanilla.

GINGER BREAD.

Two quarts of flour, 1 lb. of butter, ½ lb. of sugar, 9 eggs, 1 pint of molasses, 1 cup of ginger, 2 teaspoonfuls of soda.

MACAROONS.

Take 2 ounces of blanched almonds or peach kernels the latter must be thrown in cold water to take off the bitter taste, then drained and pounded in a mortar till they become a stiff paste; then take the white of an egg, beat it to a stiff froth and mix it with the almonds; sift in as

17

much refined sugar as will turn it to a stiff dough; form it into small cakes and put them on sheets of tin, which must be greased, and bake them in a very moderate oven; the whites of 2 eggs to 1 lb. of sugar.

CINNAMON CAKES.

Three eggs to 3 pints of flour, 1 lb. of sugar, ½ lb. of butter, 1 tablespoonful of beaten cinnamon; roll them in flour, and mould them thin; bake in a moderate oven.

CALLERS.

Take about 5 cents worth of rice, soak and pound it in a mortar; let it stand over night, then add the yolks of 3 eggs, put in a dessertspoonful of yeast powder, enough flour to make a light batter, add the whites of the eggs well beaten; have a pot of boiling lard, and cook as for fritters.

ROLL JELLY CAKE.

Three eggs, 1 cup of sugar, 1 cup of flour, yeast powder; beat the eggs well, add the sugar, then the flour; bake in a shallow square pan; when done, take it out, spread on the jelly, and roll at once.

DELICATE CAKE.

Nearly 3 cups of flour, 2 cups of powdered sugar, ¾ cup of sweet milk, whites of 6 eggs, ½ cup of butter, yeast powder; flavor with lemon.

SWEET WAFERS.

Three tablespoons of flour to 1 egg, 1 spoonful of sugar, ½ spoonful of butter; beat well and cook in wafer irons; roll up with a fork, while warm.

SPONGE CAKE.

Six eggs, 2 cups white sugar, 3½ cups of flour, ½ cup of milk, 1 tablespoon of yeast powder.

STRAWBERRY CAKE.

The above cake split, while hot, and covered between with sugared berries; place the top of cake back; the berries must stand a few minutes to make a juice.

CREAM PUFFS.

Put 1 cup of water on the fire, and when hot melt in ½ cup of best butter; when it boils beat in 1 cup of sifted flour; if lumpy, stir until perfectly smooth; place it aside to cool; when cool, stir in 1 at a time 3 eggs without first beating them; drop the batter on tins in small spoonfuls, and bake ½ hour in quick oven. For the cream put 1½ cups of milk to boil; beat yolks of 2 eggs very light, with 4 tablespoonfuls of powdered sugar; when the milk boils, pour it on the eggs, stirring all the while; wet 2 tablespoonfuls of cornstarch in fine flour, with a little cold milk; add it to the custard and replace on the fire; stir until quite thick; flavor when cold with vanilla. The cream is placed in the puff by lifting up the top with a knife and dropping in the cream with a small spoon.

ANGEL'S FOOD.

Soak 1 box gelatine in 1 quart of milk 1 hour; then let it come to a boil; beat together yolks of 3 eggs, ¾ cup of white sugar, ½ cup sherry wine, 1 teaspoon of vanilla; add to milk and gelatine, and let it boil; then add whites of the eggs, beaten with 2¼ cups of sugar; let it simmer.

ALMOND BISCUITS.

One-half lb. of almonds, blanched and pounded very fine, with as much rose or orange flower water as will prevent their oiling, the yolks of 8 and the whites of 4 eggs, beaten until very light and added to the almonds; then beat in ¾ lb. of loaf sugar; continue to beat while the oven is heating; when ready, add 3 ounces of flour, which must be stirred in and not beaten; butter the pan and fill ½ full; dust a little sugar over, as you put them in the oven.

COUSIN JANE'S BUNS.

Two quarts of flour, 1 lb. of sugar, 1 large spoonful of butter, 3 yolks and 2 whites of eggs, 2 tablespoonfuls of yeast, and 2 of spice.

SILVER CAKE.

One lb. sugar, ¾ lb. sifted flour, 6 ounces butter, whites of 14 eggs; beat the sugar and butter to a cream; add the eggs beaten to a stiff froth, and then the flour.

TEA CAKES.

Yolks of 8 eggs, and whites of 4; beat very light and add 1 lb. of brown sugar; rub 2 lbs. of flour and 6 ounces of butter well together; add a teaspoonful of soda dissolved in a little milk, and any kind of spice you like; pour the beaten eggs and sugar on the flour and butter; knead well; roll and bake in a quick oven.

SILVER CAKE.

1½ lbs. of flour, yeast powder, whites of 28 eggs, 2 lbs. of sugar, 12 ounces of butter; flavor to taste.

GOLD CAKE.

Two lbs. of sugar, yolks of 28 eggs, 2 lbs. of flour, 1½ lbs. of butter, yeast powder.

ICING.

The whites of 2 eggs, and 2 teacups of granulated sugar; boil the sugar until clear, with just enough water to moisten it; beat the eggs to a stiff froth, and pour the boiling sugar very slowly into the eggs; dissolve ½ teaspoonful of citric acid in a small tablespoonful of water, putting enough in to flavor delicately, and add a little extract of lemon.

SUNSHINE CAKE.

Yolks of 11 eggs, 2 cups of sugar, 1 cup of butter, 1 cup of milk, 1 teaspoonful of cream of tartar, ½ teaspoonful of soda, 3 cups of flour; flavor with extract of vanilla.

MARBLE CAKE.

DARK PART.

One cup of molasses, 2 cups of brown sugar, 1 cup of butter, yolks of 7 eggs, 2½ tablespoons of cinnamon, 1 tablespoon of allspice, 1 nutmeg, 2 teaspoons of cream of tartar, 1 teaspoon of soda, 4 cups of flour.

MARBLE CAKE.

LIGHT PART.

Two cups of white sugar, 1 cup of butter, 1 cup of cream, either sweet or sour; 2 teaspoons of cream of tartar, 1 teaspoon of soda, 3½ cups of flour, whites of 7 eggs; alternate layers of light and dark, and draw a knife through 2 or 3 times; then bake.

STRAWBERRY SHORT CAKE.

One cup of powdered sugar, 1 tablespoonful of butter rubbed into the sugar, 8 eggs, 1 heaping cup of flour, 2 tablespoonfuls of sweet cream, 2 teaspoonfuls of yeast powder; bake in three jelly cake pans, and when cold, lay between them nearly a quart of strawberries, sprinkling sugar over each layer, and over the top cake.

WHITE SPONGE CAKE.

Whites of 11 eggs, 10 ounces of granulated sugar, 5 ounces of flour, 1 teaspoonful of cream of tartar, 1 of extract of vanilla; sift the mixture 4 times, beat the eggs, and add the sugar and flour; bake 40 minutes.

LADY CAKE.

A light lb. of flour, and 4 of the small measures of yeast powder, 1 lb. of white sugar, ¾ lb. of butter, the whites of 20 eggs, 1 teaspoonful essence of lemon, 1½ of vanilla; cover the pan, and keep the stove hot enough to make the cake rise nicely, adding a little more fuel, if necessary; it takes about 2 hours to bake this cake.

WHITE OR SILVER CAKE.

. Whites of 20 eggs, 1¼ lbs. of flour, 1¼ lbs. of sugar, 15 ounces of butter, a little more than 1 teaspoon of almond extract, 1 level teaspoon of soda, 1 good teaspoon of cream of tartar; wash thoroughly and cream butter, roll sugar and add to it; beat the whites of eggs very stiff, and add to this; sift in the flour, and beat mixture well 10 or 15 minutes; put in the extract; last of all, pulverize soda and cream of tartar in a little flour, and sift into the mixture, beating as little as possible to mix well; bake 1¼ hours, the first 15 minutes in a very moderate oven, increasing heat gradually until the time is consumed, also covering the pan the first ½ or ¾ of the hour; this makes a good large cake, or 2 small ones.

WHITE FRUIT CAKE.

One lb. of white sugar, 1 lb. of flour, 12 eggs beaten separately, ¾ lb. of butter, creamed and stirred with the sugar, 2 lbs. of citron cut small, 2 lbs. almonds blanched and cut into strips, 2 cocoanuts grated; beat all a long time, pour into a mould and bake; ice either with almond paste, or icing into which you have stirred a grated cocoanut.

WHITE, OR BRIDE'S CAKE.

One lb. and 4 ounces of flour, 1 lb. and 2 ounces of butter, 1 lb. of sugar, the whites of 24 eggs, 2 teaspoonfuls of cream of tartar sifted in with the flour; stir the butter and flour to a cream; beat the whites very lightly, then add the sugar, and again beat well; mix all the ingredients together, and at the last add 1 teaspoonful of soda mixed with a little white of egg; season with almond essence; pour into a mould and bake; ice the cake when cold.

FRUIT CAKE.

Five lbs. of flour, 5 lbs. of sugar, 5 lbs. of butter, 10 lbs. of currants, 5 lbs. of raisins, stoned and cut, 37 eggs, 2 ounces of cloves, 2 ounces of nutmeg, 1 ounce of cinnamon, 1 ounce of mace, 2 lbs. of citron, ½ pint of brandy, ½ pint of wine, ½ pint of rose water; bake 5 hours or more.

SPICED GINGER CAKE.

Ten eggs, ½ lb. of sugar, 2 tumblerfuls of molasses, ¾ lb. of butter, 1 lb. of flour, 1 tablespoon of ground ginger, 1 of allspice, 1 of cinnamon, 2 teaspoonfuls of yeast powder.

ECONOMICAL SPONGE CAKE.

Pour 1 cup of boiling water over 2 cups of sugar; separate whites and yokes of 4 eggs, and beat well the whites to a stiff froth; add the yolks to the sugar and hot water, beating quickly; then 2 cups of flour in which 2 teaspoons of yeast powder have been mixed; it requires 2 full cups of flour measured before sifting; add a small pinch of salt and flavoring preferred; lastly, add the whites, mixing them as quickly and as lightly as possible, and bake at once in a quick oven.

DOMESTIC FRUIT CAKE.

Soak 3 cups of dried apples over night in cold water, chop them in the morning, and put them on the fire with 3 cups of molasses; stew until soft, but not pulpy; when cold, mix with 3 cups of flour, 1 cup of butter, 3 eggs and a teapoon of soda; bake in a steady oven; this will make 2 good sized loaves; the apples will cook like citron; raisins may be added, which will improve the cake; season with plenty of spice, not forgetting a little salt.

WHITE FRUIT CAKE.

Two cups of sugar, ½ cup of butter, ¾ cup of sweet milk, 2 cups of flour, 2 teaspoons of yeast powder, the whites of 9 eggs; bake in jelly pans.

FILLING FOR THE ABOVE.

For the icing, make a thick syrup of 1 lb. of sugar, and

pour over the whites of 3 eggs, which have been beaten to a stiff froth, stirring well all the time; then add ¼ lb. of citron, cut in small pieces, ¼ lb. dried figs, ½ lb. of raisins cut and stoned, 1 lb. blanched almonds cut fine; mix the fruit together; add gradually to the icing, and beat hard for some time; then spread between the layers of cake, and cover the top with grated coconut.

JELLY CAKE.

Six eggs beaten separate, very light, ½ lb. of sugar, ¼ lb. of butter, 6 ounces of flour; cream the flour and butter; beat the sugar and yolks together, and add to flour and butter; beat well, and last add the beaten whites; bake in shallow tin pans; when cool spread on the jelly; pile up; trim off the edges, and sift sugar over the top; if accustomed to using yeast powder, add 1 teaspoonful.

GINGER CAKE.

1⅛ teacups of flour, ½ cup of molasses, ½ cup of brown sugar, ¼ cup of hot water, 2 eggs, 1 teaspoon of soda, 1 heaped tablespoon of butter; mix molasses and sugar, into which put the butter, adding also hot water; beat yolks and add, also, 1 teaspoon of cinnamon, 1 of ginger, and ½ of cloves; to this add whites well beaten, and add flour last of all; dissolve the soda in a little water; place immediately in a moderate oven; about of an hour will bake it. Very simple, but good.

ANGEL'S FOOD.

The whites of 11 eggs, 1½ tumblers sifted, powdered sugar, 1 tumbler of sifted flour, 1 teaspoonful of cream of tartar; sift the flour four times, leaving the tumbler even full; then add the cream of tartar, and sift again; beat the eggs to a stiff froth on a dish, and on same dish add sugar lightly, then flour gently, then vanilla; do not stop beating until you put it in the oven to bake; bake 40 minutes in a moderately heated oven, and if too soft let it remain a few min-

utes longer; do not open the oven until it has been in 15
minutes; turn the pan upside down to cool, and when cold
take out by loosening cake with a knife; then ice. The pan
must never have been used, that is to say, greased; tumbler
must be of dimensions of 2½ gills.

ICING.

Whites of 2 eggs, and 2 teacups of granulated sugar; boil
the sugar until clear, with just enough water to moisten it;
beat the eggs to a stiff froth, and pour boiling sugar very
slowly into the eggs; dissolve ½ teaspoonful citric acid and
a small tablespoonful of water, putting enough in to flavor
delicately, and add a little extract of lemon.

18

ICE CREAM.

Thicken a quart of milk with arrowroot or cornstarch, a tablespoonful to the quart; sweeten and let it boil; when cold, add a quart of cold milk, or cream if you have it; flavor to your taste; when the cream is put into the freezer and is just beginning to thicken, whip up very light the whites of 4 to 6 eggs, and add this to the cream; (6 eggs add nearly ⅓ to the quantity), so you allow for it in seasoning.

MILK SHERBET.

One quart of fresh milk, 2 cups of white sugar, whites of 2 eggs beaten to a stiff froth; put in the freezer, and when it begins to congeal, add the juice of 3 lemons.

VELVET CREAM.

Boil a quart of milk; when boiling, stir into it the yolks of 6 eggs, 6 tablespoonfuls of sugar, 1 spoonful of flour, which has been well beaten together; when boiled, turn into a dish, and pour over it the whites beaten to a stiff froth, and mixed with 6 tablespoonfuls of powdered sugar, and brown slightly; flavor the top with vanilla and the bottom with lemon.

ICE CREAM.

One gallon of sweet milk, 1 pint of sweet cream, yolks of 8 eggs, ½ teacup of English arrowroot, sugar and vanilla to the taste.

LEMON ICE CREAM.

Boil in 1 quart of milk the peel of 2 lemons; squeeze the juice into a tumblerful of pulverized sugar, being careful to remove the seed; when the cream is cold, stir well into the sugar, and freeze immediately.

FROZEN TAPIOCA CREAM.

One teacup of pearl tapioca, soak over night in cold water, pour hot water on the soaked tapioca, and boil until a clear jelly; when cold, add the whites of 3 eggs, 1 lb. of sugar, 1 quart of cream; whip well, strain and flavor, and then freeze. Delicious.

MOCK CHARLOTTE RUSSE.

One-half box of gelatine soaked in a little cold water, and when soaked, dissolve in $\frac{1}{2}$ pint of boiling water; make a sweet custard with $1\frac{1}{2}$ pints of milk and the yolks of 6 eggs; flavor with vanilla, add gelatine to the custard, and set in a cool place to congeal; when it begins to harden, add the whites of the eggs beaten to a stiff froth, and beat well through the custard; pour into a dish lined with sponge cake.

CHARLOTTE RUSSE.

HOTEL SPLENDIDE, PARIS.

Six eggs, the yolks only, $2\frac{1}{2}$ dozen ladies' fingers, 6 ounces of granulated sugar, $\frac{1}{4}$ ounce of gelatine, 1 pint of pure sweet milk, 1 pint of thick sweet cream; put the gelatine in the milk cold, and put on to boil in a *bain Marie* (or double kettle), stirring it now and then; beat the yolks of the eggs with the sugar, and when the milk comes to a boil, add the eggs and sugar to the milk; stir this constantly, to let the custard thicken well and to prevent curdling; now strain it through a swiss muslin cloth, and set it aside in a cool place to get cold and to thicken; in the meantime, have your cream put in a pan, and put this in a larger pan which has been filled with ice and salt; after your cream gets very cold, whip it up with a fork or egg beater until it is very thick; now line your mould with ladies' fingers; gradually whip the cream into the custard, which must be quite thick, until you have used it all and the custard is free from lumps; flavor with a tablespoonful of extract of vanilla, and pour the mixture into the mould; have a cover to fit the mould, and pack this in ice and salt to stand for not less than 2 hours.

ICE CREAM.

Eight eggs to 1 box of Eagle Brand condensed milk; beat the yolks and the milk together; flavor to suit the taste; beat the whites to a froth, and sweeten to the taste; beat all the above together, and put in water enough to fill a $\frac{1}{2}$ gallon freezer.

CHARLOTTE RUSSE.

Three qunces of isinglass, put it in 1 quart of water with vanilla sufficient to flavor it; boil it down to a pint, or sufficient to make a strong jelly; when done, strain it through a sieve; take the yolks of 3 eggs, and the white of 1; beat them well, and stir them in the jelly; while hot, sweeten to your taste, and put it to cool; then take 3 pints of cream, and beat it to a high froth, and let it drain on a sieve; when the jelly is cold, stir in the froth; have the moulds buttered, have a nice sponge cake, ready to cut, and lay it round so as to fit close; cut the same in narrow pieces, and lay in the bottom, so as not move them; then pour in the froth and put it on the ice to cool; 3 hours is sufficient to let it stand; when you take it out have a cloth dipped in hot water and wipe over your mould, so as to warm the latter; then turn the mould, bottom upwards on your dish, and take it off; be careful not to make it too warm, or the shape will be spoiled.

COCOANUT CREAM.

Beat the whites of 4 eggs to a stiff froth; boil 3 pints of milk down to a quart, and pour it on the eggs, stirring it very slowly; sweeten it to the taste; after this has cooled, grate a cocoanut in it, and set it to freeze.

SEASONED CREAM.

Mix together 1 gill of rich milk and a wineglass of rose

water, and 4 ounces of powdered white sugar; then add the yolks of 2 eggs well beaten; stir all into 1 quart of good, sweet cream; set it over hot coals; let it boil, stirring it all the time; then take it off, and when cool enough, pour it into a glass bowl; when cool, eat with it any sort of preserves.

CAROMEL ICE CREAM.

Two eggs, 1 pint of milk, 2 teacups of sugar, 1 scant cup of flour, and 1 quart of cream; beat the eggs and 1 cup of sugar together; add the flour; have the milk boiling; put into the mixture and stir over the fire until it is as thick as mush; put the other cup of sugar dry into a pan and stir over the fire until it is melted; add this to the mush, and set it away to cool; when cold, strain into the cream and freeze.

VANILLA ICE.

Two pints of milk, 8 ounces of cream, 12 ounces of sugar, 4 grains of vanilla, beat it with a little sugar in a marble mortar till it becomes powdered; put it in a stewpan or skillet with the milk, cream and sugar; let them boil until the whole is sufficiently thick; then strain it through a cloth, and pour it into a bowl to cool.

CHOCOLATE ICE.

Have 6 yolks of eggs, and ¾ lb. of sugar well strained together as for cake; roll out ¼ lb. of chocolate, pour a teacupful of boiling water on it, a little at a time, until it is well mixed; boil 1 quart of cream and milk together; when it boils, mix it with the chocolate, a little at a time; then put it on the fire, and when it boils, pour it on the eggs, mixing it all the time; put it again on the fire, and stir it until it becomes thick; it must not boil; when cold, freeze it.

STRAWBERRY SHERBET.

Three lbs. of strawberries, 8 ounces of red currants, 1 pint of water; crush the strawberries and currants in a sieve and let the juice run into a deep dish or bowl; pour the water over the strawberries remaining in the sieve, melt the sugar in a little water over the fire, and add to the juice, and pour it into the mould; the taste must be the guide for the quantity of sugar.

STRAWBERRY CREAM.

Boil 1 pint of milk, well sweetened, and moisten a dessertspoonful of flour with a little of the hot milk; put the milk on the fire and stir with a wooden spoon; pour in the juice of crushed strawberries till the cream becomes a pretty color; strain the whole through a sieve.

PEACH ICE.

Pare and cut finely ½ peck of very ripe peaches; stir in well 2 lbs. of the best white sugar, let it stand for 2 or 3 hours; then stir them well together, and put into a preserving kettle to simmer for 20 minutes, stirring all the time to prevent scorching; then pour them into a pan, and when quite cold, add 1 quart of cream and 1 quart of milk; stir them together, and put instantly in the freezer to prevent curdling. This is delicious.

BLANC MANGE OF MOSS.

Take ½ ounce of " Carrigean Moss " (the white), put it into 1 quart of new milk; reduce it, by simmering, to 1 pint; flavor it with a few drops of essence of bitter almonds; add 1 glass of white wine; sweeten it to the taste; pour it into a mould, until cold and firm; serve in a glass dish.

COFFEE JELLY.

Infuse ¼ lb. of ground Mocha coffee in a glass of boiling water; when the coffee is precipitated, pour it off clear; boil ¼ lb. sugar to a rich syrup; pour the coffee to it; then set it on a slow fire, that the sugar may dissolve gently, and when it is perfectly melted, stir in gently the yolks of 8 eggs, 4 glasses of boiling milk, and 6 ounces of sugar; after which, put it on a moderate fire, stirring with a wooden spoon; when it begins to simmer, pass it through a fine sieve, and let it stand till lukewarm; then mix into it 1 ounce of clarified isinglass, and finish it by dissolving the isinglass; pour into moulds to cool.

BLANC MANGE.

Boil 2 ounces of French isinglass in 3 pints of water, 20 minutes; strain this into 1 pint of good cream, and let it simmer 5 minutes; add 1 glass of pure peach water; sweeten, and strain through a sieve into a mould.

APPLE FLOAT.

Twelve large apples, quartered, cored, and boiled in as little water as possible, and pass through a sieve; when cold, add 2 whites of eggs beaten; sweeten to the taste; beat all up with a spoon till quite stiff; have made previously a soft custard, with the 2 yolks; flavor and sweeten slightly.

ORANGE WHIPS.

Strain the juice of 6 or 8 oranges, sweetened to taste; dissolve ½ box of gelatine; put the orange juice to it, and allow it to jelly slightly; beat the whites of 2 or 3 eggs to a froth, and mix all well together; fill moulds, and set on ice.

APPLE ISLAND.

To the whites of 6 eggs put 4 tablespoonfuls of nicely stewed, seasoned apples, rich with sugar, seasoned with rose water, lemon, or nutmeg; beat till quite light; season with milk, which is prepared like boiled custard, with the apple; pour it in a dish, and put the island on it.

RICE BLANC MANGE.

Put a teacupful of the best rice into ½ pint of cold water; let it stand until the rice cracks, and looks perfectly white; then add 1 pint of new milk, and 1 tablespoonful of white sugar; stir it, and let it gently simmer until all the milk is absorbed, stirring frequently; then pour it into a mould to cool; eaten with preserves.it is very nice; the rice may be flavored with vanilla, and eaten with cream.

SUGAR CANDY CUSTARD.

Put on 1 quart of milk, with as much vanilla as will highly flavor it, the yolks of 8 eggs, beaten with a small tablespoonful of flour; mix these together as for boiled custard; put 3 ounces of white sugar into a clean frying pan; let it boil up clear; as soon as it is brown, add a little of the custard to prevent the sugar from getting in lumps; pour the whole into the custard, and sweeten it to the taste.

LEMON ICE CREAM.

The juice of 6 lemons to 2 quarts of water; steep the rinds for some time in water and strain it; then add 2 lbs. of white sugar and the whites of 24 eggs; beat until they will adhere to the bowl; the freezer must be kept in motion until the cream be of the consistency of snow.

CARRAGEEN MOSS.

To 1 quart of milk add $\frac{1}{2}$ an ounce of moss; boil it till thick; strain it, and pour it into moulds; flavor it with anything you prefer.

WINE CREAM.

Set 1 quart of cream on the fire, and when it boils, stir in very slowly 6 tablespoonfuls of white wine, taking care that the cream does not curdle; then season with nutmeg and orange flower water, and sweeten to the taste; let it stand until it is cold.

ICING.

To 1 lb. of sugar, put 2 wineglasses of water, set it on the fire and let it simmer; have 6 eggs beaten to a froth; add the syrup to the eggs after it has cooled a little; beat it 1 hour, and then use it.

BOILED ICING.

One and one-half lbs. of loaf sugar, boiled in ½ pint of water until it ropes; beat the whites of 7 eggs to a stiff froth; put the syrup on to boil, and stir it until it is milk-warm; then put in the eggs, and beat the whole 1 hour.

CUSTARD ICE.

Make your custard, allowing 5 eggs to a quart of milk, and much more sugar than for ordinary custard; flavor with whatever essence may be preferred, and freeze.

TO CLARIFY SUGAR.

To 3 lbs. of sugar allow the white of 1 egg, and 1½ pints of water; break the sugar into small lumps, put it into a saucepan, and pour the water over it; let it stand some time before it is put on the fire; then add the beaten white of the egg, stir it until the sugar is entirely dissolved, and when it boils up, pour in a pint of cold water; let it boil up a second time, then take it off the fire; let it settle for 15 minutes, remove the scum, put it on the fire again, and boil it till thick enough.

APPLE FLOAT.

One dozen large green apples boiled in as little water as possible, and passed through a fine hair sieve; when cold, sweeten to the taste; add the whites of 2 eggs well beaten, and then beat the whole with a spoon until it is quite stiff; when ready for table, grate nutmeg over it; it must be eaten with cream.

ICE CREAM.

Three quarts of sweet milk, 1 quart of cream, yolks of 6 eggs, ½ teacup of starch, 2 teacups of powdered sugar; put the milk in a porcelain or granite vessel to boil; beat the eggs and sugar till very light and free of lumps; dissolve the starch in a little cold milk and add to the

19

sugar and eggs; when the milk boils, pour it slowly into the sugar, eggs and starch, beating all the time; wash the vessel in hot water, slightly butter with the fingers, and return to the fire to thicken; stir constantly till thick, and set away to cool; when ready to freeze, add the cream whipped, and flavor to taste with vanilla.

ALMOND CREAM.

Take 1 quart of new cream, boil it with ½ nutmeg grated, a blade of mace, a bit of lemon peel, and sweeten to the taste; then blanch ¼ lb. of almonds; beat them very fine with a spoonful of rose or orange flower water; take the whites of 9 eggs well beaten and strain them to the almonds; beat them together; rub them very well through a coarse hair sieve; mix all together with the cream and set on the fire; stir it one way all the time till it boils; pour it into cups or dishes, and when cold serve it up.

ORANGE CREAM.

Take the juice of 4 oranges, and the rinds of 2, grated, the yolks of 8 eggs; mix it well together and stir it over a chafing dish of coals; add ½ a pint of cream, and stir it all one way. Excellent.

CURRANT CREAM.

Bruise currants that are quite ripe in boiled cream; put in some cinnamon, finely beaten; sweeten to the taste; then strain it through a sieve.

RICE MILK.

Milk thickened with the flour of rice, and seasoned with rose water; then put into cups.

SPANISH FLUMMERY.

One ounce of isinglass to 1 pint of water; boil it till dissolved; beat up the yolks of 8 eggs, the juice of 2 large lemons, and the rind of 1, ½ lb. of sugar; add all these to the isinglass, stirring it over the fire till it boils; add to it 1 quart of good Madeira wine; strain it through a sieve; keep stirring it till nearly cold, and then pour it into moulds. In serving it for table, you will find preserves quite an improvement.

STONE CREAM.

Put in the dish you intend sending to table, 3 spoonfuls of the lemon juice with a little of the peel grated, to apricot jam; boil together 1 pint of cream, $\frac{1}{2}$ ounce of isinglass, and some sugar; when nearly cold, pour it on the sweetmeat. A few macaroons at the bottom of the dish is an improvement; to be made a few hours before using.

LEMON JELLY.

Three ounces of isinglass dissolved in 1 pint of water, the juice of 12 large oranges and 3 lemons, well pressed; boil 3 lbs. of sugar in 1 pint of water to a syrup; strain the juice and isinglass into the boiling syrup, and stir it a little while; when nearly cold, to be poured into moulds.

BAVARIAN CREAM.

Half pint of milk, 6 eggs, 6 ounces of sugar; flavor with vanilla, or any other essence; beat till very light, and let it simmer on the fire without boiling for 15 minutes; when it becomes tepid, mix in $\frac{1}{2}$ pint of whipped cream; pour it into a mould, and surround it with ice; whip up some cream and pour it into the dish after the form is turned out.

ALMOND CUSTARDS.

One pint of cream, $\frac{1}{4}$ lb. of almonds, blanched and pounded fine, with 2 tablespoonfuls of rose water; sweeten to the taste; beat up the yolks of 4 eggs; strain all the ingredients together over the fire until the mixture is thick; then pour it into cups.

TRIFLE.

Add to 1 pint of rich cream 4 teaspoonfuls of white wine;

sweeten it with pounded loaf sugar; whisk it well and as the froth rises, lay it upon a sieve placed over a deep dish; as it drains, pour the cream into the pan in which it is whisked, till it is done.

COCOANUT CUSTARD.

One nut grated into 1 pint of milk and 3 eggs; sugar to the taste, butter the size of a walnut, the rind of 1 lemon, and a little nutmeg.

BAKED CUSTARD.

Boil 3 pints of rich milk with vanilla, and let it cool; beat the yolks of 14 eggs and the whites of 4; sweeten the milk and eggs; fill the custard cups and set them in a Dutch oven, with as much water as will reach nearly to the tops of the cups; put over the fire and make the water boil, until you perceive a scum forming on the top of the custards; put them in the stove, brown them quickly, and take them out of the water.

COTTAGE CUSTARD.

Make 1 quart of milk lukewarm, add 3 tablespoonfuls of rennet wine; after having seasoned the milk to the taste, set it by a short time, when it will be fit for use.

ALMOND CUSTARD.

Three pints of cream, 15 eggs, $\frac{1}{2}$ lb. of blanched almonds, sugar, salt and mace, or rose water, to the taste.

WHIPS.

One pint of cream, 3 gills of white wine, the juice and peel of 1 lemon, the whites of 6 or 8 eggs, sugar to the taste; whisk it well, and put in on a sieve to drain.

APPLE MERINGUE.

Fill a dish with apple compote; then whip the whites of 8 eggs to a stiff froth; sprinkle in the eggs 1 teacup of sugar, working them well together; spread this over the apple; next beat some white of eggs without sugar, and pile it high in pyramidical form, and brown it of a light fawn color.

APPLE TRIFLE.

Scald as many apples as will make, when pulped, a thick layer at the bottom of a dish; mix the rind of ½ a lemon, grated fine, and as much sugar as will sweeten to the taste; mix ½ pint of milk, the same of sweet cream, and the yolk of 1 egg; scald it over the fire, and stir it all the time; do not let it boil; add a little sugar, if required, and let it stand to cool; lay over it the apples with a spoon, and then put on a whip made the day before, as for other Trifles.

DAMSON CHEESE.

Boil the fruit in a sufficient quantity of water to cover it; strain the pulp through a very coarse sieve; to each lb. add 4 ounces of sugar; boil it till it begins to candy on the sides, then pour it into tin moulds; other kinds of plums may be treated in the same way; also cherries, and other kinds of fruit.

NOYEAU CREAM.

Dissolve 1½ ounces of isinglass; add 2 lemons and as much noyeau as pleasant to the taste; add enough cream to fill the mould, and whisk it well.

BLANC MANGE.

Whip 2 ounces of isinglass, pour a pint of boiling water over it to dissolve it; next day, break it up, add to it some bitter and sweet almonds blanched, beat them with rose water and sugar; put it on the fire and let it boil up 5 or 6 times; then take it off and strain it through a muslin bag; put 2½ quarts of cream, or a mixture of cream and milk, on the fire to simmer; stir in the isinglass which has been prepared, let them simmer together for a short time; then take it off, pour into a pitcher, and when it is sufficiently

cool, fill the moulds with it; you will find it particularly
nice to use sweet almonds coarsely beaten, and after the
blanc mange is put into the moulds, throw them over the
top, or mix the almonds (if you prefer doing so) with the
blanc mange before it is poured into the moulds, but it will
be necessary to stir it all the time, to prevent the almonds
from settling.

BISCUIT GLACÉ.

Mix together in a deep bowl or tin pail, 1 pint of rich
cream, ¼ cup of sugar, 1 teaspoon of vanilla; put this mixture in a pan of ice water, and whip to a stiff froth; stir it
down, and whip again; then skim the froth into a deep dish;
when all the cream has been whipped to a froth, fill paper
cases with it, and place these in a tin box (or a freezer will
do), that is nearly buried in ice and salt, 2 quarts of salt to
6 of ice, and is wholly covered after the cases are put in; let
them remain 2 hours; make 1 pint of strawberry sherbet;
put a thin layer of it on each, and return to the freezer for
½ hour longer, and serve. Easily made.

BISCUIT GLACÉ.

One pint of cream whipped to a froth, 1½ dozen macaroons,
3 eggs, ½ cupful water, ⅔ cup of sugar, 1 teaspoon of vanilla
extract; boil the sugar and water together for ½ hour; beat
the eggs well, and stir into the boiling syrup; place the
saucepan containing the mixture in another of boiling water,
and beat for 8 minutes; take it from the fire; place the
saucepan in a pan of cold water, and beat the mixture until
it is cold; then add the flavor and whipped cream; stir well
and fill paper cases; have the macaroons browned, and
rolled fine; put a layer of the crumbs on the cream in the
cases, and freeze as directed in the other recipe.

RICHMOND MAIDS OF HONOR.

One cup of sweet milk, 1 of sour, 1 of sugar, 1 lemon, the
yellows of 4 eggs, a little salt; put all the milk into a

double boiler, and cook until it curds; then strain, and rub the curd through a sieve; beat the sugar and eggs together, and add the rind and juice of the lemon and the curd; line little paté pans with a puff paste rolled thin; put a spoonful of the mixture in each, and bake 15 or 20 minutes in a moderate oven. Nice for lunches, suppers, or dessert.

CHOCOLATE CREAM.

One-half cupful of grated chocolate, 1 cup of water, boiled together, then 1 cupful of sweet milk, and let it boil again, add 1 heaping tablespoonful of cornstarch, dissolved in a little milk; sweeten to the taste, and flavor with vanilla.

ICE CREAM.

Twelve eggs, 3 quarts of milk; beat the eggs separately, and very light; sweeten to the taste, stirring the sugar into the yolks; then stir in the milk, and lastly the whites; flavor to the taste, and freeze.

TO MAKE SLIP.

Warm ½ gallon of new milk, and stir into it a tablespoonful of wine, in which prepared rennet has been steeped for a week; before the milk is heated, sweeten to the taste, and while warm, stir the wine round several times in the bowl in which it is to be served; then let it stand for 3 hours on ice, if the weather is very warm; season a pint of cream with wine, sugar and nutmeg, so as to make a rich syllabub; this is used with the slip.

RASPBERRY CREAM.

Put 3 or 4 tablespoonfuls of stiff raspberry jelly into a large bowl; in another bowl froth the cream, having seasoned it with sugar and wine, as you would for a Trifle; skim the froth as it rises and add it to the jelly, which must be beaten and stirred until you add frothed cream enough to make it of a handsome color, and not too sweet to the taste.

ARROWROOT JELLY.

To 1 dessertspoonful of arrowroot add as much cold water as will make it into a soft paste; then pour on ½ pint of boiling water; stir it briskly for a few minutes, when it will become a clean, smooth jelly; sweeten to the taste, and season with port or sherry wine.

ORANGE PEEL SYRUP.

The peel of 3 sweet oranges in 3 pints of cold water, to be boiled down to 1 quart, ½ lb. of loaf sugar added, and boiled together. Very nice.

CHARLOTTE RUSSE.

Dissolve ½ ounce of isinglass in a cup of sweet milk; have ready a pint of rich cream, into which stir powdered loaf sugar, until it is very sweet, as the freezing destroys the taste; flavor with vanilla, rose or any other essence; beat up the whites of 7 eggs very light; stir the dissolved isinglass into the bowl of cream, after it is sweetened and flavored; then set the bowl into a tub of ice, and stir until it thickens; then add last the whites of eggs; put the mixture into a mould lined with sponge cake, and place the mould on ice; the cake can be joined with a little isinglass to make it stick; the charlotte may be made in the morning for a late dinner, or in winter over night; turn the mould after cutting it round, and the charlotte will come out.

ITALIAN CREAM.

Put 3 quarts of cream into 2 bowls; sweeten one sweet enough for the two; add the juice of 2 lemons, and 3 glasses of white wine; then add the other quart of cream, and stir the whole very hard; boil 1½ ounces of isinglass with 4 small teacupfuls of hot water, till reduced to ½; then strain the isinglass, lukewarm, into the other ingredients, and put it into moulds.

DUTCH BLANC MANGE.

Dissolve 1 ounce of isinglass in a quart of water; let it boil down to 1 pint; add to this the yolks of 8 eggs, well beaten and seasoned highly with wine and sugar to the taste; put it in a shape, and turn it out when cold.

SYLLABUB AND CREAM.

Pare off the rinds of 4 large lemons, and put it in the bottom of a deep dish; press the juice into a bowl containing 1 pint of wine and ½ lb. loaf sugar; then, by degrees, mix in 1 quart of cream; pour the whole into the dish with the lemon peel, and let the mixture remain untouched 3 hours; then beat it with rods to a stiff froth (first taking out the peel), and having put in each of the glasses a tablespoonful of preserved fruit; heap upon it the syllabub so as to stand high on the top of the glass.

MACAROON CREAM.

Pare the rind very thin from 4 fresh lemons; squeeze the juice and strain it; pour them both into 1 quart of water; sweeten to your taste; add the whites of 6 eggs beaten to a froth; put it on the fire, and keep stirring it until it thickens, but do not let it boil; pour it into a bowl; when cold, strain it through a sieve; put it on the fire again, and add the yolks of the eggs; stir until quite thick; when cold, serve up in small glasses, and on each glass lay a nice macaroon.

CHOCOLATE CREAM.

Melt six ounces of scraped chocolate and 4 ounces of white sugar, in 1 pint of boiling milk; stir in 1 ounce of dissolved isinglass; when the whole has boiled, pour it into a mould.

ITALIAN CREAM.

Put 2 pints of cream into 2 bowls; with 1 bowl mix 6 ounces of powdered loaf sugar, the juice of two large lemons,

20

and 2 glasses of white wine; then add the other pint of cream, and stir the whole very hard; boil 2 ounces of isinglass with four small teacupfuls of water, till it is reduced to $\frac{1}{2}$; then stir the isinglass, lukewarm, into the other ingredients, and put them into a glass dish to congeal.

BISCUIT ICE CREAM.

Eight eggs, the yolks only, 8 ounces of granulated sugar, 1 pint of sweet milk, 3 pints of double sweet cream, $\frac{1}{2}$ vanilla bean, or 1 tablespoonful of Burnett's extract; break in a bowl the yolks of the eggs; stir in them the 8 ounces of sugar until they bubble (do not beat); put the milk to boil in a *bain Marie;* when it comes to a boil, stir in the eggs and sugar; do not let it boil after you put the eggs in, only simmer to let it thicken well; now strain this custard through a piece of Swiss muslin, and set aside to get cold; have 3 pints of sweet cream packed in ice and salt to get very cold; now whip it well, until it is quite thick; gradually whip the cream into the cold custard; (if vanilla bean is used, boil in the milk; if the extract, stir in the custard when cold); now freeze this until it is quite stiff, and then put in moulds and pack in ice; if you wish, you can add crystalized fruit, cut into quarters, and after the cream is partly frozen, stir the fruit in, and pack in mould.

ANGEL'S REPAST.

Stew nice apples; strain them; sweeten with white sugar; mix 4 whites of eggs; add the stewed apples and eggs beaten to a stiff froth; make a rich boiled custard; pour it into a glass dish, and drop on the custard the beaten apples and eggs.

APPLE SNOW.

Select 8 or 9 good sized apples; core them; put them into a pan and cover them with cold water; whilst they are cooking slowly, make a nice boiled custard of the yolks of

4 eggs and 1 quart of milk; set it aside to cool; when the apples are quite soft, lay them carefully on a sieve, and remove the skins; then put the pulp into a bowl, and whip to a stiff froth 4 whites of eggs and 3 large spoonfuls of pulverized sugar; then beat the apple pulp to a stiff froth, and add to it the whipped eggs (whites); beat them until they resemble snow; when done, pour the cold custard into a glass bowl and heap on the whipped snow; finish by sprinkling on colored nonpareils. This is a beautiful and very nice dessert.

ORNAMENTAL DISH.

Make the foundation of the nest of jelly, or blanc' mange; rasp the skin of 3 lemons and preserve it; then lay it around and on the jelly like the straw; take out the contents of 4 eggs through a small hole, and fill the shells with blanc mange; when cold, break off the shells and lay the mange eggs in the nest.

KISSES.

Take the whites of eggs; beat them very light, and mix with them enough sifted sugar to make them very stiff; then drop them on white paper $\frac{1}{2}$ the size you want them; let them remain in a slow oven 20 minutes; 4 eggs will make a cake basket full.

ALMOND ICE.

Two pints of milk, 8 ounces of cream, 2 ounces of orange flower water, 8 ounces of sweet almonds, 4 ounces of bitter almonds; pound all in a marble mortar, pouring in, from time to time, a few drops of water; when thoroughly pounded, add the orange flower water and $\frac{1}{2}$ the milk; pass this, tightly squeezed, through a cloth; boil the rest of the milk with the cream, and keep stirring it with a wooden spoon; as soon as it is thick enough, pour in the almond milk; give it 1 boiling, take it off, and let it cool in a bowl or pitcher, before pouring it into the mould for freezing.

MATRIMONY.

Pare and cut into small pieces 2 dozen common sized peaches; cover them thickly with sugar, and let them stand 3 or 4 hours; beat them into a quart of cream, or a rich custard (if cream, sweeten it) before freezing it.

PINEAPPLE SHERBET.

Take 2 or 3 very nice pineapples, pare and grate them into a bowl; put the grated pineapple on a sieve and let it drain well, pressing it down to get out every drop of juice; weaken it as much as you please with water, and make it very sweet, as all things, when frozen, have less sweetness.

PEACH SHERBET.

Get 2 or 3 dozen ripe, soft, free-stone peaches, peel them and pass them through a cullender; add water sufficient to weaken it, and sweeten to the taste; freeze.

LEMON SHERBET.

Make any quantity of rich lemonade (it is better made of limes); make it very sweet and freeze it.

BAKED CUSTARD.

Mix a quart of milk with 8 well beaten eggs; strain the mixture, and add· to it 5 or 6 spoonfuls of beaten sugar, a pinch of salt, with a small piece of gelatine; pour the custard into a deep dish, grate nutmeg or lemon rind over the top; bake in a moderate oven; serve it cold.

CHOCOLATE MANGE.

Three ounces of French isinglass, dissolved in a very little cold water; put on a quart of new milk to boil; grate $\frac{1}{2}$ cake of vanilla chocolate and stir in the milk; then let it simmer, and add the dissolved isinglass; let all simmer 5 minutes; then pour into a mould, and when cold and stiff, turn out and serve with cream.

WHIP FOR A TRIFLE.

One pint of cream, 1 quart of water, ¼ lb. of powdered sugar, and the juice of 4 lemons; whisk it to a strong froth; take the froth off, as it rises, with a skimmer, and lay it on a sieve to drain; continue doing so as long as you can obtain any; it must be made and kept in a cool place 4 or 5 hours before it is wanted.

GATEAU DE POMMES.

Boil ½ lb. of loaf sugar in a pint of spring water till it becomes sugar again; then pound and core 2 lbs. of apples; put all together in a stewpan, grate in the pulp of a large lemon, and stew it till it becomes a stiff jelly; put it into a mould; it will turn out when cold; if the apples are flat, you may add a little lemon juice; a custard put in the dish is an improvement; if not stiff enough, add a little isinglass; some think it better to leave out ½ lb. of sugar and reduce the water.

LEMON SALAD.

Grate the peel of 2 or 3 lemons into a dish; squeeze the juice of 3 upon it; sweeten it well; dissolve ¼ ounce of isinglass in a very little water, and strain it in a quart of cream, which you will boil; put it into a jug, and pour it as slowly as possible, that the mixture may froth; do not move the dish until the contents are quite cold; the cream should be poured in as hot as the safety of the dish will permit.

SNOW CREAM.

Put some thin slices of sponge cake in the bottom of a dish; pour in wine enough to soak it; beat up the whites of 3 eggs very hard; add to it 2 tablespoonfuls of finely powdered sugar, a glass of sweet wine, 1 pint of cream; beat well and pour over the cake.

CHARLOTTE POLONAISE.

Boil in ½ pint of sweet milk, until perfectly dissolved, 2 ounces of grated chocolate, 2 ounces of white sugar, ¼ lb. of macaroons, which must be first broken into small pieces; in another ½ pint of milk, mix 4 ounces of blanched almonds finely pounded and very sweet, 1 dozen blanched bitter almonds, 4 ounces of pounded citron, and 4 ounces of white sugar; let this mixture also boil a few minutes; then set them both away to cool; cut a sponge cake into slices ½ an inch thick; wet them well with wine and spread them alternately with the chocolate and almond mixtures; put them one upon another, until the dish is filled; then pour a rich custard over them, and, when they are well soaked, cover the whole with a floating island, made with white of egg, whipped to a froth, and sweetened and flavored with fine sugar and raspberry or other jelly; instead of the custard and floating island, you may cover the cake thickly with icing, such as is used for pound cake; the polonaise must not be put into the oven that the icing may be dried, but should be prepared an hour or two before it is wanted that the icing may become glossy.

EUGENE CREAM.

Break 5 eggs; beat the yolks with some cream and a large spoonful of finely powdered sugar; put into a saucepan 1 quart of thick cream, with a few bitter almonds, and set it on the fire; when it has once boiled, take out the almonds, and add the beaten eggs; stir all together, and keep it hot for some time, without allowing it to boil, observing to stir always the same way; when thick enough, pour it into cups for the table.

LEMON CREAM.

Take 5 large lemons; pare them as thin as possible, and steep the parings with the juice of the lemons in 20 spoonfuls of spring water; then strain into a silver saucepan through a jelly bag, and add the whites well beaten of 6 eggs, and 10 ounces of loaf sugar; set the saucepan over a very slow fire, stirring all the time one way; skim it, and when scalding hot, pour it into glasses.

MOCK ICE

Take about 3 tablespoonfuls of some good preserve; rub it through a sieve with as much cream as will fill a quart mould; dissolve ¾ ounce of isinglass in ½ pint of water; when almost cold, mix it well with the cream; put it into a mould; set it in a cool place, and turn out the next day.

DEVONSHIRE CREAM.

Set the risen cream in a warm place, and as it rises skim it off; sweeten it and grate nutmeg over it.

CHOCOLATE CUSTARD.

Make some strong chocolate, allowing ¼ lb. of the best, which is Baker's prepared cocoa, to a quart of rich milk, first fixing the milk, and scrape the chocolate to a smooth paste; boil them together hour; while warm, stir in 2 or 3 tablespoonfuls of loaf sugar; then set it away to cool; have ready 8 well beaten eggs, and stir them gradually into the chocolate; bake the mixture in cups, and serve them up with a chocolate macaroon laid on the top of each.

ALMOND AND MACAROON CUSTARD.

Boil in ½ pint of rich milk a handful of bitter almonds, blanched and broken up; when highly flavored, strain that milk and set aside; boil 1 quart of milk by itself, and when cold, stir in slowly 8 well beaten eggs, adding the flavored milk, and ½ pint of powdered sugar; stir the whole very hard at the last; bake it in cups, and when done and quite cold, put on the top of each a macaroon with 4 others placed around it.

CREAMED PINEAPPLE.

Cut into 4 pieces 2 large, ripe pineapples; stand them up successively in a deep dish, and grate them from the rind; when all is grated, transfer it to a large glass bowl, and make it very sweet by mixing it with powdered loaf sugar; whip to a stiff froth a sufficiency of rich cream, adding to it some sugar, and heap it high upon the grated pineapple.

CREAMED STRAWBERRIES.

Take fine, large, ripe strawberries; hull, or stem them, and set them on ice till just before they are wanted; then put a large quantity of powdered sugar in a bowl with a layer of strawberries and sugar, until the bowl is full; then have ready a whipped cream, which must be placed on the top of the fruit.

NOYEAU CREAM.

Dissolve 1½ ounces of isinglass; add 2 lemons and as much noyeau as is pleasant to taste, and sufficient cream to fill the mould, and whisk it well.

JELLY.

Two ounces of isinglass, 3 quarts of water, 1¼ lbs. of powdered sugar, 4 lemons, 1 pint of good wine, 3 eggs, mace to the taste.

POTATO SOUFFLÉ.

Six large, smooth potatoes, 1 cup of milk, 1 tablespoonful of butter, whites of 4 eggs, salt and pepper to taste; wash the potatoes very clean and bake them; then cut lengthwise, scrape out the insides carefully, so as not to break the skins; mash smoothly, adding the boiling milk, butter, seasoning and ½ the beaten whites of the eggs; put into potato skins, place in a pan; cover with remainder of whites, and bake a light brown.

COCOANUT SHERBET.

Two cocoanuts, ¾ lb. of best white sugar and 2 quarts of water; after taking the milk from the nuts, break and take off the dark rind; grate the white meat, and pour over it 2 quarts of water; let it stand awhile; strain through a strong piece of muslin, or use a fruit press, so that you abstract all the richness; then add the milk taken from the nuts, and the sugar; it is then ready for the freezer.

PUDDINGS.

COCOANUT PUDDING.

One quart of milk, 6 eggs, $\frac{1}{2}$ lb. sugar, $\frac{1}{4}$ lb. of butter, and 1 large cocoanut grated; put this, with the butter and sugar, over the fire; melt and cream together; next add the eggs, well beaten, then the milk; eat cold.

ICE PUDDING.

Soak $\frac{1}{4}$ lb. each of macaroons, ratifees, sponge cake, and sugar, in a light custard made with $\frac{1}{2}$ pint of milk and 1 or 2 eggs; when ready to freeze, add 1 lb. of fruit cut small (dried cherries, angelica and raisins); place in freezer; stir until partially congealed; then add a pint of whipped cream, and freeze hard. Observe the same proportions for custard and other ingredients, when increasing the quantity.

THE FAMOUS BAKEWELL PUDDING.

Lay a nice puff paste on plate, then an inch of nice preserve or jam; then mix, like pound cake, $\frac{1}{2}$ lb. of butter, beaten to cream, $\frac{1}{2}$ lb. of well boiled potatoes, pressed through a sieve; $\frac{1}{2}$ ditto of sugar, $\frac{1}{2}$ ounce each of sweet and bitter almonds, both blanched and pounded; when beaten well together, add 5 eggs well frothed, 1 tablespoon of brandy; pour over the layer of preserves and bake; $\frac{1}{4}$ lb. of ground rice may be substituted for potatoes.

FAMOUS APPLE PUDDING.

Boil until tender, 1 orange or lemon, with $\frac{1}{2}$ lb. of apples; beat until they can be passed through a wire sieve; then add the yolks of 8 eggs, $\frac{1}{2}$ lb. of sugar, $\frac{1}{4}$ lb. of butter; mix all well; fill the dish; put nice puff paste on the rim, and bake $\frac{1}{2}$ hour.

21

FIG PUDDING.

Six ounces of suet, 6 ounces of bread crumbs, 6 ounces of sugar, ½ lb. of figs chopped, 3 eggs, 1 cup milk, 1 nutmeg, ½ glass brandy, 1 teaspoonful of yeast powder; steam 3 hours, and serve with a wine sauce.

WINDSOR PUDDING.

Thicken 1 pint of milk with 2 tablespoonfuls of flour; boil and let it stand till cold; add 4 or 6 eggs, a piece of butter, 1 ounce of almonds (half bitter), a little lemon peel, the juice of 1 lemon and ¼ lb. of loaf sugar; bake in cups.

PLUM PUDDING.

One and a half lbs. of raisins, ½ lb. of currants, ¾ lb. of bread crumbs, ½ lb. of flour, ¾ lb. of beef suet, ½ lb. of citron and orange peel, ½ nutmeg, 9 eggs, 1 wineglass of brandy, a little ground ginger; chop the suet as fine as possible, and mix it with the bread crumbs and flour; add the currants, washed and dried; the citron and orange peel cut in thin slices, and the raisins stoned and divided; mix all together with the grated nutmeg and ginger; then stir in the 9 eggs well beaten, and the brandy, and again mix, so that all the ingredients may be moistened; put it into a buttered mould or cloth; tie it tightly, and boil it for six hours.

BIRD'S NEST PUDDING.

Pare and core 8 or 10 apples; place in deep flat dish; 2 eggs, 1½ cups of white sugar, 1 tablespoon of butter, 4 cups of milk, 2 cups of flour; mix well; 1 teaspoon yeast powder last; (scald apples with ½ cup of sugar); pour over the apples the above and bake.

CHEESE PUDDING.

Add to 7 ounces of good grated cheese, 2 ounces of flour, the yolks of 3 eggs, well beaten, and a little salt and pepper, all of which mix together in a pan; add ½ pint of milk; place this mixture on the fire, taking care not to let it burn, and when it has been cooking for a short time, add a little more milk and a large tablespoonful of butter; take it from the fire and allow it to cool; beat up the whites of 6 eggs, very stiff, and add it gradually to the rest; when the whole is well mixed together, put it in a dish or deep plate, and place it in a cooking stove moderately heated; as soon as the mixture has risen well, and is of a good color, serve it, and you will find it very nice—particularly for a Friday dish.

SNOW PUDDING.

One half package of Coxe's gelatine; pour over it 1 cup of cold water, and add 1½ cups of sugar; when soft, add 1 cup of boiling water, juice of 1 lemon and the whites of 4 well beaten eggs; beat all together until very light; put in glass dish, and pour over it custard made as follows: 1 pint of milk, yolks of 4 eggs and grated rind of 1 lemon; boil.

BREEZE PUDDING.

Dissolve ½ box of gelatine in 1 pint of boiling water; add 2 cupfuls of sugar and the juice of 2 lemons; after this has become cool (not cold), break into it the whites of 3 eggs; beat all to a stiff froth; pour into moulds and when ready for use, turn out, pouring over the following custard: make a soft custard with 3 eggs added to the yolks of the other eggs and a quart of milk.

BERRYMAN PUDDING.

Take 1 lb. of best white sugar, 8 eggs, 8 ounces of butter, a soup plate of cornmeal mush, and the juice and rind of 2 lemons; mix all well together till very light, and bake in a moderate oven. This is a delightful pudding, with or without paste.

SAVOY PUDDING.

Twelve eggs, all the whites taken out, ½ lb. of sugar, 5 ounces of butter, well creamed, the grating of 2 lemons and juice of 1; bake it in a thin paste.

FANCY PUDDING.

A loaf of French bread sliced, ½ pint of milk poured over it; the other ½ pint mix with 4 well beaten eggs; add sugar and cinnamon to the taste; dip each slice of bread in the mixture, and fry it in lard or butter; serve it with a sauce of sugar, wine and nutmeg.

CUSTARD AND APPLE PUDDING.

Peel and cut in slices 4 apples; put a paste in the bottom of the dish; lay a covering of apples and sugar; put a boiled custard over the top, and bake it.

APPLE BATTER PUDDING.

Six eggs, 8 tablespoonfuls of sifted flour, 1 quart of milk, 1 saltspoon of salt; stir the flour gradually into the milk, carefully dissolving all the lumps; beat the eggs very light and add them by degrees to the milk and flour; then pour the batter over a dish of pippins, pared, cored and sweetened, mixing all well together; bake it and eat it with a rich sauce, made of the yolk of 1 egg, butter, sugar and a little wine.

QUEEN MAB'S PUDDING.

Throw into a pint of new milk, the thin rind of 1 lemon, 6 or 8 bitter almonds and a pinch of salt; keep it at the boiling point till strongly flavored; add ¾ of an ounce of isinglass; when dissolved strain the milk; sugar to the taste; put it in a mould, and when cold, eat it with a rich sauce of cream, wine and sugar.

POTATO AND RAISIN PUDDING.

Mix 2 ounces of butter, 4 eggs, ½ ounce of sugar and lemon peel well together; add 6 ounces of grated potatoes; ⅛ lb. of raisins, and bake it in a form or mould by 2 degrees of heat for half an hour; serve it with or without snow (the white of eggs beaten to froth is what is meant by snow); instead of the raisins, you may mix in it 2 ounces of almonds, among which are 4 bitter ones.

GERMAN PUDDING.

To 1 pint of milk add 6 eggs, well beaten, 6 spoonfuls of flour, ½ spoonful of butter, ½ nutmeg, and 1 teaspoonful of salt; pour it into a well greased pan, and bake for ½ hour; to be eaten with wine, sugar and butter sauce.

RICE PUDDING.

Four tablespoonfuls of soft boiled rice, ¼ lb. of butter, 1 quart of milk, 8 eggs; scald the milk; add a few sticks of cinnamon, and while warm, stir into it the rice, butter, and eggs, which must be first beaten; sweeten to the taste, and bake in a dish.

ALMOND PUDDING.

Blanch ½ lb. of almonds, beat them smooth in a mortar; 1 spoonful of rose water, 1 spoonful of cream or milk thickened with 1 large spoonful of pounded biscuit, ½ lb. of sugar, 7 eggs, and 1 nutmeg; bake it carefully in a moderate oven.

EVE'S PUDDING.

Six eggs, 6 apples chopped fine, 6 ounces of suet, 6 ounces of pounded cracker, 6 ounces of currants, 6 ounces of white sugar, a little salt and nutmeg; boil it 3 hours; serve it with wine, sugar and butter sauce.

BREAD AND BUTTER PUDDING.

Cut the bread in thin slices, butter them and put a layer into a well buttered dish; strew citron and raisins, or sweetmeats, over it; then another layer of bread and fruit, and so on until the dish is filled; beat 6 eggs with 1 pint of milk, a little salt, nutmeg, and a spoonful of rose water; sweeten to the taste, and pour it over the bread; let it soak 1 or 2 hours before baking; bake ½ hour.

GROUND RICE PUDDING.

Mix 2½ large spoonfuls of rice in a little cold milk; stir it into 1 quart of boiling milk; let it boil 15 minutes, stirring it constantly; when cold, add 5 eggs, a little lemon, sugar to the taste, and bake it 1 hour; put a paste, or not, as you prefer, on the dish.

FANCY PUDDING.

A loaf of French bread sliced, ½ pint of milk poured over it; take another ½ pint of milk and mix with 4 well beaten eggs, sugar and cinnamon to the taste; dip the slices in the mixture, and fry in butter or lard.

CABINET PUDDING.

Butter a mould, and place a layer of sponge cake all around it, then citron, raisins, currants, and any spice you like; then add more cake and more fruit until the mould is filled; boil 1 quart of milk, and pour it hot on 8 well beaten eggs; then pour all into the mould; tie it in a cloth, boil it 2 hours, and serve it with cold sauce of butter and sugar, creamed well together. Delicious.

ALMOND CHEESE CAKES.

Blanch and pound 4 ounces of almonds with a spoonful of rose water; add 4 ounces of sugar pounded, a spoonful of cream, the whites of 2 eggs well beaten; mix all as quick as possible, and bake it in a warm oven 20 minutes.

SWEETMEAT PUDDING.

A layer of quinces, citron and peaches, ½ lb. of butter creamed with a spoonful of flour, ½ lb. of sugar, the yolks of 10 eggs; bake about ½ hour; preserved lemon peel is an improvement.

GOVERNOR'S PUDDING.

To 1 large cocoanut add ¼ lb. of butter, the whites of 6 eggs, nutmeg and sugar to the taste; to be baked in a rich paste.

SWEET POTATO PUDDING.

Boil 1 lb. of sweet potatoes very tender, and press them while hot through a grater (the finer the better); to this add 6 eggs well beaten, ¾ lb. of fine sugar, ¾ lb. of butter, some grated nutmeg and lemon rind, a wineglass of old brandy; put a paste in the dish, and when the pudding is done, sprinkle the top with white sugar finely pulverized.

ARROWROOT PUDDING.

Boil 1 quart of milk and make it into a thin batter with arrowroot; add 6 eggs, ½ lb. of butter, the same of sugar, ½ a nutmeg and a little grated lemon peel; put a nice paste in the dish, and bake it nicely; when done, sift sugar over it, and stick slips of citron all over the top.

INDIAN MEAL PUDDING.

Eight ounces of mush, 6 ounces of butter, 6 ounces of sugar, the yolks of 6 eggs and 1 white; mix the butter in the mush while it is warm; beat the eggs very light, mix the sugar with them, and add them to the mush when cool; season with nutmeg and mace to the taste, also a little wine.

BOILED CAKE PUDDING.

To 1 lb. of grated sponge cake, add the whites of 8 eggs and the yolks of 2, ½ lb. of butter; beat very light and boil it for 2 hours in a mould.

LEMON PUDDING.

To a dish that will hold 2½ pints, put 4 tablespoonfuls of marmalade; add 2 or 3 grated biscuits, or the same quantity of crumbled stale bread, 3 even tablespoonfuls of butter, 3 eggs beaten very light, 1 pint of milk; add some lemon chips and bake it. Delicious.

TAPIOCA PUDDING.

Wash over night 1 teacup of the best lump tapioca, and let it remain in milk to soak all night; the next morning boil 1 pint of new milk and stir in the soaked tapioca; add 1 large spoonful of butter and a little salt, 2 large spoonfuls of sugar, 1 wineglass of rose water, a little grated nutmeg; beat 4 eggs very light and stir in; mix all well together, and bake in a dish half an hour; sago is very nice prepared in the same way.

POTATO PUDDING.

Take 1½ lbs. of well mashed potatoes; while they are warm, put in ¾ lb. of butter; beat 6 eggs with ¾ lb. of sugar rolled fine; mix all well together; put in 1 glass of brandy, with nutmeg, mace, or lemon; bake it in a nice paste.

QUINCE PUDDING.

Take 6 quinces, pare them, cut them in quarters, and stew them with a little water and lemon peel; let them cook gently till soft; then rub them through a sieve; mix with sugar till very sweet; add 4 eggs, 1 pint of cream, mace and nutmeg; bake it in paste.

AMERICAN PUDDING.

Put on a pint of new milk to scald; while this is heating, stir 3 large spoonfuls of rice flour into a cup of milk; when quite smooth, stir it into the boiling milk, add a little salt and a large spoonful of butter, the rind of 1 lemon, a little nutmeg, and 1 wineglass of brandy; beat all well together, add 3 large spoonfuls of good brown sugar; beat 5 eggs very light and stir in; butter a dish and pour it in; bake it as long as custard.

WALTERIAN PUDDING.

Grate ½ lb. of pippins; stir to a cream ¼ lb. of sugar and ¼ lb. of butter, and add the apples; grate the rind of a fresh lemon, whip very light 5 eggs, and beat all well together; bake it in puff paste ½ hour.

CHANCELLOR'S PUDDING.

Butter and slice very thin 1 lb. loaf of stale bread; butter very well a large sized tin pudding dish or pan that projects out at the top, and stick raisins or almonds in the bottom and sides of the pan gracefully; then put a layer of bread; lay over it a layer of currants, raisins, sugar, and blanched almonds, well cut up, nutmeg and grated lemon peel; then lay on a layer of bread, raisins, currants, etc., in alternate layers, until you have put all in the pan; then pour over it the following batter: 4 eggs, well beaten, $\frac{3}{4}$ quart of sweet cream, or milk, a small glass of good brandy, $\frac{1}{2}$ glass of lemon juice, butter and a little more sugar; tie a strong double paper over the pan and place it in a boiling kettle of water, being careful that the water does not reach to the top of the pan; let it boil for $1\frac{1}{2}$ hours; then turn it out on a deep dessert plate or dish; pour over it boiled custard, seasoned with white wine; stick a few whole blanched almonds and serve it up for table; it is ornamental on a supper table, cold, and eaten with sweet wine.

GINGER CAKE PUDDING.

Take 1 pint of molasses, $\frac{1}{2}$ lb. of butter, 1 lb. of good brown sugar, 2 tablespoonfuls of ground ginger, and 1 gill of cream; beat these well together with a spoon; then add as much sifted flour as will make it stiff enough to bake; when done, serve it up with cold sauce of sugar and butter creamed together.

TRANSPARENT PUDDING.

Beat 8 eggs well; put them in a stewpan with $\frac{1}{2}$ lb. of white sugar pounded fine, the same quantity of butter, a little nutmeg; set it on the fire, stirring it till it thickens; then put it in a basin to cool; put a rich puff paste around the edges of the dish; pour in the pudding and bake it in a moderate oven; it will cut light and clear, when you may add candied orange and citron.

ORANGE PUDDING.

One large orange of a deep color and smooth, thin rind,

22

1 lime, $\frac{1}{4}$ lb. of powdered loaf sugar, $\frac{1}{4}$ lb. of fresh butter, 8 eggs, $\frac{1}{2}$ glass of mixed wine and brandy, 1 teaspoonful of rose water; have ready a sheet of puff paste made of 5 ounces of sifted flour and $\frac{1}{4}$ lb. of fresh butter; lay the paste in a buttered dish; trim and notch the edges, and then put in the mixture; bake it $\frac{1}{2}$ hour in a moderate oven; grate loaf sugar over it before you send it to table.   Excellent.

GOOSEBERY PUDDING.

One pint of stewed gooseberries, with all the juice made very sweet; then add $\frac{1}{4}$ lb. of white sugar, 2 lbs. of fresh butter, 2 lbs. of grated bread, 3 eggs.

PUMPKIN PUDDING.

Take $\frac{1}{2}$ lb. of stewed pumpkin, 3 eggs, $\frac{1}{4}$ lb. of fresh butter, or 1 pint of cream, $\frac{1}{4}$ lb. of powdered white sugar, $\frac{1}{2}$ glass of wine and brandy, mixed, a teaspoonful of mixed spice (mace and nutmeg), or, if you prefer it, add a little cinnamon; put a nice paste in the dish, pour the mixture in; bake it $\frac{1}{2}$ hour in a moderate oven; grate sugar over it when cool.

BAKED APPLE PUDDING.

A pint of stewed apples, which must be done in as little water as possible, and not long enough for the pieces to break and lose their shape; when cold, mix them with $\frac{1}{2}$ pint of cream, or 2 ounces of butter, $\frac{1}{4}$ lb. of powdered sugar, 1 grated nutmeg, 1 tablespoonful of rose water, 1 teaspoonful of grated lemon peel.

DANISH PUDDING.

One quart of rich milk, boil it and let stand till almost cold; beat 4 eggs for $\frac{3}{4}$ hour with $1\frac{1}{2}$ spoonfuls of flour; then mix the milk and sugar with it; tie it up in a close cloth, well floured, and boil it 1 hour; a sauce made of $\frac{1}{2}$ lb. of butter, 1 cup of sugar, with 1 wineglass of wine, the yolk of 1 egg, and a little nutmeg, is very nice with it.

COCOANUT PUDDING.

Grate 1 large, or 2 small cocoanuts, the day before, that they may dry; take 1 lb. of sugar, 10 yolks and 3 whites of eggs, beat them very light; add a tablespoonful of butter to the sugar, and put the nut in just before it is baked; season with a little brandy or wine; bake it in puff paste.

COCOANUT PUDDING.

One lb. of sugar, the yolks of 10 eggs, ½ pint of cream, ½ gill of brandy, the juice of 1 lemon, with the peel grated, ¼ lb. of the cocoanut; bake it in a nice paste.

SWEETMEAT PUDDING.

Make the paste, roll it out in square pieces; then take the preserves, and put them in with a knife (any kind of jam or marmalade); have each layer different; do this till you have a sufficient quantity; roll it round; then sprinkle the cloth with flour and put the pudding on to boil.

ADELAIDE'S PUDDING.

Pare and core 6 apples; fill up the cores with sugar and cinnamon; make a batter of 1 egg, a little flour, 1 teaspoonful of salt; pour around it and bake; serve hot with wine and sugar sauce.

PLUM PUDDING.

One quart of flour, 1 pint of milk, 1 lb. of suet chopped fine, 1 lb. of brown sugar, 8 eggs, 1 lb. of stoned raisins, ¼ lb. of currants, ½ lb. of citron; sauce of sugar and butter creamed together, with wine and nutmeg; boil it 6 hours.

SODA CRACKER PUDDING.

Four soda crackers, soaked in 3 teacups of cold water, 2 lemons and 2 teacups of sugar.

ORANGE PUDDING.

Pare the yellow rinds of 2 fine oranges very thin; beat it extremely fine in a marble mortar; add to it ½ lb. of sugar,

¼ lb. of butter, free of salt; beat the yolks of 16 eggs very light, and add to them the other ingredients, which you must mix and beat until they are all of a color; lay a puff paste with a double rim in a dish; pour in the pudding and bake it.

VICTORIA PUDDING.

Blanch ½ lb. of best almonds; rub them in a mortar with rose water to prevent their oiling; (they must be rubbed together to a smooth paste); cream ½ lb. of good butter, ½ lb. of white sugar; when smooth and light, stir in the almonds, add 1 wineglass of wine and brandy mixed, 1 wineglass of rose water; beat separately the whites from the yolks of 7 eggs; first add the yolks, then the whites; beat all well together; line the dish with puff paste, and bake as long as a custard.

PEACH PUDDING.

Five eggs, beaten with 2 cupfuls of sugar, well mixed together, a dinner plate full of peaches, peeled and cut up fine; add the peaches to the sugar and eggs, with 3 or 4 tablespoonfuls of milk, and as much flour, a pinch of salt, and a dessertspoon of butter; bake in a slow oven; eaten hot or cold.

FRUIT PUDDING.

Take a pint of hot milk, and stir in sifted indian meal till the batter is stiff; add a teaspoonful of salt and a little molasses; then stir in a pint of whortleberries or chopped sweet apple; tie in a cloth that has been wet, and leave room for it to swell, or put it in a pudding pan, and tie a cloth over; boil 3 hours; the water must boil when it is put in; you can use cranberries, and use sweet sauce.

LEMON PUDDING.

Three lemons grated and the juice of 1, 3 cups of sugar, 7 soda crackers, soaked 1 hour in 3 cups of cold water; bake in a nice paste.

ALMOND PUDDING.

Steep 4 ounces of crumbs of bread, sliced, in 1½ pints of cream, or grate the bread; then beat ½ lb. of blanched almonds very fine, till they become a paste, with 2 teaspoonfuls of orange flower water; beat up the yolks of 8 eggs and the whites of 4; mix all well together, put in ¼ lb. of loaf sugar, and stir in 3 or 4 ounces of melted butter; put it over the fire, stirring it until it is thick; lay a sheet of paper at the bottom of a dish, and pour in the ingredients; bake ½ hour.

MURANGUE PUDDING.

Six large, nice apples, stewed, and mashed through a sieve, ¼ lb. of butter, ¼ lb. of sugar, 6 eggs beaten very light, the juice and grated rind of 1 lemon; save out the whites of 3 eggs, beat them up with 3 tablespoonfuls of sifted sugar to a stiff froth; after the pudding is baked and nearly cold, lay the sugar and egg over the top, and set it in a cool oven for a few minutes, until it is crusted, but not browned. Excellent.

NUTMEG PUDDING.

Three-fourths lb. of butter, 1 lb. of sugar, the yolks of 10 eggs and the whites of 5, 2 nutmegs; bake either with or without paste.

FLIRTATION PUDDING.

Make a rich boiled custard, and when cold, beat to a froth the whites of 2 eggs, and drop it in spoonfuls on the top of the custard; set it before the fire to brown the whites slightly.

AUNT MARY'S PUDDING.

One lb. of stoned raisins; currants nicely washed, suet finely minced, bread and apples grated, and brown sugar, ¼ lb. of each; 4 well beaten eggs, a teaspoonful of pounded ginger, ½ teaspoonful of salt, ½ a nutmeg grated, a wineglass

of brandy; mix all the ingredients well, and boil it in a
cloth for 2 hours; serve with a sauce of melted butter, a
glass of wine, and sugar to the taste.

GINGER PUDDING.

Five cups of flour, 2 cups of sugar, 1 cup of molasses, ½
cup butter, 1 teaspoonful of soda in ½ cup of sour milk, 3
eggs, 1 tablespoonful of ginger; to be eaten with sauce; but
just as good cold, without the sauce.

PLUM PUDDING.

One lb. of flour, 1 lb. of beef suet, 1 lb. of raisins, 1 lb. of
currants, 4 eggs, 1 pint of milk, and spicing to the taste; tie
it in a bag; allow no room for swelling and boil 4 hours.

DOMESTIC PUDDING.

Sweeten 1½ pints of cream, and boil it with the peel of a
small lemon; cut the crumbs of a small loaf of bread; put
it in the cream; boil it for 8 minutes, stirring constantly;
when thick, add ¼ lb. of fresh butter beaten to a cream; 1
teaspoonful of grated nutmeg, and 4 well beaten eggs; beat
all well together for some minutes; it may be baked or
boiled.   In boiling a pudding the water should boil quick
when it is put in, and moved for a minute, to cause the ingredients to mix; when the pudding is done, a pan of cold
water should be ready, and the pudding dipped into it, as
soon as it comes out of the pot, which will prevent its ad-
hering to the cloth in which it is boiled.

CHEAP PUDDING.

Four eggs well beaten with a tumbler of brown sugar, ¼
lb. of melted butter, 1 quart of flour, 1 tumbler of milk with
1 teaspoonful of soda; mix all well together; pour into a
pan, and bake in a quick oven; when done, serve it, with
wine and sugar sauce.

ALMOND GUST.

Two ounces of almonds, blanched and pounded to a paste with a large spoonful of orange flower water, or rose water, to prevent oiling; put on a pint of new milk to boil; beat the yolks of 6 eggs with ¼ lb. of crushed sugar, and when the milk boils, stir in the eggs and sugar, and then add the almonds; mix all together, and set it aside to cool; then whip 1 quart of cream to a stiff froth, with ¼ lb. of fine sugar; drain the froth; lay some slices of sponge cake in a dish; spread apple or quince jelly on it; on this pour the cold custard; then add the whipped cream. This is a handsome dessert.

RIZ AU LAIT.

This pudding, if properly prepared, is better without eggs; wash a coffee cupful of rice well; put it into 1 quart of new milk over night to soak; in the morning add a large spoonful of butter, a little salt, grated nutmeg, a little ground cinnamon, 1 pint more of new milk; then put it into the oven, and when it is warm, stir the pudding without removing it from the oven; stone ¼ lb. of raisins, and add at this time; then let it cook until the rice is perfectly done.

APPLE CORNMEAL PUDDING.

Pare and core 12 pippin apples; slice them very thin; then stir into 1 quart of new milk, 1 quart of sifted cornmeal; add a little salt, then the apples, 4 spoonfuls of chopped suet and a teacup of good molasses; mix these well together; pour into a buttered dish, and bake 4 hours; serve hot, with sugar and wine sauce.

SWISS PUDDING.

Beat together the yolks of 5 eggs; add 1 quart of milk; sweeten with white sugar to the taste; flavor with extract of vanilla, or nutmeg; if baked in cups, let there be cold water poured in a pan, and the cups placed in that for the oven; if in a dish, cut bread very thin; butter it, and lay on the top.

LEMON PUDDING.

One nice lemon, with a smooth thin rind, 3 eggs, ¼ lb. of
fine white sugar, the same of fresh butter, 1 tablespoonful
of wine and brandy mixed, 1 teaspoonful of rose water;
grate the rind of the lemon; then cut it in half, and squeeze
the juice of the lemon into the plate with the grated rind,
taking out all the seeds; mix the juice and rind well together; stir the sugar and butter with a spoon till it
is perfectly light and of the consistency of cream; beat
the eggs until they are quite smooth and as thick as a
boiled custard; then stir the eggs gradually into the pan of
butter and sugar; add the seasoning by degrees; then the
juice and rind of the lemon; mix all the ingredients well
together; have ready a nice puff paste, enough to cover the
edges and bottom of the dish; pour the mixture in and bake
the pudding ½ hour, in a moderate oven.

SOUFFLÉ PUDDING.

Three ounces of sifted flour, 2½ ounces of granulated
sugar, 1 pint of sweet milk, 1 tablespoon of butter, 5 eggs
beaten separately; put on your milk to boil, reserving
about a gill to wet the flour; when the milk comes to a
boil, add the flour which has been wet with the milk, also
the butter and sugar; let this thicken well; now put it in a
bowl to get cold, at least for 1 or 2 hours before you are ready
to use it; about ½ hour before you are ready to use, have
the yolks well beaten, which you add by degrees to the cold
paste; and last of all, add the whites, which have been
whipped until very light; have a yellow bowl buttered, put
the paste in it, and bake in a hot oven a good ½ hour; serve
with a hard sauce of butter and sugar, flavored as you wish.
This pudding must be served immediately, as it will fall by
standing.

BISCUIT PUDDING.

Pour a pint of boiling milk over 3 Naples biscuits grated;
cover it close; when cold, add the yolks of 4 eggs and the

whites of 2, nutmeg, a little brandy, a spoonful of sugar and flour; boil it 1 hour in a bowl.

HINDOO BALLS.

Blanch ¼ lb. of almonds, and fry them in a small table-spoonful of fresh butter, until they are of a light brown; then wipe with a towel and put them into a bowl or pan; make a syrup with 1 lb. of sugar and 3 gills of water; boil it to a thread; care must be taken to boil it to the exact candying point; pour it boiling upon the almonds, and stir them until the sugar hardens around them; groundnuts are very nice prepared in the same way.

ELYSIAN PUDDING.

Grate ½ lb. of pippins; stir to a cream ¼ lb. of sugar, the same of butter; add the grated apples and the rind of 1 fresh lemon; whip very light 5 eggs; beat all well together; line a dish with puff paste; pour in the batter, and bake ½ an hour.

WELLINGTON PUDDING.

Beat to a cream 1 cup of good brown sugar and 2½ large spoonfuls of good butter; then stir in 1 well whipped egg, a little grated nutmeg, and a large spoonful of orange flower water; sift into a pan 1 pint of flour, and stir in 2 teaspoon-fuls of cream of tartar; dissolve in a cup of new milk 1 tea-spoonful of soda; beat these well together; then add the milk and soda with the flour, eggs and spice; butter a bak-ing dish, and pour in the pudding; bake ½ an hour; serve with wine sauce. This makes a delightful cake by adding 2 eggs.

SOUTHERN PUDDING.

Lay alternately in a baking dish slices of nice tart apples; on these sprinkle sugar, and the grated oily rind of 1 lemon, and then crumbs of stale rusks which have been soaked in

23

milk; then more slices of apples, sugar and crumbs of rusks; cut very thin slices of butter and lay thinly on the top; over this sift thickly pulverized sugar; bake 1 hour, and send to table in the same dish.

HOMINY PUDDING.

Take from the hominy, when nearly done, 1 pint of the liquor; put into it, while hot, a lump of fresh butter, 4 eggs, the juice of half a lemon with the rind grated; sweeten to the taste with powdered loaf sugar, and bake it in a rich paste.

SPONGE CAKE PUDDING.

Grate 3 stale sponge cakes and with them ½ the peel of a lemon, and all the juice; mix them in cold milk until they are quite soft; beat 3 eggs together, and stir them by degrees into the biscuits; add a teacupful of orange juice, and a little sugar, a thick slice of butter well melted; mix all well together; put it in a dish with paste round the edges; bake it slowly.

ALMOND FLORENDINE.

Beat ½ lb. of blanched sweet almonds with rose water; beat the yolks of 8 eggs and add them, with a gill of cream, and sugar to the taste; lay a sheet of puff paste in a plate or dish; put the mixture on it, cover it with another sheet of paste, and bake 1½ hours in a slow oven.

BAKED ARROWROOT PUDDING.

One quart of milk, 2 large tablespoonfuls of butter, same of rose water, the yolks of 8 eggs, ½ lb. of sugar, and 1 stick of cinnamon; boil the milk and cinnamon together; then take the saucepan from the fire, and stir in quickly the arrowroot, which must be previously rubbed smooth in a little water or cold milk; pour it into the dish in which it is to be baked, and while warm stir in the butter; beat the eggs and sugar together until very light, and add them to the other ingredients; bake for 15 or 20 minutes in rather a quick oven; the stick of cinnamon must be taken out of the pap as soon as it is turned into the dish, before the butter is mixed with it.

BAKED BATTER PUDDING.

One quart of milk, 1 teaspoonful of salt, 6 eggs beaten separately and very light, 9 tablespoonfuls of flour, stirred in gradually while the milk is boiling hot; bake $\frac{1}{2}$ hour in a quick oven; serve with wine and sugar sauce; this pudding must be sent to the table as soon as it is done.

ALMOND PUDDING.

Four ounces of rice, well washed, put into a milk or rice boiler containing $1\frac{1}{2}$ pints of rich milk or cream; let them boil gently until the rice is swollen and is quite soft; blanch 40 sweet and 6 bitter almonds, pound them into a smooth paste; grate the rind of a lemon, or a small piece of vanilla bean, into a small quantity of new milk; boil this until soft; when the rice is done, put it into a dish or pan; when a little cooled, throw into it 2 ounces of butter and as much sugar as suits the taste, mixing it well; add the almonds, beating it well; to this add the yolks of 5 eggs beaten very light; butter the dish it is to be baked in; take the 5 whites of the eggs and beat in a very light whip, add to each a tablespoonful of sifted sugar; the moment the oven is ready, quickly lay over the pudding the icing of eggs and bake 15 minutes; it should be served immediately.

BREAD PUDDING.

Pour on a loaf of bread a pint of boiled milk; mix into it when soft the yolks of 6 eggs and the whites of 3 eggs well beaten, 2 tablespoons of flour, nutmeg, and 1 lb. of raisins; boil 2 hours and serve with sauce.

SAUCE FOR BATTER PUDDINGS.

Beat the yolks of 6 eggs with 4 spoonfuls of sifted sugar

and butter mixed together; have ready a pint of boiling cream to mix with the yolks; afterwards, put it on the fire and stir it until it is of the consistency of sauce; then add to it a wineglass of brandy. Delicious.

POTATO PONE.

Take 2 good sized sweet potatoes, wash well; then grate, and season with 2 eggs, a good spoonful of butter, 2 coffee-cups of sugar, milk enough to make it soft, and powdered ginger; bake, and eat hot with butter; or, when cold, sliced and fried.

APPLE PIE.

To ½ lb. of apples, well boiled and pounded, add, while warm, ¼ lb. of butter beaten to a cream; to this add 6 eggs, the whites well beaten, ¼ lb. of powdered sugar, and the peel of 2 lemons, well boiled and pounded; put thin crust at the bottom and round the sides of the dish, and bake ½ hour.

LEMON MINCE.

Squeeze 2 large lemons; boil the peel till tender enough to beat to a mush; 6 large apples, ½ lb. of suet, 1 lb. of currants, ½ lb. of sugar, and candied fruit, as for other mince pies.

CUSTARD FOR PIES.

In 1 pint of new milk, put 2 or 3 bitter almonds, a stick of cinnamon, a piece of lemon peel, and 7 or 8 good sized lumps of sugar; let the whole simmer gently till the flavor is extracted; then strain, and stir till cool; beat the yolks of 6 eggs, and mix well with the milk; then stir the whole over a slow fire, till it is the thickness of rich cream; flavor it with almond or rose water, of which 1 ounce will be sufficient.

APPLE FRITTERS.

The yolks of 3 eggs, beat up with wheat flour to a batter; the whites beaten separately and added to it; pare the apples, core, and cut them in slices; lay them in a bowl in brandy and sugar about 3 hours before dressing them; dip each piece in batter, and fry in lard; sprinkle white sugar over them; peach fritters are made in the same way.

COCOANUT TARTS.

Take 6 cocoanuts, yolks of 10 eggs, $\frac{1}{2}$ lb. of white sugar, $\frac{1}{2}$ lb. of butter; season with rose water; put the butter in cold, and bake in a nice puff paste.

BAKED APPLE DUMPLING.

Large sized cooking apples, pare and core, (be careful not to make holes through); enclose each in the usual pie paste; place in a pan, fill apples with a little nutmeg, butter and sugar; leave the tops of apples open; flute with the fingers the top of crust; this is an ornamental dish when baked; eat with hard sauce.

MINCE MEAT.

One fresh beef tongue, boiled and chopped very fine, 2 lbs. of suet, picked and chopped fine, 4 lbs. of raisins, 2 lbs. of Sultana plums, 3 lbs. of currants, washed and dried, 2 lbs. of white sugar, 1 pint of brandy, 1 bottle of wine, nutmeg, cinnamon and mace to the taste; also add a little allspice; the day you bake the pie, add a few apples cut up very fine; line the dish with light paste, covering the top with the same and bake in a moderate oven; the ingredients must be well mixed together, and kept in a closely covered jar.

MINCE PIES WITHOUT MEAT.

Six lbs. of the best apples, cored and minced, 3 lbs. of raisins stoned and minced, 3 lbs. of hard boiled eggs, cut very fine, 3 lbs. of powdered sugar, $\frac{3}{4}$ ounce of salt, $\frac{1}{2}$ ounce of cinnamon, the same of nutmeg and mace, 8 finely powdered cloves, the grated peel of 4 lemons, and the juice of 2, $\frac{1}{2}$ pint of brandy, the same of wine; mix all well together, and put

14

it into a deep pan; have ready, washed and dried, 4 lbs. of currants, and as you make the pies, add them with candied fruit.

CHEESE CAKES.

Six ounces of butter, 6 of sugar; beat to a cream; 4 eggs, a glass of brandy or wine, a little rose water, a teaspoonful of nutmeg or mace, with a handful of currants; bake it in a puff paste.

LEMON CHEESE CAKES.

Grate with care the oily rind of 3 fresh lemons; rub this with ¼ lb. of loaf sugar pounded, until perfectly incorporated with sugar; then add by degrees ½ lb. of good fresh butter; beat very light the yolks of 6 eggs; mix all well together; then line a dish with puff paste, and put in the above mixture; bake ¾ hour; serve hot.

MINCE MEAT.

Two lbs. raisins, 1½ lbs. suet, 2¾ lbs. acid apples, 6 ounces preserved lemon peel, ½ ounce mace, ⅛ ounce of cloves, 1 large nutmeg, 2 lbs. sugar, 1 pint of French brandy, and ½ pint of wine.

PRESERVES, ETC.

PRESERVED PINEAPPLE.

Pare the pineapples and cut them in thick slices; weigh the slices, and to each lb. of fruit put 1 lb. of sugar; dissolve the sugar in a very small quantity of water; stir it and set it over the fire in a kettle; boil it 10 minutes; put in the fruit, letting it remain ½ hour; after this process, put the preserve in a pan or dish to cool; have the jars ready to put away for use; cover it well with the jelly; exclude it well from the air, and it will keep some time.

JELLY.

Those who would make fine jelly, should always avoid boiling the juice of the fruit, when it is desirable to have the article retain the flavor of the fruit from which it is prepared. After the juice is pressed from the fruit, and the proper quantity of sugar is added to it, let it be heated until the sugar is dissolved; after this is effected, no further heat is required.

PRESERVED CRANBERRIES

Wash the fruit, weigh it, and to each lb. of cranberries allow 1 lb. of loaf sugar, dissolved, ½ pint of water to 1 lb. of sugar; set it on the fire in a preserving kettle, boiling it 10 minutes; then put in the fruit and boil slowly till it is soft and a ruby color; put away in glass jars, with brandied paper on the top; exclude the air with kid tightly sealed over the jars.

PRESERVED ORANGE PEEL.

Put the peels in salt and water for 3 days, changing it each day; then put them in fresh water until they are tender; make a rich syrup, and finish as other preserves.

PINEAPPLE SYRUP FOR ICE CREAM.

Pare and slice the pineapples, and to each lb. of fruit add 1 lb. of white sugar; put in the jar first a layer of sugar pulverized, then a layer of pines; then one of sugar and another of pines, until the jar is full; tie up tight, to exclude the light and air; this is delicious, and keeps well; not to be scalded.

LEMON CITRON.

Turn water on nice, fresh lemon peels; soak them till all the white pulp can be scraped off; boil till soft; preserve them in $\frac{1}{2}$ their weight in sugar; they are a good substitute for citron.

RICH SYRUP.

One pint of cold water to 2 lbs. of white sugar; when it is dissolved, set it over a moderate fire; beat $\frac{1}{2}$ the white of an egg, and put it to the sugar before it gets warm; watch it, and when it is ready to run over, put in 1 teaspoonful of cold water; after the boiling ceases, put it on the fire again; do this 3 times, and the last time take it off and let it settle; take off the scum, and strain the syrup through a jelly bag.

BAKED QUINCES.

Gather the quinces when ripe, wash them nicely and put them in an oven to bake; when quite soft, take them out, cut them open, and serve with butter, sugar, and a little nutmeg, while hot; this is a nice dish for dessert or tea.

ORANGE WAFERS.

Take the best oranges, cut them in half, and take out the seeds and juice; boil them in 3 or 4 waters (always hot) until they are tender, and then beat them to pulp in a marble mortar, and rub them through a hair sieve; to 1 lb. of this pulp allow $1\frac{1}{2}$ lbs. of loaf sugar; take $\frac{1}{2}$ of the sugar and boil it with the oranges till it becomes ropy; then take it from the fire, and when cold, make it up in paste with the other ½ of the sugar; make but a little at a time, for it will dry fast; then with a rolling pin roll them out as thin as tiffery, upon paper; cut them round with a wineglass; let them dry, and they will look clear.

PRESERVED FIGS.

Pick the white or brown figs when a little more than half ripe; peel them very thin, and to 1 lb. of fruit put ¾ lbs. of sugar; make a syrup, and put the figs into it with lemon peel and ginger; let them boil till clear, stirring frequently.

PRESERVED TOMATOES.

Take the tomatoes while small and green, put them in cold clarified syrup, with 1 orange, cut in slices, to every 2 lbs. of tomatoes; but if very superior preserves are wanted, add, instead of the oranges, 2 fresh lemons to 3 lbs. of tomatoes; simmer them over a slow fire for 2 or 3 hours.

QUINCE CHEESE.

Take fine ripe quinces, pare and core them, cut them into pieces and weigh them; to each lb. of the cut quinces allow ½ lb. of the best brown sugar; put the cores and parings into a kettle with water enough to cover them, keeping the lid of the kettle closed; when you find they are all boiled to pieces and quite soft, strain off the water over the sugar, and when it is entirely dissolved, put it over the fire and boil it to a thick syrup, skimming it well; when no more scum rises, put in the quinces; cover them closely, and boil them all day over a slow fire, stirring them and mashing them down with a spoon till they are a thick smooth paste; then take it out and put it into buttered deep pans or dishes; let it set to get cold; it will then turn out so firm that you may cut it into slices like cheese; keep it in a dry place in broad stone pots. It is intended for the tea table.

24

PRESERVED PEPPERS.

Take the small round peppers while they are green, extract the seeds and cores with a sharp penknife, and then put the outsides into a kettle with vine leaves and a little alum to give them firmness, and assist in keeping them green; flavor with lemon or ginger. Water melon rind is done in the same way: allow 1 pint of water to 1½ lbs. of sugar mixing with it some white of egg beaten to a stiff froth; boil and skim it, and when the scum ceases to rise, put in the fruit.

TOMATO JELLY.

Fill a large jar with slices of the ripest and best tomatoes; lay a cloth over the jar, and over that put a piece of dough, to keep in the heat; place the jar in a large pot of water, and boil 4 or 5 hours constantly; then strain the juice through a coarse hair sieve, and to every pint of juice add 1 lb. of the best brown sugar, if you wish the jelly very sweet, or half that quantity, if to eat with meat; add the whites of 8 eggs to every gallon of juice; skim it and boil till nearly half evaporated; then put it into glasses, and keep them in the sun till sufficiently thick. A very good jelly may be made to eat with meat, by putting salt, pepper, mace and nutmeg, instead of sugar.

GRAPE JELLY.

Pick the grapes from the stems; wash and drain them; mash them with a spoon; put them in the preserving kettle, and cover them closely with a large plate; boil them 10 minutes; then pour them into the jelly bag, and squeeze out the juice; allow a pint of juice to 1 lb. of sugar; put the sugar and juice into the kettle, and boil them 20 minutes, skimming them well; fill the glasses while the jelly is warm, and tie them up with brandy papers.

PEACH JELLY.

Wipe your peaches perfectly dry, after washing them,

(they should be free-stones and perfectly ripe); cut them in quarters; crack the stones and break the kernels small; put the peaches and the kernels into a covered jar; set them in boiling water, and let them boil till they are soft; strain them through a jelly bag; add 1 lb. of loaf sugar to 1 pint of juice; put all in the preserving kettle; boil them 20 minutes.

RASPBERRY JAM.

Take the weight of raspberries and sugar; pick the berries very carefully, and lay them, with the sugar, in a stone jar over night; in the morning boil it until it begins to jelly; the great secret of making nice jam, and preserving the raspberry flavor, is to boil it enough; in this particular, however, housekeepers differ.

TO STEW APRICOTS.

Put your fruit on in bell metal with plenty of water to cover them; lay grape vine leaves or grass on top; let them boil till tender, by which time they will probably become green; put your sugar in another skillet, allowing $\frac{1}{2}$ pint of water, or more (if you wish a great deal of syrup) and boil it till quite clear; then take the fruit from the water, and put them into the syrup to boil together till the syrup is as thick as you wish.

STEWED APPLES.

To $2\frac{1}{2}$ lbs. of apples put $1\frac{1}{4}$ lbs. of coarse white sugar, which must be clarified with the whites of 3 eggs, after having put more than a quart of water to the beaten sugar; as the apples are peeled, they must be dropped in water; when the syrup is sufficiently clear, put them in; when half done, add orange peel and cut citron.

WHITE COMPOTE OF PEARS.

Blanch as many pears as you intend to use, whole, with the skins on, in boiling water; take them out when soft,

peel and put into cold water; have your syrup ready in the
stewpan; when it is boiling hot, put in the pears, with a
slice of lemon, to keep them white; when thoroughly
stewed take them out and serve in the syrup; they may
be served hot or cold.

WHITE COMPOTE OF APPLES.

Cut 6 large apples in half, peel and take out the seeds;
stew them in 1 pint of water, the juice of $\frac{1}{2}$ a lemon and
sugar; when the apples are sufficiently tender take them out
and arrange them in the dessert dish; let the syrup keep on
boiling till it is clear and rich; then pour it over the apples.

DRIED CHERRIES.

Stew the cherries with a little sugar for a short time; then
spread them on dishes and set them in the sun; as they
dry pour the syrup over them, a little at a time, for 3 or 4
days; when dry, pack them away in boxes or jars, putting
a layer of cherries with a layer of sugar, and a little whisky
sprinkled between.

CHERRY JAM.

Stone the cherries (they should be the short stem); take
equal quantities of sugar and fruit, and boil slowly
till it is almost a jelly; it is delicious and keeps well.

BAKED APPLES.

Take 1 dozen large juicy apples, pare and core them, but
do not cut them in pieces; put them side by side into a large
baking pan, and fill up with white sugar the holes from
whence you have extracted the cores; pour into each a little lemon juice, and stick in everyone a long piece of lemon
peel evenly cut; into the bottom of the pan put a very little
water, just enough to prevent the apples from burning; bake
them about 1 hour, or till they are tender through, but not
till they break; when done, set them away to get cold; if
closely covered they will keep 2 days; they are very nice

with cream, eaten at tea, or at dinner, with boiled custard poured over them.

BAKED PEARS.

The best for baking are the large pound pears; remove the skins; cut them in half, and take out the cores; lay them in a deep dish, with a thin slip of lemon peel in the place from which each core was taken; sprinkle them with sugar, and strew some cloves or pounded cinnamon among them; pour into the dish some port wine; to 1 dozen large pears allow 1 lb. of sugar, and 1 pint of wine; cover the dish with a large sheet of brown paper, tied on; set it in a moderate oven and let them bake till tender all through, which you may ascertain by sticking a straw through them; you must not let them remain long enough in the oven to break to pieces.

CHARLOTTE DES POMMES.

Pare, core and mince 14 or 15 very nice apples; put them into a frying pan with some loaf sugar, a little pounded cinnamon, grated lemon peel, and 2½ ounces of fresh butter; fry them ¼ hour over a quick fire, stirring them constantly; butter a shape of the size the charlotte is intended to be; cut strips of bread 2 inches wide, and long enough to reach from the bottom to the rim of the shape, so that the whole be lined with bread; dip each bit into melted butter, and then put a layer of the fried apples, and one of apricot jam or marmalade, and one of bread dipped into butter; begin and finish with it; bake it in an oven for nearly 1 hour; turn it out to serve it; it may be boiled and served with a sweet sauce.

PEACH TART.

Take ripe, juicy, free-stone peaches, pare them and cut them into small pieces, (leaving out the stones, half of which must be cracked, and the kernels blanched and mixed with the peaches); mix in a sufficient quantity of sugar, to make them very sweet, and set the peaches away till the sugar draws out the juice; then stew them (without water) till quite soft; take them out, mash them with the back of a spoon, and set them away to cool; have ready some shells of fine puff paste baked a light brown; when cool, put the peaches into the shells; having first mixed the stewed fruit with cream; grate white sugar over them.

TO PRESERVE STRAWBERRIES.

To 1 lb. of strawberries add 1 lb. of sugar, strew it over them, and let them remain until they have made a syrup; put them in a skillet, and let them simmer over a fire until they are half or two-thirds done; take them off and spread them in dishes; they must remain in the sun, until they are sufficiently cooled, to keep the summer; be careful not to bruise the strawberries in stirring them.

QUINCE JAM.

Put equal weight of loaf sugar with the fruit; mash them well together, and stew them until they become sufficiently thick, which you can ascertain by cooling a little; if stewed too long, the color of the fruit will change; if put away in moulds, it forms a pretty dish for a tea table.

PRESERVED APPLES.

Take equal weights of white sugar and apples; peel, core and chop the apples fine; allow to every 3 lbs. of sugar 1 pint of water; then boil the sugar quite thick, skimming it well; add the apples to the grated peel of 1 or 2 lemons and 2 pieces of white ginger; boil until the apples look clear and yellow; this will keep for years.

PRESERVED FIGS.

The white figs must be nearly ripe; score them across, as deep as the outside skin; make a syrup of white sugar, equal weight with the figs, which you may clarify, if you see proper; after this process put in the figs and boil them gently, until they look clear; then take them off the fire and again boil the syrup, till very thick and rich; pour it over the figs hot.

PRESERVED TOMATOES.

To 1 lb. of tomatoes put 2 lbs. of sugar; make the syrup first, and then put the fruit in, and let it remain a short time over a slow fire; they do not require a great deal of cooking.

ORANGE MARMALADE.

Take fine, large, ripe oranges, with thin deep colored skins; weigh them, and allow to each lb. of oranges, 1 lb. of loaf sugar; pare off the yellow outside of the rind from half of the oranges as thin as possible, and put it into a pan with plenty of cold water; cover it closely to keep in the steam, and boil it slowly until it is so soft that the head of a pin will pierce it; in the meantime, grate the rind from the remaining oranges, and take out all the pulp and juice, removing the seeds and core; put the sugar into a preserving kettle, with ½ pint of clear water to each pound, and mix it with some beaten white of egg, allowing 1 white of egg to every 2 lbs. of sugar; when the sugar is all dissolved, put it on the fire and boil, and skim it till it is quite clear and thick; next take the boiled parings and pound them to a paste in a mortar; put this paste into the sugar, and boil and stir it 10 minutes; then put it into the pulp and juice of the oranges, and the grated rind (which will much improve the color); boil all together for ½ hour, till it is a transparent mass; when cold, put it up in glass jars with brandy paper on the top.

APPLE JELLY.

One lb. of ripe apples, pared and cut thin; stew them until quite soft with lemon peel; then add ¾ lb. of white sugar, and stew it ½ hour.

MIXED MARMALADE.

Take 1 peck of quinces, pare and cut them in small

pieces; take the rinds and cores and boil them in water; strain it, and boil the quinces till quite soft; then add 1 peck of pears; when done, 1 peck of peaches; when quite done, 1 peck of apples; and lastly, 3 lbs. of good sugar to each peck of fruit.

STRAWBERRIES WHOLE.

Take an equal weight of fruit and double refined sugar; lay the former in a large dish and sprinkle ½ the sugar in fine powder; give a gentle shake to the dish, that the sugar may reach the under side of the fruit; the next day make a thin syrup with the remainder of the sugar, and allow 1 pint of red currant juice to every 3 lbs. of strawberries; in this simmer them till sufficiently jellied; choose the largest scarlets, not dead ripe.

STRAWBERRY JELLY.

Take 4 lbs. of the juice of strawberries and 2 lbs. of sugar; boil down.

RASPBERRY JELLY.

Pick all the leaves and stems from the raspberries; put them on in bell metal skillets; mix a little powdered sugar with them, and mash them well; stew only a short time; then take them off, pass them well through a clean sieve, so as to extract as much of the pulp as possible; then, when you have a sufficient quantity of juice, to every pint put 1 lb. (dead weight) of loaf sugar; return it to the skillet, and stew until you think it sufficiently thick, which you may discover by cooling a little.

QUINCE JELLY.

Prepare the quinces as before directed; take off the stems and blossoms; wash them clean, and cut them in slices, without paring; fill the pan, and pour in water to cover them; stew them gently, putting in a little water occasionally, till they are quite soft; then pour them in a jelly bag; let all the juice run through, pressing it.

ORANGE JELLY.

The juice of 8 oranges and 6 lemons; grate the peel of $\frac{1}{2}$ the fruit and steep it in a pint of cold water; when the flavor is extracted, mix the water with the juice; add $\frac{3}{4}$ lb. of loaf sugar, $1\frac{1}{4}$ ounces of isinglass, and the beaten whites of 7 eggs; put all into a saucepan and stir till it boils; let it boil a few minutes; strain it till clear, through a jelly bag; put it into a mould or glasses.

PEACH JAM.

Gather the peaches when ripe; peel and stone them; put them into a preserving pan and put them over the fire till hot; rub them through a sieve, and add to 1 lb. of pulp the same weight of powdered loaf sugar, and $\frac{1}{2}$ ounce of bitter almonds, blanched and pounded; let it boil 10 or 12 minutes; stir and skim well.

25

PICKLES.

PICKLED CUCUMBERS.

Make a brine of salt and water strong enough to bear an egg; pour it over the cucumbers and cover them with cabbage leaves; let them stand for a week, until they are quite yellow; pour off the water; take a porcelain kettle, cover the bottom with fresh leaves; put in the cucumbers with a piece of alum; cover them closely with vine leaves and then with a dish or cloth, to keep in the steam; fill up kettle with clear water and hang it over the fire, but not in a blaze; the fire under the kettle must be moderate; keep them over the fire in a slow heat for several hours; if they are not then a pretty green, repeat the process; when they are well greened, take them out of the kettle, drain them on a sieve and put them into a clean stone jar; then spice the vinegar with cloves, mace, mustard seed and sugar; boil well for 5 or 6 minutes, when they will be fit for use.

PICKLED CHERRIES.

Morella cherries are the best, if you can get them; remove the stems and prepare the vinegar with mace and cinnamon, with a sufficient quantity of brown sugar, (say 2 large tablespoonfuls to 1 quart of vinegar); boil all together for a few minutes, and put it over the cherries when cold; put them away in jars, carefully excluding the air. Damsons or blue plums may be done in the same way.

PICKLED LEMONS.

Wipe 6 large lemons; put on them 1 lb. of salt, 6 large cloves of garlic, 2 ounces of horse radish sliced thin; $\frac{1}{2}$ ounce of cloves, mace, nutmeg, and cayenne; 2 ounces of flour of mustard; then add 2 quarts of vinegar; boil $\frac{1}{4}$

hour; set the jar by and stir it daily for 6 weeks; it must be kept closed.

PICKLED DAMSONS.

Do these in the same way as the plums; but as they are much more acid, allow brown sugar of the best kind; plums or damsons may be pickled plain, and with little trouble if full ripe, pricked with a needle, and packed down in a stone jar, with profuse layers of brown sugar between the layers of fruit, the jars filled up with cold cider vinegar, and putting sweet oil at the top.

PICKLED CAULIFLOWERS.

Take large, ripe, fullblown cauliflowers; remove the leaves and stalks, and divide the blossom into pieces or clusters of equal size; throw them into a porcelain kettle of boiling water (adding a little salt); let them simmer, and skim them well; when they come to a boil, take them up with a perforated skimmer, and lay them on a sieve to drain; put them into stone jars (3 parts full); season with mace and nutmeg infused in sufficient of the best cider vinegar, and simmer it for $\frac{1}{4}$ hour; when it comes to boil, take it off the fire, and pour it hot over the cauliflower in the jar, filling it quite up to the top, and adding sweet oil at the last; cover it while warm, and tie leather over the top.

NASTURTION SEEDS.

Keep a large glass jar of cold cider vinegar, and put in the green seeds of nasturtions after the flowers are off, and the seeds full grown, but not hard; remove the stalks; in this simple way nasturtions will keep perfectly well, and are an excellent substitute for capers, with boiled mutton; they can be raised profusely in a city garden; to flavor them with spice, boil the vinegar with a bag of spice in it, and pour it on hot, leaving the spice in the jar.

SWEET PICKLE TOMATOES.

Peel the tomatoes and put 1 lb. of brown sugar to 2 lbs.

of tomatoes; sprinkle it on, and let it stand 2 hours; boil them till the scum ceases to rise, skimming it off as fast as it rises; then add ½ pint of vinegar to 1 lb. of tomatoes; add cinnamon, allspice, mace, cloves and black pepper; boil them slowly until transparent; you must be very careful to take off the scum, as it is that which prevents its keeping.

AUGUSTINE MANGOES.

One lb. of horse radish, 1 lb. of white mustard seed, 1 lb. of white pepper, and 1 lb. of celery seed, 2 ounces of mace, 2 ounces of cloves, 2 ounces of nutmeg, 1 lb. of garlic, ¼ lb. of tumeric, 1 bottle of pure sweet oil, 1 bottle of mustard; mix all well together, and after you have greened your mangoes for three days, wipe them dry; then stuff them with the prepared ingredients and pour boiling vinegar over them; cork them closely and put away for use; all the ingredients must be well beaten.

TO PICKLE WALNUTS WHITE.

Pare green walnuts very thin till the white appears; then throw them into spring water with a handful of salt; keep them under water 6 hours; then put them in a stewpan to simmer 5 minutes, but do not let them boil; take them out and put them in cold water and salt, keeping them quite under the water with a board, otherwise they will not pickle white; then lay them on a cloth and cover them with another to dry; carefully rub them with a soft cloth and put them into the jar with blades of mace and nutmeg cut in slices; pour strong vinegar over them and put away for use.

PICKLED ENGLISH WALNUTS.

Put the nuts in strong salt and water for 12 days, changing the water several times; after which put them in fresh water a short time; then wipe them dry and put them in the sun until they become black; put them in common vinegar for several weeks; after that time, spice the good vinegar with allspice and cloves, horse radish, made mustard, red pepper, garlic, and a little salt must be added; boil. the vinegar and pour it over the nuts while hot.

TOMATO CATSUP (FRENCH).

Take a quantity of tomatoes, put them into a tub; a layer of tomatoes and a layer of salt till all are in; let them stand 24 hours; then strain off all the juice, squeezing the pulp well, and when all the juice is extracted, put it on to boil; reduce it to $\frac{1}{2}$, and to every gallon of liquor put 2 ounces cloves, $\frac{1}{2}$ ounce of allspice, 1 ounce of mace, and boil it down well; then to every 3 quarts add 1 bottle of port wine, and boil it a little longer; put it away to cool and settle, then bottle it. If there is not enough spice, pound a fresh nutmeg and put it in.

PICKLED PEACHES.

Wash your peaches in weak lye; rub them with a coarse cloth to remove the fur; put them in strong salt and water for 7 or 8 days; wipe them dry; put them carefully into the jars; cover them with strong vinegar; add mace, cloves, horse radish, white mustard seed and turmeric, (if you like it); the color of the peach is improved by it and it sharpens the vinegar.

PICKLED ONIONS.

Put the onions in salt and water strong enough to bear an egg; change the water every day; then make a strong brine, pour it on boiling hot for 3 days; then lay them on a sieve to drain; put them in the jar; fill it with good vinegar, add mace and horse radish; if you wish them white, put salt and oil over the top; if you prefer them yellow, add from 2 to 3 tablespoonfuls of turmeric with the vinegar; tie them up very close and they will keep any length of time for table use.

SPICED PEACHES.

Nine lbs. of nice peaches, 4 lbs. of sugar, 1 pint of good vinegar; boil the peaches in water till tender, then put in vinegar and sugar, with a little whole allspice till done; pare, stone and halve the peaches first; apples are very nice done in the same way, for immediate use, and a very good embellishment for cold meats.

PICKLED CUCUMBERS.

Wipe and put them in salt and water, strong enough to bear an egg, in which let them remain 6 or 7 days; then scald in vinegar to green them, after which put them in cold spiced vinegar. Snaps are done in the same way.

PICKLED TOMATOES.

Prick the skins of fair, ripe tomatoes, spread them in layers, and on each layer put pounded mace, cloves and cinnamon, pouring cold vinegar over the whole. The vinegar from tomatoes, thus prepared, is a very good catsup.

OIL MANGOES.

One lb. of race ginger, well soaked and dried; 1 lb. of horse radish done in the same way; 1 lb. of mustard seed, well washed; ½ lb. of garlic, soaked and bleached; 2 ounces black pepper, 2 ounces of cloves, ½ ounce of mace. The mangoes should be laid in salt and water till they are yellow, and then scalded until they are green; soak the ingredients well and beat them together in a mortar, and mix them with a pint of made mustard and as much sweet oil as will make the ingredients into a paste; then fill the mangoes, and what is left put between the layers; then pour over them as much boiling vinegar as will cover them. This recipe will answer for cantelope.

PICKLED CUCUMBERS.

Make a strong brine and let it boil in a bell metal skillet; pour over your cucumbers (which have been placed in a jar) with layers of fig and grape leaves, alternately, until filled; then cover up closely, and repeat the next day with the same brines, but fresh leaves; if sufficiently green, scald with vinegar and water on the day following; let them remain 24 hours; then boil strong vinegar with a small piece of alum, horse radish and garlic, with 2 lbs. of brown sugar and a small quantity of turmeric, cloves, mace, and nutmeg, allspice, celery seed and cayenne pepper, say ½ ounce of each.

PICKLED PLUMS.

Take large fine plums, perfect and quite ripe; to every quart of plums allow ½ lb. of the best white sugar powdered, and a large pint of the best cider vinegar; melt the sugar in the vinegar, and put it, with the fruit, in a porcelain kettle; all the plums having been previously pricked to the stone with a large needle; lay among them some small muslin bags filled with broken nutmeg, mace, and cinnamon; give them one boil up, skimming them well; put them warm into stone jars, with the bags interspersed, and cork them immediately; green gages may be done in the same way, first rendering them greener, by boiling with vine leaves in the usual way.

BUTTON TOMATOES.

The small round tomatoes, either red or yellow, will keep perfectly, if put whole into cold vinegar of the best quality; you may add a bag of spice, if you choose.

TOMATO CATSUP.

One peck of tomatoes sliced and washed; boil or stew them with a little salt, until perfectly soft; then strain them through a hair sieve, and press as much of the pulp through as possible; after which, add 2 tablespoonfuls of scraped horse radish, 1 large onion stuck full of cloves, ground allspice, red pepper and salt, to the taste; put all on together, boiling, until the catsup looks rich and thick; when done,

add 1 pint of strong vinegar, and 1 teacup of made mustard ;
let the catsup be cold, before you bottle it; let it be free of
the onion and horse radish ; rosin the bottles tightly, and
put away for use.

WINTER TOMATOES.

Peel and cut all of the hard part of the tomatoes ; add a
little salt and red pepper ; let them stew until thick enough
to bottle; after which, put all the bottles in an oven with
straw placed around them (so as to prevent their breaking) ;
fill the oven with lukewarm water; let it boil 10 minutes ;
cork the bottles tightly, whilst in the oven, so as to make
them air tight ; rosin them also.

TOMATO CATSUP.

To one gallon of skinned tomatoes, put 4 spoonfuls of
salt, 4 of black pepper, 3 of mustard, $\frac{1}{2}$ a spoonful of allspice, 8 pods of red pepper; all the ingredients made fine,
and simmer slowly in sufficient sharp vinegar to have 2
quarts of catsup ; after simmering it 3 or 4 hours, and straining it through a wire sieve, (those who like it), may add 2
spoonfuls of the juice of garlic, after the simmering is
somewhat over, and the ingredients are cool. This is superior to West India catsup.

GREEN TOMATO SOY.

Take $\frac{1}{2}$ bushel of green tomatoes, 1$\frac{1}{2}$ dozen of white onions ;
slice them thin and put them in jars, with a tablespoonful
of salt between each layer; let them stand 24 hours; then
drain off the water and boil them 10 or 15 minutes in
vinegar; then take them out and put them again in jars,
a layer of tomatoes and onions, spice, a little sugar, and a
tablespoonful of sweet oil, until the jar is filled ; mix a box
of mustard in the vinegar, and pour over them till all are
covered ; use black pepper, mace, cloves, allspice, mustard
seed, coriander and celery seed ; spices to be bruised.

PEPPER MANGOES.

Take large, green peppers and put them in salt and water and let them stand 9 days; the day before you are to take them out, get nice white cabbages and chop them very fine; sprinkle them well with salt and let them stand all night; in the morning drain off the water, and mix with them celery seed, mustard seed, and a little turmeric, and all kinds of spice, and moisten the whole with pure sweet oil; then take the seed out of the peppers and stuff the pods with the above mixture; cover them with boiling vinegar and tie them up closely.

A QUICK WAY OF PICKLING CABBAGE.

Take 2 nice white cabbages and quarter them; if very large more than quarter them; and put them in salt and water to remain 24 hours; then boil them till tender in weak vinegar with a little turmeric in it; then put them in jars and pour over them good cold vinegar and tie them up.

SWEET DAMSONS.

To 5 lbs. of fruit add 3 lbs. of sugar, 1 quart of vinegar; boil the sugar and vinegar, with mace, cloves and cinnamon, and pour it boiling over the fruit; repeat this when it gets cold.

SWEET PLUMS.

Take 1 peck of damsons, or prune plums, and stone them; put into a kettle 3½ pints of vinegar, 7 lbs. of brown sugar; boil, and skim it well; then put in the fruit, with a tablespoonful of cloves, mace and cinnamon powdered; boil it 2 hours; then take out the fruit and let it boil some time longer; remove it from the fire, and when cold mix all together.

LEMON PICKLE.

Cut 12 lemons into 6 pieces each; put on them 2 lbs. of salt,
26

8 or 9 cloves of garlic, with mace, nutmeg, cayenne and all-spice, ½ ounce of each, and ¼ lb. of flour of mustard; to these ingredients add 1 gallon of good vinegar; boil the whole for ½ hour; then put it in a jar, and set it by for 8 weeks, stirring it every day; after which, pour it into small bottles, and close them very tight. To be eaten with meat.

CIDER APPLE SAUCE.

Boil down new sweet cider, till about as thick as good molasses; when cold, strain it through a sieve; as soon as it boils put in the apples, pared, quartered and cored; stew over a slow fire till the fruit is perfectly tender.

GERMAN PICKLE.

Take sound, ripe cucumbers; peel and remove the seeds; cut lengthways into strips an inch wide; to 3 quarts of the pieces add 3 cups of vinegar, and 4 of water; soak 24 hours, stirring once or twice; put 1 quart of vinegar on the fire; add 1 pint of sugar, a little cinnamon bark, 1 teaspoonful of pimento, tied in a piece of cloth; scald all together; add the cucumbers and boil till soft; put in glass jars.

SWEET PICKLE PEACHES.

Six lbs. of peaches to 3 lbs. of sugar, 1 quart of vinegar; in making the syrup add allspice, cloves and mace to the taste; after the syrup is formed, throw in the fruit and cook it, but not as much as usual with preserves; some prefer them with the skins on, in which case, the fur should be rubbed off with a coarse napkin.

SWEET PEACHES.

Cover 1 peck of cling-stone peaches with salt and water; let them remain all night; in the morning, take them out, and to 1 gallon of vinegar add 4 lbs. of brown sugar, with allspice, cloves, nutmeg and mace to the taste; boil it, and pour it over the peaches hot; do the same 4 days in succession; the Heath peach is the best. (Philadelphia receipt.)

PICKLED CABBAGE.

Lay slices of red cabbage into a jar, and strew salt over each layer; put 2 tablespoonfuls of whole black pepper, all-spice, cloves and cinnamon in a bag, and scald them in 2 quarts of vinegar, which, pour over the cabbage, and cover it tight; it will be fit for use in 3 days.

PICKLED RADISH PODS.

Put the pods, which must be gathered when very young, into salt and water all night; boil the salt and water they were laid in; pour it upon the pods, and cover the jar close, to keep in the steam; when it is nearly cold, pour it on again, and continue to do so till the pods are green; then drain them on a sieve and make a pickle for them of white vinegar, mace, black pepper and horse radish; pour it boiling hot upon the pods; tie them down, and put them away for use.

SOY.

Take a common size jar of anchovies; bruise and strain them; add a quart of mushroom catsup, a quart of walnut pickle, a gallon of Maderia wine and a little black mustard seed; boil $\frac{1}{2}$ hour; bottle and cork tight; seal with wax and in 10 days the soy will be fit for use.

PICKLED CABBAGE.

Take nicely headed cabbages and quarter them; put them in a porcelain skillet of cold water with 1 gill of salt, and let them boil until they may be pierced easily with a straw; then place them on a dish carefully to drain; while drain-ing, take a jar of cold vinegar and stir in 2 tablespoonfuls of turmeric; in this vinegar place the cabbage and let it remain 48 hours; then take 2 gallons of the best vinegar, 2 lbs. of brown sugar, 1 tablespoonful best cayenne pepper, 2 ounces of turmeric (which should be divided equally) and tied up in 6 muslin bags; two of these bags must be boiled with the sugar and pepper in the vinegar, and while boiling, pour upon the cabbage, after having been placed in a dry place with the other bags of turmeric. Made and fit for use in one week.

GERMAN PICKLE.

Stick the damsons with a fork to prevent splitting them, then weigh 1 lb. of brown sugar to every 3 lbs. of damsons, making a syrup by letting them boil a very short time with the spices, and pour into a jar when cold; the syrup must be poured from the damsons for 3 mornings and made boiling hot, then poured over the fruit, but not until nearly cold; on the 4th morning the fruit must be put into the jars also, and remain till quite done (but not too much); the spices used and boiled in the vinegar are 1 ounce of cinnamon, 2 ounces of mace, 2 of allspice, 2 of cloves, to a ½ bushel of damsons.

CREOLE SAUCE.

(For Fish). Worcestershire sauce, 1 tablespoonful; cayenne pepper, ¼ teaspoonful; butter, 1 ounce; tomatoes, 2; onions, 1 tablespoonful; parsley, 1 tablespoonful; chop the tomatoes, onions and parsley very fine; boil all together 10 minutes and strain.

The two following receipts were taken from a cookery book, "The gift of Mrs. Francis Dandridge to Anna Maria Dandridge," 15th December, 1756, having belonged to Mrs. Washington, and now in the library at Mount Vernon.

CHICKENS ROYAL.

Lard them, and force the bellies and pass them off; then store them in good gravy and broth, gold color; make a ragoo of mushrooms, morels, truffles and cocks-combs; and when your chickens are done enough dish them up, lay your ragoo over and garnish with petty-patties and fried sweet-breads.

FOWLS IN FILLETS WITH PISTACHOES.

Spit your fowls and let them roast; they being done take them off, and cut off the wings, and the white of the breasts; keep a small sauce ready in a stewpan, made with sweet herbs, a little good butter, small champignons cut in slices; put it over the fire, with a dust of flour in it; stir and moisten it with a ladleful of good broth; see it be of a good taste; the pistachoes being scalded and cut into slices, put them in and make a thick sauce with 4 or 5 yolks of eggs; beat the same up with cream; then put in the white and legs of fowls, with juice of a lemon; you must cut your wings only in two, then place the slices of your fowls in the bottom of the dish with your sauce over it, and serve up hot for an entry.

MRS. JOY'S CHOW-CHOW PICKLE.

Two large heads of cabbage, cut as for slaw, but not so fine, 8 large onions sliced; mix the onions with the cut cabbage, and sprinkle about 2 teacups of salt over them; mix the salt thoroughly in the cabbage, and let them stand not less than 12 hours; drain all the water from the cabbage through a muslin cloth; now put the cabbage in a porcelain kettle and cover it with a gallon of vinegar, 1 teacup of white mustard seed, $\frac{1}{2}$ teacup of celery seed, 1 teacup of grated horse radish, 1 whole garlic minced fine, 2 or 3 pods of green or red peppers cut fine; let this come to a boil, and add 2 teacups of brown sugar; set this aside until the next day to get cold; when ready to put away, have a paste made of 1 teacup of the best sweet oil, 2 ounces of turmeric and $\frac{1}{2}$ teacup of mustard, made quite thick and stirred into the oil; now mix this paste in well with the hand into the vinegar and cabbage; it is now ready to put away, and will be fit for use in 10 days.

STUFFED PEACHES.

Take free-stone peaches of the finest kind (let them be full grown, but not quite ripe) and lay them in salt and water for 2 days, covered with a board to keep them down; after which, wipe them dry; cut them open, and extract the stones; then prepare the stuffing to the taste: minced garlic, scraped horse radish, bruised mustard seed, and cloves, a little ginger root, soaked in water to soften it, and then sliced; fill the peaches with the mixture, tying them round to secure the stuffing; season the vinegar with broken cinnamon, fresh made mustard, a little ginger and nutmeg; having mixed this all well together, fill up the jar with the pickle.

OIL MANGOES.

One-quarter of garlic, 1 lb. of scraped horse radish, 1 lb. of white mustard seed, 1 lb. of black mustard seed, 1 ounce of long pepper, 2 ounces of black pepper, 2 ounces of turmeric, 1 ounce of mace, 1 ounce of cloves, ¼ lb. of race ginger cut up fine, 4 ounces of olive oil; fill the mangoes with salt, let them stand 24 hours; then wipe them clear from salt; mix the prementioned articles together, put them in the mangoes and sew them up; have some vinegar spiced well with common spices, such as black pepper, allspice, horse radish and mustard, boil it well pour it over the mangoes, and tie the jar closely.

YELLOW PICKLE.

One lb. of ginger sliced and dried, 1 lb. of horse radish scraped, 1 lb. of white mustard seed washed and dried, 1 lb. of garlic salted, sliced and dried, ½ lb. of nutmegs, 1 ounce of long peppers, ½ ounce of turmeric, to 1½ gallons of vinegar; put the vegetables intended for the pickle into a a kettle, pour the vinegar and spices over them and set them over a clear fire; let them boil a few moments; put them in jars and tie them up tightly.

CHOCOLATE CARAMELS.

Two cups of molasses, 1 cup of grated chocolate, 1 cup of milk, 2 teaspoonfuls of vanilla, 1 tablespoon of butter; boil 25 minutes; set to cool in buttered pans, mark in squares.

CANDY.

One gallon of good molasses, 5 lbs. of brown sugar, and ¼ lb. of butter; boil together until they candy well; then pour into buttered dishes, and pull until very white.

CHOCOLATE CARAMELS.

Three cups of sugar, 1 cup of water, and ¼ lb. of chocolate; dissolve the chocolate in the water; then add 1 cup of milk, and ½ cup of butter; let it boil till it will drop from a spoon, generally about ½ hour; pour in a flat dish and cut in squares.

COCOANUT DROPS.

Twelve eggs to 5 cocoanuts; grate the nuts fine, and dry it in a moderate oven; beat up the whites of the eggs; then add the sugar, allowing 1 cup to 2 of the cocoanuts, and beat to a paste; then stir in the cocoanut, and drop in a pan or on a sheet of paper, and bake for 10 minutes.

BROWN TAFFY.

Six lbs. of New Orleans sugar, water sufficient to dissolve it, ½ lb. of butter; boil until it cracks; when almost done, stir constantly to prevent burning; when done pour on a marble slab, or in a flat dish, and when cool, pull till light brown.

COCOANUT MERINGUE.

One lb. of powdered sugar, the whites of 9 eggs, beaten to a froth; the sugar should be worked in slowly with a wooden spoon; have ready a pan well greased and floured; drop a tablespoonful and sprinkle well with grated cocoanut; bake in a slow oven till a light brown.

COCOANUT DROPS.

One lb. of grated cocoanut, $\frac{1}{2}$ lb. of white powdered sugar, whites of 6 eggs, beaten to a stiff froth; drop in buttered pans and bake.

MISCELLANEOUS.

REIZ DE VEAU.

Fry slightly, putting in a little flour before it becomes too brown, as the sauce must be a pale yellow; add water to the sauce; then put in a little onion, thyme and parsley, chopped very fine; 2 or 3 cloves and allspice; let the whole simmer till well done; then add the juice of a lemon, and a little of the peel, and at last stir in the yolks of 2 eggs well beaten; you may use the same receipt for making nims.

COTELETTES EN PAPILOTTES.

Trim the cutlets nicely; prepare a stuffing of dry, stale bread crumbs, mixed with the yolks of some raw eggs; season highly with thyme, parsley, marjoram, onion and celery leaves or seed, etc.; cut up 1 dozen olives fine, and mix in; put plenty of the dressing on each cutlet, and wrap it carefully in letter paper; lay them side by side in a flat, common pot; add a little lard and let them sweat for ½ hour; then broil quickly on hot coals, and serve and eat with lemon juice.

CURRY.

Put ½ tablespoonful of fresh butter into a saucepan; let it boil; add a medium sized onion, cut into thin slices; fry the onion a deep brown ; have ready a chicken jointed and cut up into small pieces, or 2 lbs. of mutton, lamb or veal without fat, cut into pieces about ½ inch square; to the fried onion now add a whole tablespoonful of butter and 1 of curry powder; stir well and cook for a few moments; then add the meat; stir the whole over the fire; add a teacup of water; let the whole simmer over a gentle fire for 20 minutes, stirring occasionally; then remove the saucepan to the top of

27

the stove, and let the contents simmer for 1½ to 2 hours; must not let it boil; the addition of a pineapple takes the place of the gum mango in India; then add cocoanut, potato, green peas to taste, only just long enough before the curry is done to insure their being thoroughly cooked; all fat and flour should be eschewed; rice should be served separately, having been well drained and put into cold water to boil.

BISQUE POTAGE.—MADAME EUGÈNE.

Take 50 or more shrimp; wash them in 5 or 6 waters; put them in a saucepan, adding salt and big black pepper, a little nutmeg (grated) and a bit of butter, on a brisk fire; stir with a spoon for ½ hour; when cooked let the shrimp drain; remove the meats and mash in mortar; boil rice in bouillon ¼ hour; strain, and put it in mortar with the shrimp; when well pounded, put in saucepan, and thin with bouillon, and pass through a sieve; thin this purée (cream) so that it be neither too thick nor too thin; then mash the shrimp shells, add juice or butter in which the shrimps have been cooked, and strain the purée in a cullender; it should then be of reddish color; put this in a saucepan on a moderate fire; do not let come to a boil, but should be quite hot; put crust of bread in soup dish and pour on a little broth, hot, and when ready to serve add a little Maderia.

SPICED PEACHES.

Nine lbs. of good, ripe peaches, rub with a coarse towel, and halve them; put 4 lbs. of sugar and 1 pint of vinegar in a kettle with cloves, mace and cinnamon, each 1 ounce; when the syrup is formed throw in the peaches, a few at a time, so as to keep them whole; when clear, take out and put in more until all are done; boil the syrup till quite rich; then pour over the peaches.

HERB GUMBO.

Herbs to be thoroughly boiled together; then chopped fine; put in a pot a tablespoonful of lard; when hot, put in

1 lb. of brisket of veal; smother slowly for ½ hour; add a pinch of flour; let veal fry brown; add onions to taste; then ½ lb. of raw ham cut in small pieces; put in herbs for a little while; then add boiling water, say about 1½ pints; let stew together for about ¾ hour; add red or green pepper and serve with rice in separate dish; herbs, spinach, lettuce and mustard tops predominate; green cabbage, raddish, and turnip tops in small quantities.

CROQUETTES.

Two lbs. veal, boiled till done; then take out the bones, skins and strings; chop very fine; take enough of the broth the veal was boiled in and ½ loaf of bread to make a panada as thick as mush; stir into this while on the fire, 3 eggs and 2 heaping tablespoons of butter, till the whole looks like thin scrambled eggs; then turn this out on the meat, stirring it well; add part of a nutmeg or powdered mace and salt and pepper, in fact, any seasoning to taste; a little parsley, thyme and sage chopped very fine, and a little onion chopped and fried is an improvement. Excellent.

SAVORY FRIAR'S OMELET.

Have 1 lb. of nice potatoes boiled, and also ½ lb. of carrots; when cooked quite tender, rub the potatoes and carrots through a wire sieve with a wooden spoon; then add the yolk of an egg, salt and pepper to taste, and about a teaspoonful of butter; rub and beat all up into a thick paste; have a pudding dish well buttered and scattered all over with fine bread crumbs; put in the mixture; add bread crumbs on the top, and 1 or 2 small pieces of butter, and bake for about ½ hour, or till the crumbs are nice and brown; turn out the whole on a dish, and serve hot.

TO BOIL HAMS.

Soak all night in water enough to cover the ham; put the ham into a large vessel full of cold water, and simmer 20 minutes to each lb. of meat; when done, take off the skin,

and grate bread crumbs over the top ; sprinkle 1 tablespoonful of brown sugar over the bread crumbs, and pour over
them 1 tablespoonful of wine vinegar; bake for 1 hour;
serve cold.

FIG PICKLES.

Gather the figs when fully swollen, but not quite ripe,
leaving the stems on; soak them 10 or 12 hours in moderately strong brine (salt and water); take them out of this
brine; rinse with clear water and place in glass or stone
jars; have a kettle of pure, strong vinegar; add a gallon of
light brown sugar to each gallon of vinegar, with such spices
as you prefer for flavoring, cinnamon and a few cloves;
place this kettle of vinegar over the fire, stirring and dissolving the sugar, and when the vinegar comes to a simmer,
pour it over the figs, covering them about an inch; this process of scalding the vinegar and pouring over figs should be
repeated about 3 times; a small piece of horse radish is an
improvement.

POTATO SALAD.

Boiled potatoes (Irish) sliced, 5 large hard boiled eggs
(sliced), 4 potted ham, 2 tablespoons sweet pickle, 2 tablespoons salt and pepper; mix thoroughly before making the
dressing; a good deal of salt, the potatoes absorb so much;
for the dressing, 2 tablespoons of Prince of Wales salad
sauce; 2 yolks (raw) and 1 cooked, 1 tablespoon Worcester
sauce, 1 teaspoon sugar, pepper to the taste, sweet oil about
1 pint, use neither mustard nor vinegar, the salad sauce contains all that is necessary of each; after mixing thoroughly,
squeeze a few drops of lemon juice, and then add the whites
beated stiff; pour the dressing on the potatoes, 1 spoonful
or more at a time; mix well, and then garnish with eggs,
pickles, etc., according to your taste; stir the oil into the
raw yolk as you do for mayonnaise dressing; then add the
other ingredients.

MANGOES.

Put the mangoes into salt and water and let them remain for nine days; split them, take out the insides, put them in a kettle, cover them with vinegar and water; put in a lump of alum the size of a hickory nut; put cabbage leaves around them; put them on the stove where they will keep warm, but not boil, and keep them there until green; take 1 lb. of ginger, crack it but don't powder it fine, 1 lb. of grated horse radish, ½ lb. of garlic, 2 ounces of black mustard seed, 2 ounces of white mustard seed, 2 ounces of celery seed, 2 ounces of ground mace, 2 ounces of ground cloves; in each mango put a small cucumber and a long white pepper; mix the stuffing with olive oil, fill the mangoes, tie them with a worsted string (yarn), pour boiling vinegar over them two or three times; put a whole red pepper in each jar, fill the spaces with cucumbers; put a little unmixed mustard and brown sugar in the top of each jar; seal them up and put them away for a year or more; this quantity of stuffing will fill thirty or forty mangoes.

USEFUL RECEIPTS.

How to test fish when thoroughly cooked: lift it upon the dish and insert a thin bladed knife in the thickest part close to the bone; if the bone readily divides from the fish, it should be taken from the fire; it is done.

When boiling puddings have the water boiling when the pudding is put in, and do not let it stop till you take out; dip the cloth in cold water, and it will release the pudding easily.

Whites of eggs should always be beaten till they become a heap of stiff froth, without any liquid at the bottom and till it hangs from the folk without dropping.

A few drops of glycerine in a bottle of mucilage will cause the mucilage to adhere to glass, when used upon labels.

Before you cut an iced cake cut the icing by itself with a small sharp knife.

Carbonate of soda applied to the bite of a spider or any venomous creature will neutralize the poisonous effect almost instantly; it acts like a charm in case of a snake bite.

Cement for broken glass: slake some quicklime with boiling water, and collect some of the fine powder of the lime; take the white of an egg well beaten, with an equal bulk of water, and add the slaked lime to it to form a thin paste; use quickly, and it will resist, when dry, boiling water.

SPONGE CAKE.

Whites of 14 eggs, yolks of 7 eggs, 10 ounces of flour; 1 lb. of sugar.

OMELETTE SOUFFLÉ.

Put the yolks of 6 eggs in a large basin; a dessert-spoonful of potato flour, 1 dessertspoonful of orange flower water ; add a very little salt; stir these together with a wooden spoon for about 10 minutes; then whip the 6 whites and mix them in lightly with the batter; next put 2 ounces of butter into a saucepan; set it on the fire, and as soon as the butter begins to sputter, pour the batter into it; set the pan over the fire and as the batter becomes partially set round the sides and at the bottom, toss it over gently and then turn the omelette out neatly in the form of a dome on a silver dish greased with butter; put it in the oven and bake it for about 12 minutes; when it is ready to send to table, shake some sugar over it and serve immediately.

TO BOIL FISH.

In boiling fish use invariably cold water. If a fish is put into boiling water, the flesh being softer than the meat of animals, the act of boiling causes it to break up. When water is boiling in which the fish has been placed, remove it from the fire and let the fish simmer; a boiled fish is done when the fins can be easily removed.

NEUTRALIZING POISON WITH SWEET OIL.

A poison of any description may be rendered almost instantly harmless, by swallowing 2 gills of sweet oil. An individual with a strong constitution should take nearly twice that quantity. The oil will neutralize almost every form of vegetable, animal or mineral poison with which physicians and chemists are acquainted.

DRAWN BUTTER.

Two teaspoonfuls of flour, ¼ lb. of butter; stir this into 4 tablespoons of boiling water, stirring until all of the butter is melted. This is the foundation of most of the sauces for mutton fish, and poultry. Egg sauce is made by adding to the drawn butter, the yolks of 4 hard boiled eggs and a little more boiling water.

BEEF TEA FOR INVALIDS.

One pound of the best beef; take off all the fat and cut the lean into small pieces; pour over it 1 pint of cold water and let it stand 3 or 4 hours; then put it over a brisk fire and let it boil 20 minutes.

HOME MADE YEAST POWDER.

Mix thoroughly 2 lbs. of cream of tartar and 1 lb. of soda; use 1 teaspoonful of the mixture to 1 pint of flour, sifting it into the dry flour.

KENTUCKY CORN PUDDING.

One dozen ears of corn; cut the grains down through the middle; scrape out the heart; mix this with 1 teacup of milk, 3 eggs, ½ cup of butter with 1 teaspoonful of sugar; mix well and bake in a moderate oven. This is delicious.

WEIGHTS AND MEASURES.

10 eggs is equal to 1 lb.

1 lb. of sugar is equal to 1 quart.

1 lb. of butter, when soft, is 1 quart.

1 lb. 2 ounces of flour is equal to 1 quart.

4 tablespoonfuls to $\frac{1}{2}$ gill.

16 tablespoonfuls to $\frac{1}{2}$ pint.

A common sized wineglass, $\frac{1}{2}$ a gill.

A common sized tumbler, $\frac{1}{2}$ pint.

2 ordinary teacups, 1 pint.

The Daily Picayune.

The leading paper of New Orleans, and of the South, equal to any in circulation and second to none in merit. is THE NEW ORLEANS DAILY PICAYUNE, published by Nicholson & Co. This great daily newspaper, established nearly fifty years ago, by practical enterprising men, as a step forward in American Journalism at the South, has grown with the growth of the city and is a power in the land. Through all the years of its life the PICAYUNE has had the confidence and support of the business community, whose interest is the good of the City and State, morality and commercial prosperity. Many papers have come up to foster factions, support rings, and carry out the plans of selfish adventurers. THE DAILY PICAYUNE has remained fearless and independent, and it has been rewarded with success. Its news gathering system is perfect—it is edited with ability—and is frank and outspoken on all subjects concerning the public welfare. Naturally the comprehensive and impartial reports of exhibits, and all things concerning the World's Exposition, found in the DAILY PICAYUNE, are the best made, and have been the subject of many compliments from visitors and the press of the North and West. Being a family paper, widely circulated. the DAILY PICAYUNE is also the best advertising medium in the South, as well as the best newspaper.

THE WEEKLY PICAYUNE.

THE WEEKLY PICAYUNE, made up of the most important matter that appears in the daily, with an original synopsis of the news of the week, is intended for country circulation. Its condensed news, literary features, correspondence, devotion to agricultural interests, makes it the most desirable home paper to be found—certainly in the South—for the low price of one dollar and fifty cents per year. The WEEKLY PICAYUNE, fifty-two papers in a year, is a library of information and pleasant reading, and a history of the events of each week. It should be found in every Southern home.

THE SUNDAY PICAYUNE.

Although included in the daily subscription, THE NEW ORLEANS SUNDAY PICAYUNE has special features, and may be received separately by subscribers when desired. It is usually a mammoth paper of sixteen pages, and in addition to the full telegraphic, home, foreign and local news reports, THE SUNDAY PICAYUNE contains regular Paris and New York correspondence, with the best information on fashions, household matters, science, the drama, society news and gossip, in New Orleans and out of town, and choice selections of poetry, stories, and miscellaneous matter, and original contributions from " Catherine Cole," Jenny June, Mollie E. Moore, J. H. Haynie, " Vidette," and many others. THE SUNDAY PICAYUNE is deservedly a popular favorite with all classes.

TERMS OF SUBSCRIPTION.—*Postage prepaid.*

DAILY.

Twelve Months	$12 00
Six Months	6 00
Three Months	3 00

WEEKLY.

Twelve Months	$1 50
Six Months	75
Three Months	50

SUNDAY PICAYUNE BY MAIL.

Twelve Months	$2 00
Six Months	1 00